50% OFF Online SAT Prep Course!

Dear Customer,

We consider it an honor and a privilege that you chose our SAT Study Guide. As a way of showing our appreciation and to help us better serve you, we are offering **50% off their online SAT Prep Course.** Many SAT courses are needlessly expensive and don't deliver enough value. With their course, you get access to the best SAT prep material, and **you only pay half price**.

Mometrix has structured their online course to perfectly complement your printed study guide. The SAT Prep Course contains **in-depth lessons** that cover all the most important topics, **220+ video reviews** that explain difficult concepts, over **350 practice questions** to ensure you feel prepared, and more than **350 digital flashcards**, so you can study while you're on the go.

Online SAT Prep Course

Topics Covered:

- Reading
  - Common Organizations of Texts
  - Using Contexts to Determine Meaning
  - Reading Informational Texts
- Writing and Language
  - The Writing Process
  - Common Types of Writing
  - Common Sentence Errors
- Mathematics
  - Foundational Math Concepts
  - Passport to Advanced Math
  - Student-Produced Response

Course Features:

- SAT Study Guide
  - Get content that complements our best-selling study guide.
- Full-Length Practice Tests
  - With over 350 practice questions, you can test yourself again and again.
- Mobile Friendly
  - If you need to study on the go, the course is easily accessible from your mobile device.
- SAT Flashcards
  - Their course includes a flashcards mode with over 350 content cards for you to study.

To receive this discount, visit their website: mometrix.com/university/sat or simply scan this QR code with your smartphone. At the checkout page, enter the discount code: **TPBSAT50**

If you have any questions or concerns, please contact Mometrix at support@mometrix.com.

Sincerely,

in partnership with

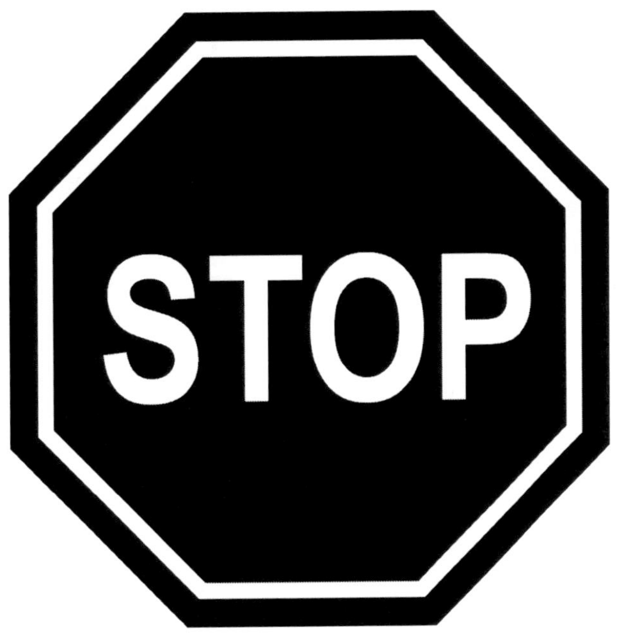

FREE Test Taking Tips Video/DVD Offer

To better serve you, we created videos covering test taking tips that we want to give you for FREE. **These videos cover world-class tips that will help you succeed on your test.**

We just ask that you send us feedback about this product. Please let us know what you thought about it—whether good, bad, or indifferent.

To get your **FREE videos**, you can use the QR code below or email freevideos@studyguideteam.com with "Free Videos" in the subject line and the following information in the body of the email:

a. The title of your product

b. Your product rating on a scale of 1-5, with 5 being the highest

c. Your feedback about the product

If you have any questions or concerns, please don't hesitate to contact us at info@studyguideteam.com.

Thank you!

Digital SAT Study Guide 2025 and 2026

7 Practice Tests and SAT Prep Book
[Updated for the New Exam Outline]

Lydia Morrison

Written and edited by TPB Publishing.

Interested in buying more than 10 copies of our product? Contact us about bulk discounts:
bulkorders@studyguideteam.com

ISBN 13: 9781637754054

Table of Contents

Welcome

Dear Reader,

Welcome to your new Test Prep Books study guide! We are pleased that you chose us to help you prepare for your exam. There are many study options to choose from, and we appreciate you choosing us. Studying can be a daunting task, but we have designed a smart, effective study guide to help prepare you for what lies ahead.

Whether you're a parent helping your child learn and grow, a high school student working hard to get into your dream college, or a nursing student studying for a complex exam, we want to help give you the tools you need to succeed. We hope this study guide gives you the skills and the confidence to thrive, and we can't thank you enough for allowing us to be part of your journey.

In an effort to continue to improve our products, we welcome feedback from our customers. We look forward to hearing from you. Suggestions, success stories, and criticisms can all be communicated by emailing us at info@studyguideteam.com.

Sincerely,
Test Prep Books Team

FREE Videos/DVD OFFER

Doing well on your exam requires both knowing the test content and understanding how to use that knowledge to do well on the test. We offer completely FREE test taking tip videos. **These videos cover world-class tips that you can use to succeed on your test.**

To get your **FREE videos**, you can use the QR code below or email freevideos@studyguideteam.com with "Free Videos" in the subject line and the following information in the body of the email:

a. The title of your product
b. Your product rating on a scale of 1-5, with 5 being the highest
c. Your feedback about the product

If you have any questions or concerns, please don't hesitate to contact us at info@studyguideteam.com.

Quick Overview

As you draw closer to taking your exam, effective preparation becomes more and more important. Thankfully, you have this study guide to help you get ready. Use this guide to help keep your studying on track and refer to it often.

This study guide contains several key sections that will help you be successful on your exam. The guide contains tips for what you should do the night before and the day of the test. Also included are test-taking tips. Knowing the right information is not always enough. Many well-prepared test takers struggle with exams. These tips will help equip you to accurately read, assess, and answer test questions.

A large part of the guide is devoted to showing you what content to expect on the exam and to helping you better understand that content. In this guide are practice test questions so that you can see how well you have grasped the content. Then, answer explanations are provided so that you can understand why you missed certain questions.

Don't try to cram the night before you take your exam. This is not a wise strategy for a few reasons. First, your retention of the information will be low. Your time would be better used by reviewing information you already know rather than trying to learn a lot of new information. Second, you will likely become stressed as you try to gain a large amount of knowledge in a short amount of time. Third, you will be depriving yourself of sleep. So be sure to go to bed at a reasonable time the night before. Being well-rested helps you focus and remain calm.

Be sure to eat a substantial breakfast the morning of the exam. If you are taking the exam in the afternoon, be sure to have a good lunch as well. Being hungry is distracting and can make it difficult to focus. You have hopefully spent lots of time preparing for the exam. Don't let an empty stomach get in the way of success!

When travelling to the testing center, leave earlier than needed. That way, you have a buffer in case you experience any delays. This will help you remain calm and will keep you from missing your appointment time at the testing center.

Be sure to pace yourself during the exam. Don't try to rush through the exam. There is no need to risk performing poorly on the exam just so you can leave the testing center early. Allow yourself to use all of the allotted time if needed.

Remain positive while taking the exam even if you feel like you are performing poorly. Thinking about the content you should have mastered will not help you perform better on the exam.

Once the exam is complete, take some time to relax. Even if you feel that you need to take the exam again, you will be well served by some down time before you begin studying again. It's often easier to convince yourself to study if you know that it will come with a reward!

Test-Taking Strategies

1. Predicting the Answer

When you feel confident in your preparation for a multiple-choice test, try predicting the answer before reading the answer choices. This is especially useful on questions that test objective factual knowledge. By predicting the answer before reading the available choices, you eliminate the possibility that you will be distracted or led astray by an incorrect answer choice. You will feel more confident in your selection if you read the question, predict the answer, and then find your prediction among the answer choices. After using this strategy, be sure to still read all of the answer choices carefully and completely. If you feel unprepared, you should not attempt to predict the answers. This would be a waste of time and an opportunity for your mind to wander in the wrong direction.

2. Reading the Whole Question

Too often, test takers scan a multiple-choice question, recognize a few familiar words, and immediately jump to the answer choices. Test authors are aware of this common impatience, and they will sometimes prey upon it. For instance, a test author might subtly turn the question into a negative, or he or she might redirect the focus of the question right at the end. The only way to avoid falling into these traps is to read the entirety of the question carefully before reading the answer choices.

3. Looking for Wrong Answers

Long and complicated multiple-choice questions can be intimidating. One way to simplify a difficult multiple-choice question is to eliminate all of the answer choices that are clearly wrong. In most sets of answers, there will be at least one selection that can be dismissed right away. If the test is administered on paper, the test taker could draw a line through it to indicate that it may be ignored; otherwise, the test taker will have to perform this operation mentally or on scratch paper. In either case, once the obviously incorrect answers have been eliminated, the remaining choices may be considered. Sometimes identifying the clearly wrong answers will give the test taker some information about the correct answer. For instance, if one of the remaining answer choices is a direct opposite of one of the eliminated answer choices, it may well be the correct answer. The opposite of obviously wrong is obviously right! Of course, this is not always the case. Some answers are obviously incorrect simply because they are irrelevant to the question being asked. Still, identifying and eliminating some incorrect answer choices is a good way to simplify a multiple-choice question.

4. Don't Overanalyze

Anxious test takers often overanalyze questions. When you are nervous, your brain will often run wild, causing you to make associations and discover clues that don't actually exist. If you feel that this may be a problem for you, do whatever you can to slow down during the test. Try taking a deep breath or counting to ten. As you read and consider the question, restrict yourself to the particular words used by the author. Avoid thought tangents about what the author *really* meant, or what he or she was *trying* to say. The only things that matter on a multiple-choice test are the words that are actually in the question. You must avoid reading too much into a multiple-choice question, or supposing that the writer meant something other than what he or she wrote.

5. No Need for Panic

It is wise to learn as many strategies as possible before taking a multiple-choice test, but it is likely that you will come across a few questions for which you simply don't know the answer. In this situation, avoid panicking. Because most multiple-choice tests include dozens of questions, the relative value of a single wrong answer is small. As much as possible, you should compartmentalize each question on a multiple-choice test. In other words, you should not allow your feelings about one question to affect your success on the others. When you find a question that you either don't understand or don't know how to answer, just take a deep breath and do your best. Read the entire question slowly and carefully. Try rephrasing the question a couple of different ways. Then, read all of the answer choices carefully. After eliminating obviously wrong answers, make a selection and move on to the next question.

6. Confusing Answer Choices

When working on a difficult multiple-choice question, there may be a tendency to focus on the answer choices that are the easiest to understand. Many people, whether consciously or not, gravitate to the answer choices that require the least concentration, knowledge, and memory. This is a mistake. When you come across an answer choice that is confusing, you should give it extra attention. A question might be confusing because you do not know the subject matter to which it refers. If this is the case, don't eliminate the answer before you have affirmatively settled on another. When you come across an answer choice of this type, set it aside as you look at the remaining choices. If you can confidently assert that one of the other choices is correct, you can leave the confusing answer aside. Otherwise, you will need to take a moment to try to better understand the confusing answer choice. Rephrasing is one way to tease out the sense of a confusing answer choice.

7. Your First Instinct

Many people struggle with multiple-choice tests because they overthink the questions. If you have studied sufficiently for the test, you should be prepared to trust your first instinct once you have carefully and completely read the question and all of the answer choices. There is a great deal of research suggesting that the mind can come to the correct conclusion very quickly once it has obtained all of the relevant information. At times, it may seem to you as if your intuition is working faster even than your reasoning mind. This may in fact be true. The knowledge you obtain while studying may be retrieved from your subconscious before you have a chance to work out the associations that support it. Verify your instinct by working out the reasons that it should be trusted.

8. Key Words

Many test takers struggle with multiple-choice questions because they have poor reading comprehension skills. Quickly reading and understanding a multiple-choice question requires a mixture of skill and experience. To help with this, try jotting down a few key words and phrases on a piece of scrap paper. Doing this concentrates the process of reading and forces the mind to weigh the relative importance of the question's parts. In selecting words and phrases to write down, the test taker thinks about the question more deeply and carefully. This is especially true for multiple-choice questions that are preceded by a long prompt.

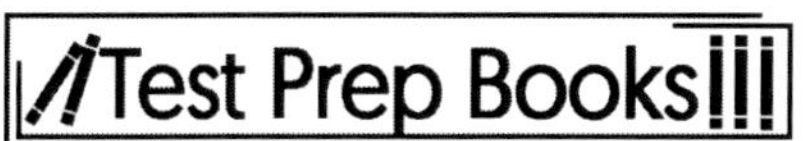

9. Subtle Negatives

One of the oldest tricks in the multiple-choice test writer's book is to subtly reverse the meaning of a question with a word like *not* or *except*. If you are not paying attention to each word in the question, you can easily be led astray by this trick. For instance, a common question format is, "Which of the following is...?" Obviously, if the question instead is, "Which of the following is not...?," then the answer will be quite different. Even worse, the test makers are aware of the potential for this mistake and will include one answer choice that would be correct if the question were not negated or reversed. A test taker who misses the reversal will find what he or she believes to be a correct answer and will be so confident that he or she will fail to reread the question and discover the original error. The only way to avoid this is to practice a wide variety of multiple-choice questions and to pay close attention to each and every word.

10. Reading Every Answer Choice

It may seem obvious, but you should always read every one of the answer choices! Too many test takers fall into the habit of scanning the question and assuming that they understand the question because they recognize a few key words. From there, they pick the first answer choice that answers the question they believe they have read. Test takers who read all of the answer choices might discover that one of the latter answer choices is actually *more* correct. Moreover, reading all of the answer choices can remind you of facts related to the question that can help you arrive at the correct answer. Sometimes, a misstatement or incorrect detail in one of the latter answer choices will trigger your memory of the subject and will enable you to find the right answer. Failing to read all of the answer choices is like not reading all of the items on a restaurant menu: you might miss out on the perfect choice.

11. Spot the Hedges

One of the keys to success on multiple-choice tests is paying close attention to every word. This is never truer than with words like *almost*, *most*, *some*, and *sometimes*. These words are called "hedges" because they indicate that a statement is not totally true or not true in every place and time. An absolute statement will contain no hedges, but in many subjects, the answers are not always straightforward or absolute. There are always exceptions to the rules in these subjects. For this reason, you should favor those multiple-choice questions that contain hedging language. The presence of qualifying words indicates that the author is taking special care with his or her words, which is certainly important when composing the right answer. After all, there are many ways to be wrong, but there is only one way to be right! For this reason, it is wise to avoid answers that are absolute when taking a multiple-choice test. An absolute answer is one that says things are either all one way or all another. They often include words like *every*, *always*, *best*, and *never*. If you are taking a multiple-choice test in a subject that doesn't lend itself to absolute answers, be on your guard if you see any of these words.

12. Long Answers

In many subject areas, the answers are not simple. As already mentioned, the right answer often requires hedges. Another common feature of the answers to a complex or subjective question are qualifying clauses, which are groups of words that subtly modify the meaning of the sentence. If the question or answer choice describes a rule to which there are exceptions or the subject matter is complicated, ambiguous, or confusing, the correct answer will require many words in order to be expressed clearly and accurately. In essence, you should not be deterred by answer choices that seem excessively long. Oftentimes, the author of the text will not be able to write the correct answer without offering some qualifications and modifications. Your job is to read the answer choices thoroughly and completely and to select the one that most accurately and precisely answers the question.

13. Restating to Understand

Sometimes, a question on a multiple-choice test is difficult not because of what it asks but because of how it is written. If this is the case, restate the question or answer choice in different words. This process serves a couple of important purposes. First, it forces you to concentrate on the core of the question. In order to rephrase the question accurately, you have to understand it well. Rephrasing the question will concentrate your mind on the key words and ideas. Second, it will present the information to your mind in a fresh way. This process may trigger your memory and render some useful scrap of information picked up while studying.

14. True Statements

Sometimes an answer choice will be true in itself, but it does not answer the question. This is one of the main reasons why it is essential to read the question carefully and completely before proceeding to the answer choices. Too often, test takers skip ahead to the answer choices and look for true statements. Having found one of these, they are content to select it without reference to the question above. The savvy test taker will always read the entire question before turning to the answer choices. Then, having settled on a correct answer choice, he or she will refer to the original question and ensure that the selected answer is relevant. The mistake of choosing a correct-but-irrelevant answer choice is especially common on questions related to specific pieces of objective knowledge.

15. No Patterns

One of the more dangerous ideas that circulates about multiple-choice tests is that the correct answers tend to fall into patterns. These erroneous ideas range from a belief that B and C are the most common right answers, to the idea that an unprepared test-taker should answer "A-B-A-C-A-D-A-B-A." It cannot be emphasized enough that pattern-seeking of this type is exactly the WRONG way to approach a multiple-choice test. To begin with, it is highly unlikely that the test maker will plot the correct answers according to some predetermined pattern. The questions are scrambled and delivered in a random order. Furthermore, even if the test maker was following a pattern in the assignation of correct answers, there is no reason why the test taker would know which pattern he or she was using. Any attempt to discern a pattern in the answer choices is a waste of time and a distraction from the real work of taking the test. A test taker would be much better served by extra preparation before the test than by reliance on a pattern in the answers.

Bonus Content

We host multiple bonus items online, including all seven practice tests in digital format. Scan the QR code or go to this link to access this content:

testprepbooks.com/bonus/sat

The first time you access the tests, you will need to register as a "new user" and verify your email address.

If you have any issues, please email support@testprepbooks.com.

Introduction to the SAT

Function of the Test

The SAT is a standardized test taken by high school students across the United States and internationally for college placement, designed by the College Board, a not-for-profit organization that owns and publishes the SAT. The test is designed to assess a student's aptitude with reading, writing, and math skills. The SAT also serves as a qualifying measure to identify students for college scholarships, depending on the college being applied to. All colleges in the US accept the SAT and, in addition to admissions and scholarships, use SAT scores for course placement as well as academic counseling.

Most of the high school students who take the SAT each year are seniors. In 2023, the number of students who took the SAT was over 1.9 million. That same year, approximately 40 percent of students met the College Board's "college and career readiness" benchmark in both major categories of the test.

Test Administration

The SAT is offered on seven days throughout the year at schools throughout the United States and internationally. There are thousands of testing centers worldwide. Test takers can view the test centers in their area when they register for the test, or they can view testing locations at the College Board website.

The SAT is entirely digital, administered through the Bluebook testing application. If test takers do not have access to an appropriate device, the College Board has a SAT device lending program to ensure access.

Beginning August 24, 2024, the SAT registration fee is $68, although a fee waiver is available to eligible test takers. Also note that students outside the US may have to pay an extra processing fee. Possible additional fees include a test center fee, cancel fee, late registration fee, or a fee for additional score reports.

Test Format

The SAT gauges a student's proficiency in two areas. The **Reading and Writing** section measures English reading comprehension and use of language. The **Math** section measures fluency in mathematical problem solving, conceptual understanding of equations, and real-world applications of content. Each overall section is divided into two modules, each of which includes half of the section's the total questions.

The digital SAT tailors itself to the test taker's level of aptitude. After the first module of each section (Reading and Writing or Math), the second module will be adjusted to include questions which will be more or less difficult, based on the test taker's performance in the first module.

The SAT contains 98 questions, most of which are multiple-choice, with each module comprising over 20 questions. Each module is allotted just over half an hour, with a total test length of two hours and fourteen minutes. The current SAT is shorter than previous versions, both in terms of time allotted and the number of questions. One effect of this is that test takers will have more time to answer each question, allowing for more thoughtful answers.

Section	**Time (In Minutes)**	**Number of Questions**
Reading and Writing: Module 1	32	27
Writing and Language: Module 2	32	27
Math: Module 1	35	22
Math: Module 2	35	22
Total	**134**	**98**

Scoring

SAT test scores are released two to four weeks after the test is taken. Scores are based on a scale from 400 to 1600, which combines a range from 200 to 800 for Reading and Writing and 200 to 800 for Math. The SAT does not penalize for incorrect answers. On the College Board website, there are indicators to determine what the "college and career readiness" benchmark scores are. The College and Career Readiness benchmark for the Reading and Writing section is a score of 480 or higher, while the Math section has a benchmark score of 530 or higher.

Study Prep Plan for the SAT

1 **Schedule** - Use one of our study schedules below or come up with one of your own.

2 **Relax** - Test anxiety can hurt even the best students. There are many ways to reduce stress. Find the one that works best for you.

3 **Execute** - Once you have a good plan in place, be sure to stick to it.

One Week Study Schedule

Day 1	Reading
Day 2	Writing and Language
Day 3	Mathematics
Day 4	Additional Topics in Math
Day 5	SAT Practice Tests #1, #2, & #3
Day 6	SAT Practice Tests #4, #5, #6, & #7
Day 7	Take Your Exam!

Two Week Study Schedule

Day 1	Reading	Day 8	SAT Practice Test #2
Day 2	Writing and Language	Day 9	SAT Practice Test #3
Day 3	Capitalization Rules	Day 10	SAT Practice Test #4
Day 4	Problem Solving and Data Analysis	Day 11	SAT Practice Test #5
Day 5	Passport to Advanced Math	Day 12	SAT Practice Test #6
Day 6	Additional Topics in Math	Day 13	SAT Practice Test #7
Day 7	SAT Practice Test #1	Day 14	Take Your Exam!

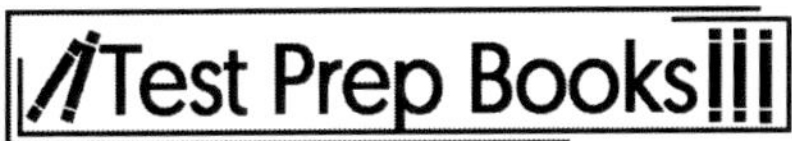

One Month Study Schedule

Day 1	Reading	Day 11	Creating Equivalent Forms of Expressions	Day 21	Answer Explanations #3
Day 2	Words in Context	Day 12	Rewriting Simple Rational Expressions	Day 22	SAT Practice Test #4
Day 3	Interpreting Data and Considering Implications	Day 13	Additional Topics in Math	Day 23	Answer Explanations #4
Day 4	Writing and Language	Day 14	Congruence and Similarity	Day 24	SAT Practice Test #5
Day 5	Standard English Conventions	Day 15	Essay	Day 25	Answer Explanations #5
Day 6	Capitalization Rules	Day 16	SAT Practice Test #1	Day 26	SAT Practice Test #6
Day 7	Sentence Fragments	Day 17	Answer Explanations #1	Day 27	Answer Explanations #6
Day 8	Mathematics	Day 18	SAT Practice Test #2	Day 28	SAT Practice Test #7
Day 9	Problem Solving and Data Analysis	Day 19	Answer Explanations #2	Day 29	Answer Explanations #7
Day 10	Comparing Linear and Exponential Growth	Day 20	SAT Practice Test #3	Day 30	Take Your Exam!

Build your own prep plan by visiting:
testprepbooks.com/prep

Math Reference Sheet

Symbol	Phrase
+	added to, increased by, sum of, more than
-	decreased by, difference between, less than, take away
×	multiplied by, 3 (4, 5 . . .) times as large, product of
÷	divided by, quotient of, half (third, etc.) of
=	is, the same as, results in, as much as
x, *t*, *n*, etc.	a variable which is an unknown value or quantity
<	is under, is below, smaller than, beneath
>	is above, is over, bigger than, exceeds
≤	no more than, at most, maximum; less than or equal to
≥	no less than, at least, minimum; greater than or equal to
√	square root of, exponent divided by 2

Geometry	Description
$P = 2l + 2w$	for perimeter of a rectangle
$P = 4 \times s$	for perimeter of a square
$P = a + b + c$	for perimeter of a triangle
$A = \frac{1}{2} \times b \times h = \frac{bh}{2}$	for area of a triangle
$A = b \times h$	for area of a parallelogram
$A = \frac{1}{2} \times h(b_1 + b_2)$	for area of a trapezoid
$A = \frac{1}{2} \times a \times P$	for area of a regular polygon
$C = 2 \times \pi \times r$	for circumference (perimeter) of a circle
$A = \pi \times r^2$	for area of a circle
$c^2 = a^2 + b^2; c = \sqrt{a^2 + b^2}$	for finding the hypotenuse of a right triangle
$SA = 2xy + 2yz + 2xz$	for finding surface area
$V = \frac{1}{3}xyh$	for finding volume of a rectangular pyramid
$V = \frac{4}{3}\pi r^3;\ \frac{1}{3}\pi r^2 h;\ \pi r^2 h$	for volume of a sphere; a cone; and a cylinder

Radical Expressions	Description
$\sqrt[n]{a} = a^{\frac{1}{n}}, \sqrt[n]{a^m} = (\sqrt[n]{a})^m = a^{\frac{m}{n}}$	*a* is the radicand, *n* is the index, *m* is the exponent
$\sqrt{x^2} = (x^2)^{\frac{1}{2}} = x$	to convert square root to exponent
$a^m \times a^n = a^{m+n}$	multiplying radicands with exponents
$(a^m)^n = a^{m \times n}$	multiplying exponents
$(a \times b)^m = a^m \times b^m$	parentheses with exponents

Property	Addition	Multiplication
Commutative	$a + b = b + a$	$a \times b = b \times a$
Associative	$(a + b) + c = a + (b + c)$	$(a \times b) \times c = a \times (b \times c)$
Identity	$a + 0 = a;\ 0 + a = a$	$a \times 1 = a;\ 1 \times a = a$
Inverse	$a + (-a) = 0$	$a \times \frac{1}{a} = 1;\ a \neq 0$
Distributive	$a(b + c) = ab + ac$	

Data	Description
Mean	equal to the total of the values of a data set, divided by the number of elements in the data set
Median	middle value in an odd number of ordered values of a data set, or the mean of the two middle values in an even number of ordered values in a data set
Mode	the value that appears most often
Range	the difference between the highest and the lowest values in the set

Graphing	Description
(x, y)	ordered pair, plot points in a graph
$y = mx + b$	slope-intercept form; *m* represents the slope of the line and *b* represents the *y*-intercept
$f(x)$	read as *f* of *x*, which means it is a function of *x*
(x_2, y_2) and (x_2, y_2)	two ordered pairs used to determine the slope of a line
$m = \frac{y_2 - y_1}{x_2 - x_1}$	to find the slope of the line, *m*, for ordered pairs
$Ax + By = C$	standard form of an equation, also for solving a system of equations through the elimination method
$M = (\frac{x_1 + x_2}{2}, \frac{y_1 + y_2}{2})$	for finding the midpoint of an ordered pair
$y = ax^2 + bx + c$	quadratic function for a parabola
$y = a(x - h)^2 + k$	quadratic function for a parabola with vertex
$y = ab^x; y = a \times b^x$	function for exponential curve
$y = ax^2 + bx + c$	standard form of a quadratic function
$x = \frac{-b}{2a}$	for finding axis of symmetry in a parabola; given quadratic formula in standard form
$f = \sqrt{\frac{\Sigma(x - \bar{x})^2}{n - 1}}$	function for standard deviation of the sample; where $\bar{x}$ = sample mean and *n* = sample size

Proportions and Percentage	Description
$\frac{\text{gallons}}{\text{cost}} = \frac{\text{gallons}}{\text{cost}} : \frac{7 \text{ gallons}}{\$14.70} = \frac{x}{\$20}$	written as equal ratios with a variable representing the missing quantity
$\frac{y_1}{x_1} = \frac{y_2}{x_2}$	for direct proportions
$(y_1)(x_1) = (y_2)(x_2)$	for indirect proportions
$\frac{\text{change}}{\text{original value}} \times 100 = \text{percent change}$	for finding percentage change in value
$\frac{\text{new quantity} - \text{old quantity}}{\text{old quantity}} \times 100$	for calculating the increase or decrease in percentage

Reading and Writing

The Reading and Writing section of the SAT measures test takers' mastery of the English language. Some questions assess the test taker's the ability to read, understand, and interpret the types of texts they will encounter in higher education and their vocational pursuits; some questions are designed to assess the test taker's command of standard conventions of English language and their ability to edit errors appropriately. The Reading and Writing section contains 54 questions, which are divided into two modules of 27 questions each. The questions in each module must be answered in the allotted 32 minutes (64 minutes total).

Some of the brief passages included in this section are drawn from previously published literary or informational texts. Some passages include graphics such as charts, graphs, and tables, which the test taker must interpret alongside the written text to correctly answer the questions. Other questions will follow two passages that are paired for the test taker to compare and contrast. All of the information needed to answer the questions is provided within the passages, and test takers do not need to have prior knowledge of the passages' content to obtain the correct answers.

In addition to encountering a variety of topics in the passages, test takers will need to employ their comprehension skills pertaining to understanding texts written for different purposes. Some texts may tell a story or describe a process. Others will present an argument and support for an opinion, while still other passages may delineate the purpose of a study or experiment. The text complexity or reading level of each passage also varies; passages may span the gamut from a ninth-grade reading level to that expected of a first-year university student or post-secondary scholar.

Each question in the Reading and Writing section will fall into one of four principal categories: craft and structure, information and ideas, standard English conventions, and expression of Ideas. **Craft and Structure** looks at comprehension and vocabulary, and it may include paired texts that require the test taker to make cross-text connections. As the name implies, **Information and Ideas** questions focus on the direct or indirect ideas or facts that the passage presents. The answers to some of these questions will not necessarily be explicitly revealed in the passage; rather, test takers must use their inferential skills to uncover the author's implied meaning. **Standard English Conventions** questions address one's skill in identifying the best choice for sentence structure, word usage, grammar, and punctuation. For the **Expression of Ideas** questions, test takers will select answers that improve a text's organization, topic development, and the effectiveness of the language used. The scope of these questions assesses one's understanding of text structure and organization, ability to analyze evidence and arguments and strengthen them with designated improvements, and use transition words and phrases effectively.

While the vast majority of questions in the Reading and Writing section address the test taker's ability to understand written language and ideas, a small number of questions will also assess the test taker's ability to interpret graphs, tables, and charts. For this reason, in addition to studying reading comprehension techniques and honing skills related to synthesis and inference, test takers should practice reading and interpreting tables, graphs, and charts.

Craft and Structure

Words in Context

In order to successfully complete the Reading and Writing section of the SAT, the test taker should be able to identify the meaning of words in context. This involves a set of skills that requires the test taker to answer questions about unfamiliar words within a particular text passage. Additionally, the test taker may be asked to answer critical thinking questions based on unfamiliar word meanings. Identifying the meaning of different words in context is very much like solving a puzzle. By using a variety of techniques, a test taker should be able to correctly identify the meaning of unfamiliar words and concepts with ease.

Using Context Clues

A context clue is a hint that an author provides to the reader in order to help define difficult or unique words. When reading a passage, a test taker should take note of any unfamiliar words, and then examine the sentence around them to look for clues to the word meanings. Let's look at an example:

> He faced a *conundrum* in making this decision. He felt as if he had come to a crossroads. This was truly a puzzle, and what he did next would determine the course of his future.

The word *conundrum* may be unfamiliar to the reader. By looking at context clues, the reader should be able to determine its meaning. In this passage, context clues include the idea of making a decision and of being unsure. Furthermore, the author restates the definition of conundrum in using the word *puzzle* as a synonym. Therefore, the reader should be able to determine that the definition of the word *conundrum* is a difficult puzzle.

Similarly, a reader can determine difficult vocabulary by identifying antonyms. Let's look at an example:

> Her *gregarious* nature was completely opposite of her twin's, who was shy, retiring, and socially nervous.

The word *gregarious* may be unfamiliar. However, by looking at the surrounding context clues, the reader can determine that *gregarious* does not mean shy. The twins' personalities are being contrasted. Therefore, *gregarious* must mean sociable, or something similar to it.

At times, an author will provide contextual clues through a cause and effect relationship. Look at the next sentence as an example:

> The athletes were *elated* when they won the tournament; unfortunately, their off-court antics caused them to forfeit the win.

The word *elated* may be unfamiliar to the reader. However, the author defines the word by presenting a cause and effect relationship. The athletes were so elated at the win that their behavior went overboard, and they had to forfeit. In this instance, *elated* must mean something akin to overjoyed, happy, and overexcited.

Cause and effect is one technique authors use to demonstrate relationships. A **cause** is why something happens. The **effect** is what happens as a result. For example, a reader may encounter text such as *Because he was unable to sleep, he was often restless and irritable during the day.* The cause is insomnia due to lack of sleep. The effect is being restless and irritable. When reading for a cause and effect relationship, look for words such as *if, then, such,* and *because*. By using cause and effect, an author can describe direct relationships, and convey an overall theme, particularly when taking a stance on their topic.

An author can also provide contextual clues through **comparison and contrast**. Let's look at an example:

> Her *torpid* state caused her parents, and her physician, to worry about her seemingly sluggish well-being.

The word *torpid* is probably unfamiliar to the reader. However, the author has compared *torpid* to a state of being and, moreover, one that's worrisome. Therefore, the reader should be able to determine that *torpid* is not a positive, healthy state of being. In fact, through the use of comparison, it means sluggish. Similarly, an author may contrast an unfamiliar word with an idea. In the sentence *Her torpid state was completely opposite of her usual, bubbly self,* the meaning of *torpid*, or sluggish, is contrasted with the words *bubbly self*.

A test taker should be able to critically assess and determine unfamiliar word meanings through the use of an author's context clues in order to fully comprehend difficult text passages.

Relating Unfamiliar Words to Familiar Words

The Reading section of the SAT will test a reader's ability to use context clues, and then relate unfamiliar words to more familiar ones. Using the word *torpid* as an example, the test may ask the test taker to relate the meaning of the word to a list of vocabulary options and choose the more familiar word as closest in meaning. In this case, the test may say something like the following:

> Which of the following words means the same as the word *torpid* in the above passage?

Then they will provide the test taker with a list of familiar options such as happy, disgruntled, sluggish, and animated. By using context clues, the reader has already determined the meaning of *torpid* as slow or sluggish, so the reader should be able to correctly identify the word *sluggish* as the correct answer.

One effective way to relate unfamiliar word meanings to more familiar ones is to substitute the provided word in each answer option for the unfamiliar word in question. Although this will not always lead to a correct answer every time, this strategy will help the test taker narrow answer options. Be careful when utilizing this strategy. Pay close attention to the meaning of sentences and answer choices because it's easy to mistake answer choices as correct when they are easily substituted, especially when they are the same part of speech. Does the sentence mean the same thing with the substituted word option in place or does it change entirely? Does the substituted word make sense? Does it possibly mean the same as the unfamiliar word in question?

How an Author's Word Choice Shapes Meaning, Style, and Tone

Authors choose their words carefully in order to artfully depict meaning, style, and tone, which is most commonly inferred through the use of adjectives and verbs. The **tone** is the predominant emotion present in the text, and represents the attitude or feelings that an author has towards a character or event.

To review, an **adjective** is a word used to describe something, and usually precedes the noun, a person, place, or object. A **verb** is a word describing an action. For example, the sentence "The scary woodpecker ate the spider" includes the adjective "scary," the noun "woodpecker," and the verb "ate." Reading this sentence may rouse some negative feelings, as the word "scary" carries a negative charge. The **charge** is the emotional connotation that can be derived from the adjectives and verbs and is either positive or negative. Recognizing the charge of a particular sentence or passage is an effective way to understand the meaning and tone the author is trying to convey.

Many authors have conflicting charges within the same text, but a definitive tone can be inferred by understanding the meaning of the charges relative to each other. It's important to recognize key conjunctions, or words that link sentences or clauses together. There are several types and subtypes of conjunctions. Three are most important for reading comprehension:

1. **Cumulative conjunctions** add one statement to another.
   Examples: and, both, also, as well as, not only
   e.g. The juice is sweet *and* sour.
2. **Adversative conjunctions** are used to contrast two clauses.
   Examples: but, while, still, yet, nevertheless
   e.g. She was tired, *but* she was happy.
3. **Alternative conjunctions** express two alternatives.
   Examples: or, either, neither, nor, else, otherwise
   e.g. He must eat, *or* he will die.

Identifying the meaning and tone of a text can be accomplished with the following steps:

- Identify the adjectives and verbs.
- Recognize any important conjunctions.
- Label the adjectives and verbs as positive or negative.
- Understand what the charge means about the text.

To demonstrate these steps, examine the following passage from the classic children's poem, "The Sheep":

> Lazy sheep, pray tell me why
>
> In the pleasant fields you lie,
>
> Eating grass, and daisies white,
>
> From the morning till the night?
>
> Everything can something do,
>
> But what kind of use are you?

–Taylor, Jane and Ann. "The Sheep."

This selection is a good example of conflicting charges that work together to express an overall tone. Following the first two steps, identify the adjectives, verbs, and conjunctions within the passage. For this example, the adjectives are <u>underlined</u>, the verbs are in **bold**, and the conjunctions *italicized*:

> <u>Lazy</u> sheep, pray **tell** me why
>
> In the <u>pleasant</u> fields you **lie**,
>
> **Eating** grass, and daisies <u>white,</u>
>
> From the morning till the night?
>
> Everything can something do,
>
> *But* what kind of use are you?

For step three, read the passage and judge whether feelings of positivity or negativity arose. Then assign a charge to each of the words that were outlined. This can be done in a table format, or simply by writing a + or – next to the word.

The word <u>lazy</u> carries a negative connotation; it usually denotes somebody unwilling to work. To **tell** someone something has an exclusively neutral connotation, as it depends on what's being told, which has not yet been revealed at this point, so a charge can be assigned later. The word <u>pleasant</u> is an inherently positive word. To **lie** could be positive or negative depending on the context, but as the subject (the sheep) is lying in a pleasant field, then this is a positive experience. **Eating** is also generally positive.

After labeling the charges for each word, it might be inferred that the tone of this poem is happy and maybe even admiring or innocuously envious. However, notice the adversative conjunction, "but" and what follows. The author has listed all the pleasant things this sheep gets to do all day, but the tone changes when the author asks, "What kind of use are you?" Asking someone to prove their value is a rather hurtful thing to do, as it implies that the

person asking the question doesn't believe the subject has any value, so this could be listed under negative charges. Referring back to the verb **tell**, after reading the whole passage, it can be deduced that the author is asking the sheep to tell what use the sheep is, so this has a negative charge.

+	−
Pleasant • Lie in fields • From morning to night	• Lazy • Tell me • What kind of use are you

Upon examining the charges, it might seem like there's an even amount of positive and negative emotion in this selection, and that's where the conjunction "but" becomes crucial to identifying the tone. The conjunction "but" indicates there's a contrasting view to the pleasantness of the sheep's daily life, and this view is that the sheep is lazy and useless, which is also indicated by the first line, "lazy sheep, pray tell me why."

It might be helpful to look at questions pertaining to tone. For this selection, consider the following question:

The author of the poem regards the sheep with a feeling of what?

a. Respect
b. Disgust
c. Apprehension
d. Intrigue

Considering the author views the sheep as lazy with nothing to offer, Choice *A* appears to reflect the opposite of what the author is feeling.

Choice *B* seems to mirror the author's feelings towards the sheep, as laziness is considered a disreputable trait, and people (or personified animals, in this case) with unfavorable traits might be viewed with disgust.

Choice *C* doesn't make sense within context, as laziness isn't usually feared.

Choice *D* is tricky, as it may be tempting to argue that the author is intrigued with the sheep because they ask, "pray tell me why." This is another out-of-scope answer choice as it doesn't *quite* describe the feelings the author experiences and there's also a much better fit in Choice *B.*

Reading for Tone, Message, and Effect

The SAT does not just address a test taker's ability to find facts within a historical reading passage; it also evaluates a reader's ability to determine an author's viewpoint through the use of tone, message, and overall effect. This type of reading comprehension requires inference skills, deductive reasoning skills, the ability to draw logical conclusions, and overall critical thinking skills. Reading for factual information is straightforward. Reading for an author's tone, message, and overall effect is not. It's key to read carefully when asked test questions that address a test taker's ability to identify and analyze these writing devices. These are not questions that can be easily answered by quickly scanning for the right information.

Tone

An author's **tone** is the use of particular words, phrases, and writing style to convey an overall meaning. Tone expresses the author's attitude towards a particular topic. For example, a historical reading passage may begin like the following:

> The presidential election of 1960 ushered in a new era, a new Camelot, a new phase of forward thinking in US politics that embraced brash action and unrest and responded with admirable leadership.

From this opening statement, a reader can draw some conclusions about the author's attitude towards President John F. Kennedy. Furthermore, the reader can make additional, educated guesses about the state of the Union during the 1960 presidential election. By close reading, the test taker can determine that the repeated use of the word *new* and words such as *admirable leadership* indicate the author's tone of admiration regarding the President Kennedy's boldness. In addition, the author assesses that the era during President Kennedy's administration was problematic through the use of the words *brash action* and *unrest.* Therefore, if a test taker encountered a test question asking about the author's use of tone and their assessment of the Kennedy administration, the test taker should be able to identify an answer indicating admiration. Similarly, if asked about the state of the Union during the 1960s, a test taker should be able to correctly identify an answer indicating political unrest.

When identifying an author's tone, the following list of words may be helpful. This is not an inclusive list. Generally, parts of speech that indicate attitude will also indicate tone:

- Comical
- Angry
- Ambivalent
- Scary
- Lyrical
- Matter-of-fact
- Judgmental
- Sarcastic
- Malicious
- Objective
- Pessimistic
- Patronizing
- Gloomy
- Instructional
- Satirical
- Formal
- Casual

Message

An author's **message** is the same as the overall meaning of a passage. It is the main idea, or the main concept the author wishes to convey. An author's message may be stated outright, or it may be implied. Regardless, the test taker will need to use careful reading skills to identify an author's message or purpose.

Often, the message of a particular passage can be determined by thinking about why the author wrote the information. Many historical passages are written to inform and to teach readers established, factual information. However, many historical works are also written to convey biased ideas to readers. Gleaning bias from an author's message in a historical passage can be difficult, especially if the reader is presented with a variety of established facts as well. Readers tend to accept historical writing as factual. This is not always the case. Any discerning reader

who has tackled historical information on topics such as United States political party agendas can attest that two or more works on the same topic may have completely different messages supporting or refuting the value of the identical policies.

Therefore, it is important to critically assess an author's message separate from factual information. One author, for example, may point to the rise of unorthodox political candidates in an election year based on the failures of the political party in office while another may point to the rise of the same candidates in the same election year based on the current party's successes. The historical facts of what has occurred leading up to an election year are not in refute. Labeling those facts as a failure or a success is a bias within an author's overall *message*, as is excluding factual information in order to further a particular point. In a standardized testing situation, a reader must be able to critically assess what the author is trying to say separate from the historical facts that surround their message.

Using the example of Lincoln's Gettysburg Address, a test question may ask the following:

> What message is the speaker trying to convey through this address?

Then they will ask the test taker to select an answer that best expresses Lincoln's message to his audience. Based on the options given, a test taker should be able to select the answer expressing the idea that Lincoln's audience should recognize the efforts of those who died in the war as a sacrifice to preserving human equality and self-government.

Effect

An author may want to challenge a reader's intellect, inspire imagination, or spur emotion. An author may present information to appeal to a physical, aesthetic, or transformational sense. Take the following text as an example:

> In 1963, Martin Luther King stated "I have a dream." The gathering at the Lincoln Memorial was the beginning of the Civil Rights movement and, with its reference to the Emancipation Proclamation, Dr. King's words electrified those who wanted freedom and equality while rising from hatred and slavery. It was the beginning of radical change.

The test taker may be asked about the effect this statement might have on King's audience. Through careful reading of the passage, the test taker should be able to choose an answer that best identifies an effect of grabbing the audience's attention. The historical facts are in place: King made the speech in 1963 at the Lincoln Memorial, kicked off the civil rights movement, and referenced the Emancipation Proclamation. The words *electrified* and *radical change* indicate the effect the author wants the reader to understand as a result of King's speech. In this historical passage, facts are facts. However, the author's message goes beyond the facts to indicate the effect the message had on the audience and, in addition, the effect the event should have on the reader.

When reading historical passages, the test taker should perform due diligence in their awareness of the test questions and answers up front. From there, the test taker should carefully, and critically, read all historical excerpts with an eye for detail, tone, message (biased or unbiased), and effect. Being able to synthesize these skills will result in success in a standardized testing situation.

Standardized test questions that ask for factual information are usually straightforward. These types of questions will either ask the test taker to confirm a fact by choosing a correct answer, or to select a correct answer based on a negative fact question.

For example, the test taker may encounter a passage from Lincoln's Gettysburg Address. A corresponding test question may ask the following:

> Which war is Abraham Lincoln referring to in the following sentence?
>
> > Now we are engaged in a great civil war, testing whether that nation, or any nation so conceived and so dedicated, can long endure.

This type of question is asking the test taker to confirm a simple fact. Given options such as World War I, the War of Spanish Succession, World War II, and the American Civil War, the test taker should be able to correctly identify the American Civil War based on the words "civil war" within the passage itself, and, hopefully, through general knowledge. In this case, reading the test question and scanning answer options ahead of reading the Gettysburg Address would help quickly identify the correct answer. Similarly, a test taker may be asked to confirm a fact based on a negative fact question. For example, a passage's corresponding test question may ask the following:

> Which option is FALSE based on the above passage?

Given a variety of choices speaking about which war Abraham Lincoln was addressing, the test taker would need to eliminate all correct answers pertaining to the American Civil War and choose the answer choice referencing a different war. In other words, the correct answer is the one that contradicts the information in the passage.

It is important to remember that reading for factual information is straightforward. The test taker must distinguish fact from bias. **Factual statements** can be proven or disproven independent of the author and from a variety of other sources. Remember, successfully answering questions regarding factual information may require the test taker to re-read the passage, as these types of questions test for attention to detail.

Information and Ideas

Command of Evidence

Command of evidence, or the ability to use contextual clues, factual statements, and corroborative phrases to support an author's message or intent, is an important part of the Information and Ideas section of the SAT. A test taker's ability to parse out factual information and draw conclusions based on evidence is important to critical reading comprehension. The test will ask students to read text passages, and then answer questions based on information contained in them. These types of questions may ask test takers to identify stated facts. They may also require test takers to draw logical conclusions, identify data based on graphs, make inferences, and to generally display analytical thinking skills.

Finding Evidence in a Passage

The basic tenet of reading comprehension is the ability to read and understand a text. One way to understand a text is to look for information that supports the author's main idea, topic, or position statement. This information may be factual, or it may be based on the author's opinion. This section will focus on the test taker's ability to identify factual information, as opposed to opinionated bias. The test will ask test takers to read passages containing factual information, and then logically relate those passages by drawing conclusions based on evidence.

In order to identify factual information within a text passage, test takers should begin by looking for statements of fact. **Factual statements** can be either true or false. Identifying factual statements as opposed to opinion statements is important in demonstrating full command of evidence in reading. For example, the statement *The temperature outside was unbearably hot* may seem like a fact; however, it's not. While anyone can point to a temperature gauge as factual evidence, the statement itself reflects only an opinion. Some people may find the

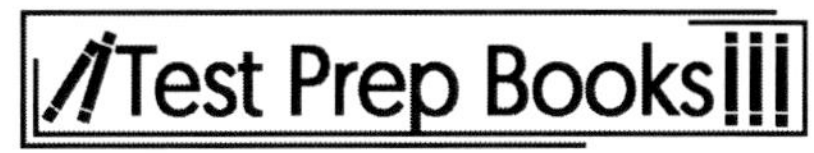

temperature unbearably hot. Others may find it comfortably warm. Thus, the sentence, *The temperature outside was unbearably hot,* reflects the opinion of the author who found it unbearable. If the text passage followed up the sentence with atmospheric conditions indicating heat indices above 140 degrees Fahrenheit, then the reader knows there is factual information that supports the author's assertion of *unbearably hot*.

In looking for information that can be proven or disproven, it's helpful to scan for dates, numbers, timelines, equations, statistics, and other similar data within any given text passage. These types of indicators will point to proven particulars. For example, the statement, *The temperature outside was unbearably hot on that summer day, July 10, 1913,* most likely indicates factual information, even if the reader is unaware that this is the hottest day on record in the United States. Be careful when reading biased words from an author. Biased words indicate opinion, as opposed to fact. The following list contains a sampling of common biased words:

Remember, most of what is written is actually opinion or carefully worded information that seems like fact when it isn't. To say, *duplicating DNA results is not cost-effective* sounds like it could be a scientific fact, but it isn't. Factual information can be verified through independent sources.

The simplest type of test question may provide a text passage, then ask the test taker to distinguish the correct factual supporting statement that best answers the corresponding question on the test. However, be aware that some questions may ask the test taker to identify which answer choice best supports an author's topic. While the ability to identify factual information is critical, these types of questions require the test taker to identify chunks of details, and then relate them to one another.

Displaying Analytical Thinking Skills

Analytical thinking involves being able to break down visual information into manageable portions in order to solve complex problems or process difficult concepts. This skill encompasses all aspects of command of evidence in reading comprehension.

A reader can approach analytical thinking in a series of steps. First, when approaching visual material, a reader should identify an author's thought process. Is the line of reasoning clear from the presented passage, or does it require inference and coming to a conclusion independent of the author? Next, a reader should evaluate the author's line of reasoning to determine if the logic is sound. Look for evidentiary clues and cited sources. Do these hold up under the author's argument? Third, look for bias. Bias includes generalized, emotional statements that will not hold up under scrutiny, as they are not based on fact. From there, a reader should ask if the presented evidence is trustworthy. Are the facts cited from reliable sources? Are they current? Is there any new factual information that has come to light since the passage was written that renders the argument useless? Next, a reader should carefully think about information that opposes the author's view. Do the author's arguments guide the reader to identical thoughts, or is there room for sound arguments? Finally, a reader should always be able to identify an author's conclusion and be able to weigh its effectiveness.

The ability to display analytical thinking skills while reading is key in any standardized testing situation. Test takers should be able to critically evaluate the information provided, and then answer questions related to content by using the steps above.

Making Inferences

Simply put, an **inference** is an educated guess drawn from evidence, logic, and reasoning. The key to making inferences is identifying clues within a passage, and then using common sense to arrive at a reasonable conclusion. Consider it "reading between the lines."

One way to make an inference is to look for main topics. When doing so, pay particular attention to any titles, headlines, or opening statements made by the author. Topic sentences or repetitive ideas can be clues in gleaning inferred ideas. For example, if a passage contains the phrase *While some consider DNA testing to be infallible, it is an inherently flawed technique,* the test taker can infer the rest of the passage will contain information that points to problems with DNA testing.

The test taker may be asked to make an inference based on prior knowledge but may also be asked to make predictions based on new ideas. For example, the test taker may have no prior knowledge of DNA other than its genetic property to replicate. However, if the reader is given passages on the flaws of DNA testing with enough factual evidence, the test taker may arrive at the inferred conclusion that the author does not support the infallibility of DNA testing in all identification cases.

When making inferences, it is important to remember that the critical thinking process involved must be fluid and open to change. While a reader may infer an idea from a main topic, general statement, or other clues, they must be open to receiving new information within a particular passage. New ideas presented by an author may require the test taker to alter an inference. Similarly, when asked questions that require making an inference, it's important to read the entire test passage and all of the answer options. Often, a test taker will need to refine a general inference based on new ideas that may be presented within the test itself.

Author's Use of Evidence to Support Claims

Authors utilize a wide range of techniques to tell a story or communicate information. Readers should be familiar with the most common of these techniques. Techniques of writing are also commonly known as rhetorical devices, and they are some of the evidence that authors use to support claims.

In nonfiction writing, authors employ argumentative techniques to present their opinion to readers in the most convincing way. Persuasive writing usually includes at least one type of appeal: an appeal to logic (**logos**), emotion (**pathos**), or credibility and trustworthiness (**ethos**). When a writer appeals to logic, they are asking readers to agree with them based on research, evidence, and an established line of reasoning. An author's argument might also appeal to readers' emotions, perhaps by including personal stories and **anecdotes** (a short narrative of a specific event). A final type of appeal, appeal to authority, asks the reader to agree with the author's argument on the basis of their expertise or credentials. Consider three different approaches to arguing the same opinion:

Logic (Logos)

Below is an example of an appeal to logic. The author uses evidence to disprove the logic of the school's rule (the rule was supposed to reduce discipline problems, but the number of problems has not been reduced; therefore, the rule is not working) and call for its repeal.

> Our school should abolish its current ban on cell phone use on campus. This rule was adopted last year as an attempt to reduce class disruptions and help students focus more on their lessons. However, since the rule was enacted, there has been no change in the number of disciplinary problems in class. Therefore, the rule is ineffective and should be done away with.

Emotion (Pathos)

An author's argument might also appeal to readers' emotions, perhaps by including personal stories and anecdotes.

The next example presents an appeal to emotion. By sharing the personal anecdote of one student and speaking about emotional topics like family relationships, the author invokes the reader's empathy in asking them to reconsider the school rule.

> Our school should abolish its current ban on cell phone use on campus. If they aren't able to use their phones during the school day, many students feel isolated from their loved ones. For example, last semester, one student's grandmother had a heart attack in the morning. However, because he couldn't use

his cell phone, the student didn't know about his grandmother's accident until the end of the day—when she had already passed away, and it was too late to say goodbye. By preventing students from contacting their friends and family, our school is placing undue stress and anxiety on students.

All three examples begin from the same opinion—the school's phone ban needs to change—but rely on different argumentative styles to persuade the reader.

Credibility (Ethos)

Finally, an appeal to authority includes a statement from a relevant expert. In this case, the author uses a doctor in the field of education to support the argument.

> Our school should abolish its current ban on cell phone use on campus. According to Dr. Bartholomew Everett, a leading educational expert, "Research studies show that cell phone usage has no real impact on student attentiveness. Rather, phones provide a valuable technological resource for learning. Schools need to learn how to integrate this new technology into their curriculum." Rather than banning phones altogether, our school should follow the advice of experts and allow students to use phones as part of their learning.

Quantitative Information

As mentioned, some passages in the test contains **infographics** such as charts, tables, or graphs. In these cases, interpret the information presented and determine how well it supports the claims made in the text. For example, if the writer makes a case that seat belts save more lives than other automobile safety measures, they might want to include a graph (like the one below) showing the number of lives saved by seat belts versus those saved by air bags.

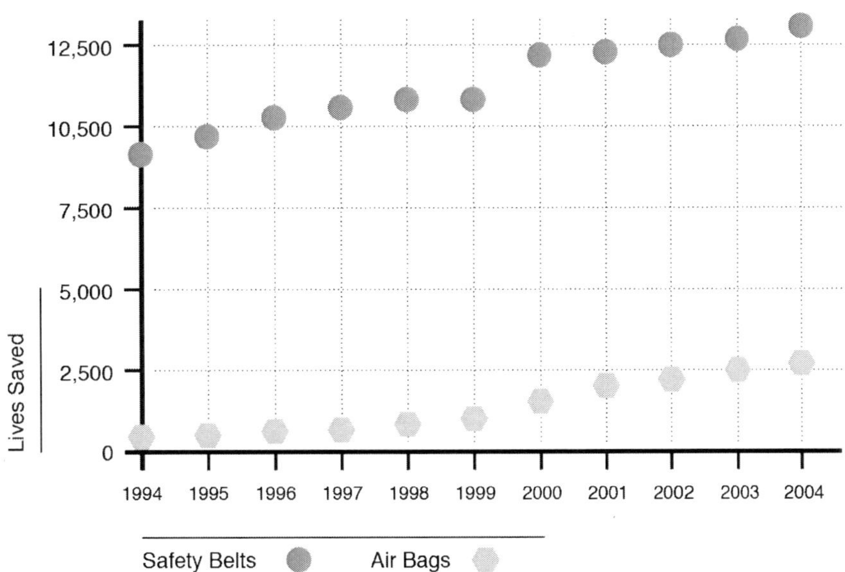

Based on data from the National Highway Traffic Safety Administration

If the graph clearly shows a higher number of lives are saved by seat belts, then it's effective. However, if the graph shows air bags save more lives than seat belts, then it doesn't support the writer's case.

Finally, graphs should be easy to understand. Their information should immediately be clear to the reader at a glance. Here are some basic things to keep in mind when interpreting infographics:

- In a **bar graph**, higher bars represent larger numbers. Lower bars represent smaller numbers.
- **Line graphs** often show trends over time. Points that are higher represent larger numbers than points that are lower. A line that consistently ascends from left to right shows a steady increase over time. A line that consistently descends from left to right shows a steady decrease over time. A line that bounces up and down represents instability or inconsistency in the trend. When interpreting a line graph, determine the point the writer is trying to make, and then see if the graph supports that point.
- **Pie charts** are used to show proportions or percentages of a whole but are less effective in showing change over time.
- **Tables** present information in numerical form, not as graphics. When interpreting a table, make sure to look for patterns in the numbers.

There can also be timelines, illustrations, or maps on the test. When interpreting these, keep in mind the writer's intentions and determine whether or not the graphic supports the case.

Interpreting Data and Considering Implications

In general, there are two types of data: qualitative and quantitative. Science passages may contain both, but simply put, **quantitative** data is reflected numerically and qualitative is not. **Qualitative** data is based on its qualities. In other words, qualitative data tends to present information more in subjective generalities (for example, relating to size or appearance). Quantitative data is based on numerical findings such as percentages. Quantitative data will be described in numerical terms. While both types of data are valid, the test taker will more likely be faced with having to interpret quantitative data through one or more graphic(s), and then be required to answer questions regarding the numerical data. The section of this study guide briefly addresses how data may be displayed in line graphs, bar charts, circle graphs, and scatter plots. A test taker should take the time to learn the skills it takes to interpret quantitative data.

Line Graphs

Cell Phone Use in Kiteville, 2000-2006

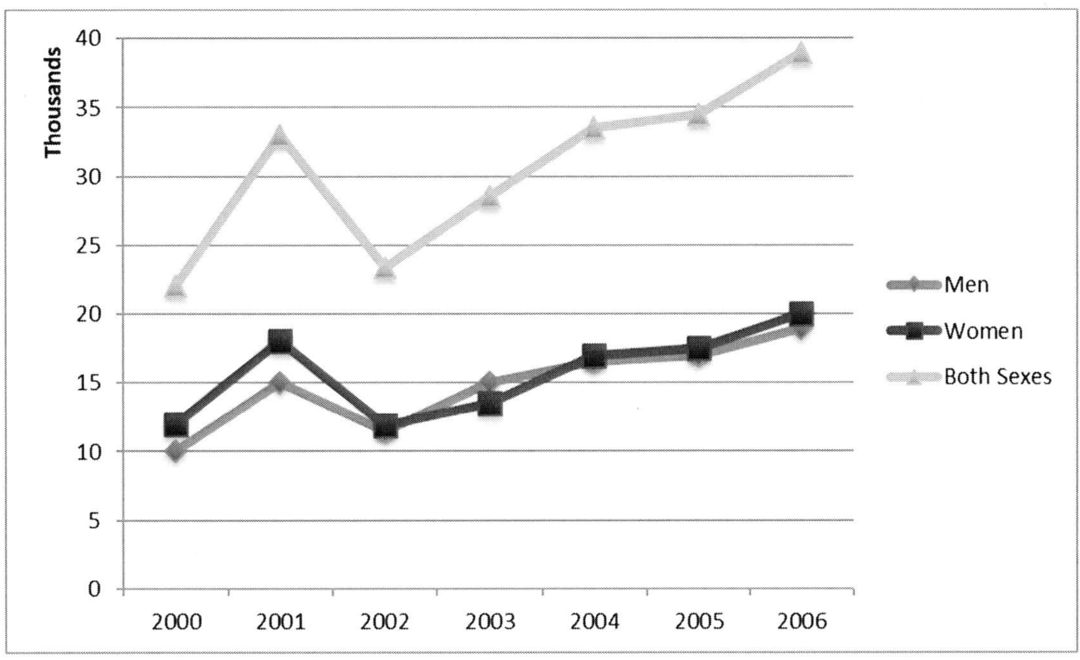

A **line graph** presents quantitative data on both horizontal (side to side) and vertical (up and down) axes. It requires the test taker to examine information across varying data points. When reading a line graph, a test taker should pay attention to any headings, as these indicate a title for the data it contains. In the above example, the test taker can anticipate the line graph contains numerical data regarding the use of cellphones during a certain time period. From there, a test taker should carefully read any outlying words or phrases that will help determine the meaning of data within the horizontal and vertical axes. In this example, the vertical axis displays the total number of people in increments of 5,000. Horizontally, the graph displays yearly markers, and the reader can assume the data presented accounts for a full calendar year. In addition, the line graph also uses different shapes to mark its data points. Some data points represent the number of men. Some data points represent the number of women, and a third type of data point represents the number of both sexes combined.

A test taker may be asked to read and interpret the graph's data, then answer questions about it. For example, the test may ask, *In which year did men seem to decrease cellphone use?* then require the test taker to select the correct answer. Similarly, the test taker may encounter a question such as *Which year yielded the highest number of cellphone users overall?* The test taker should be able to identify the correct answer as 2006.

Bar Graphs

A **bar graph** presents quantitative data through the use of lines or rectangles. The height and length of these lines or rectangles corresponds to the magnitude of the numerical data for that particular category or attribute. The data presented may represent information over time, showing shaded data over time or over other defined parameters. A bar graph will also utilize horizontal and vertical axes. An example of a bar graph is as follows:

Population Growth in Major US Cities

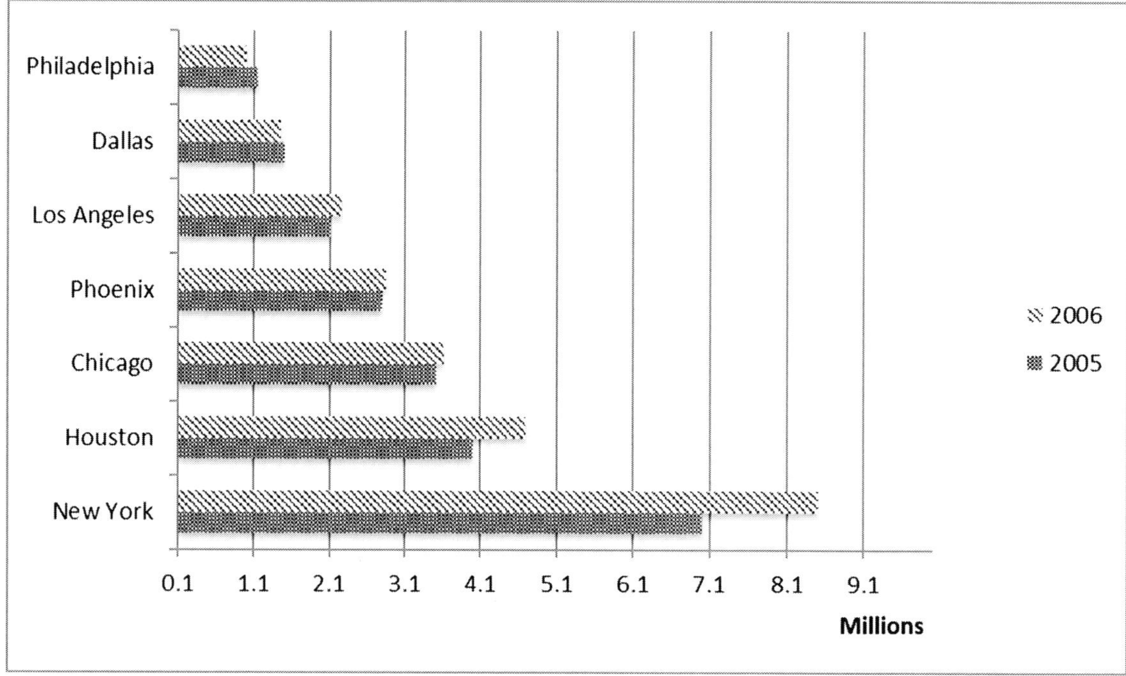

Reading the data in a bar graph is similar to the skills needed to read a line graph. The test taker should read and comprehend all heading information, as well as information provided along the horizontal and vertical axes. Note that the graph pertains to the population of some major US cities. The "values" of these cities can be found along the left side of the graph, along the vertical axis. The population values can be found along the horizontal axes. Notice how the graph uses shaded bars to depict the change in population over time, as the heading indicates. Therefore, when the test taker is asked a question such as, *Which major US city experienced the greatest amount of population growth during the depicted two year cycle,* the reader should be able to determine a correct answer of New York. It is important to pay particular attention to color, length, data points, and both axes, as well as any outlying header information in order to be able to answer graph-like test questions.

Circle Graphs

A **circle graph** (also sometimes referred to as a **pie chart**) presents quantitative data in the form of a circle. The same principles apply: the test taker should look for numerical data within the confines of the circle itself but also note any outlying information that may be included in a header, footer, or to the side of the circle. A circle graph will not depict horizontal or vertical axis information, but will instead rely on the reader's ability to visually take note of segmented circle pieces and apply information accordingly.

An example of a circle graph is as follows:

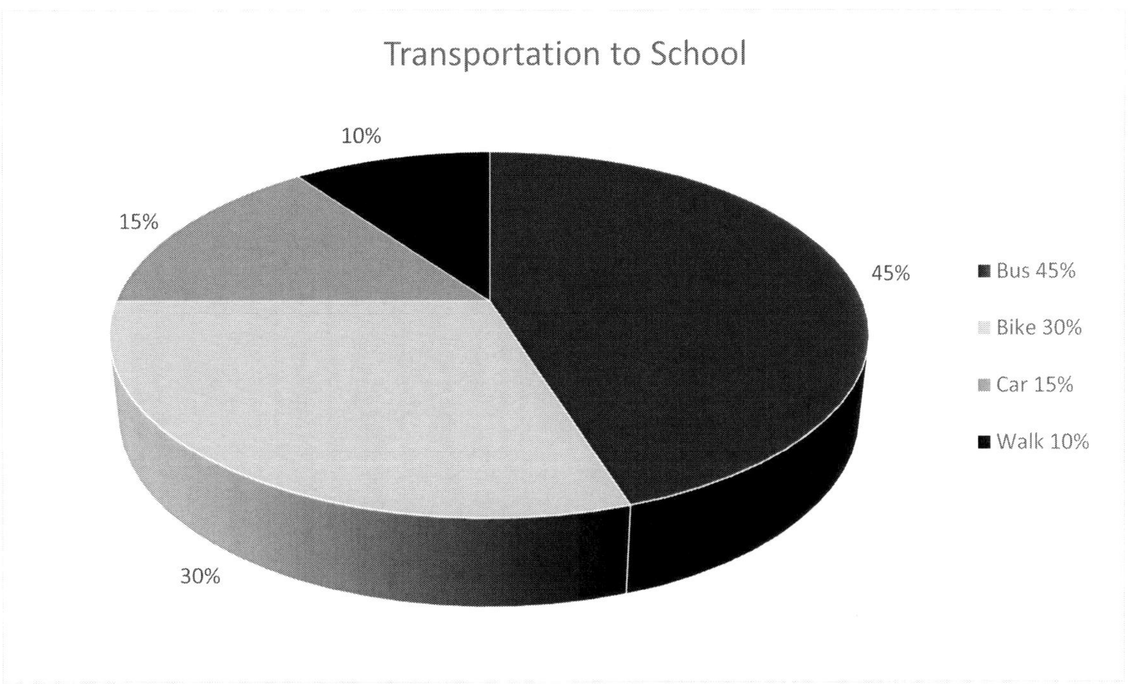

Notice the heading "Transportation to School." This should indicate to the test taker that the topic of the circle graph is how people traditionally get to school. To the right of the graph, the reader should comprehend that the data percentages contained within it directly correspond to the method of transportation. In this graph, the data is represented through the use shades and pattern. Each transportation method has its own shade. For example, if the test taker was then asked, *Which method of school transportation is most widely utilized,* the reader should be able to identify school bus as the correct answer.

Be wary of test questions that ask test takers to draw conclusions based on information that is not present. For example, it is not possible to determine, given the parameters of this circle graph, whether the population presented is of a particular gender or ethnic group. This graph does not represent data from a particular city or school district. It does not distinguish between student grade levels and, although the reader could infer that the typical student must be of driving age if cars are included, this is not necessarily the case. Elementary school students may rely on parents or others to drive them by personal methods. Therefore, do not read too much into data that is not presented. Only rely on the quantitative data that is presented in order to answer questions.

Scatter Plot

A **scatter plot** or **scatter diagram** is a graph that depicts quantitative data across plotted points. It will involve at least two sets of data. It will also involve horizontal and vertical axes.

An example of a scatter plot is as follows:

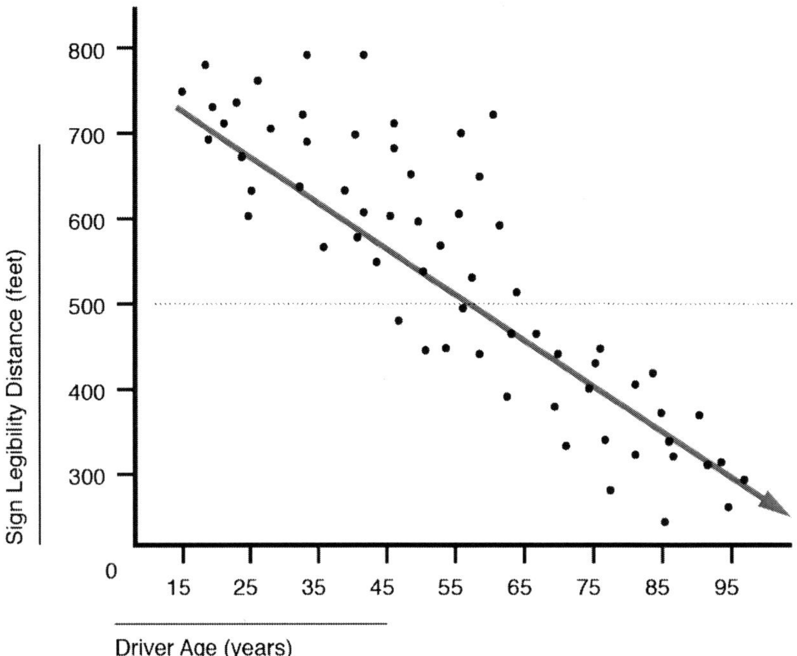

The skills needed to address a scatter plot are essentially the same as in other graph examples. Note any topic headings, as well as horizontal or vertical axis information. In the sample above, the reader can determine the data addresses a driver's ability to correctly and legibly read road signs as related to their age. Again, note the information that is absent. The test taker is not given the data to assess a time period, location, or driver gender. It simply requires the reader to note an approximate age to the ability to correctly identify road signs from a distance measured in feet. Notice that the overall graph also displays a trend. In this case, the data indicates a negative one and possibly supports the hypothesis that as a driver ages, their ability to correctly read a road sign at over 500 feet tends to decline over time. If the test taker were to be asked, *At what approximation in feet does a sixteen-year-old driver correctly see and read a street sign,* the answer would be the option closest to 700 feet.

Reading and examining scientific data in excerpts involves all of a reader's contextual reading, data interpretation, drawing logical conclusions based only on the information presented, and their application of critical thinking skills across a set of interpretive questions. Thorough comprehension and attention to detail is necessary to achieve test success.

Standard English Conventions

Types of Sentences

There isn't an overabundance of absolutes in grammar, but here is one: every sentence in the English language falls into one of four categories.

- **Declarative:** a simple statement that ends with a period

    The price of milk per gallon is the same as the price of gasoline.

- **Imperative:** a command, instruction, or request that ends with a period

    Buy milk when you stop to fill up your car with gas.

- **Interrogative:** a question that ends with a question mark

    Will you buy the milk?

- **Exclamatory:** a statement or command that expresses emotions like anger, urgency, or surprise and ends with an exclamation mark

    Buy the milk now!

Declarative sentences are the most common type, probably because they are comprised of the most general content, without any of the bells and whistles that the other three types contain. They are, simply, declarations or statements of any degree of seriousness, importance, or information.

Imperative sentences often seem to be missing a subject. The subject is there, though; it is just not visible or audible because it is *implied*. Look at the imperative example sentence.

Buy the milk when you fill up your car with gas.

You is the implied subject, the one to whom the command is issued. This is sometimes called **the understood you** because it is understood that *you* is the subject of the sentence.

Interrogative sentences—those that ask questions—are defined as such from the idea of the word **interrogation**, the action of questions being asked of suspects by investigators. Although that is serious business, interrogative sentences apply to all kinds of questions.

To exclaim is at the root of **exclamatory** sentences. These are made with strong emotions behind them. The only technical difference between a declarative or imperative sentence and an exclamatory one is the exclamation mark at the end. The example declarative and imperative sentences can both become an exclamatory one simply by putting an exclamation mark at the end of the sentences.

The price of milk per gallon is the same as the price of gasoline!
Buy milk when you stop to fill up your car with gas!

After all, someone might be really excited by the price of gas or milk, or they could be mad at the person that will be buying the milk! However, as stated before, exclamation marks in abundance defeat their own purpose! After a while, they begin to cause fatigue! When used only for their intended purpose, they can have their expected and desired effect.

Parts of Speech

Nouns

A **noun** is a person, place, thing, or idea. All nouns fit into one of two types, common or proper.

A **common noun** is a word that identifies any of a class of people, places, or things. Examples include numbers, objects, animals, feelings, concepts, qualities, and actions. *A, an,* or *the* usually precedes the common noun. These parts of speech are called *articles*. Here are some examples of sentences using nouns preceded by articles.

A building is under construction.
The girl would like to move to *the* city.

A **proper noun** (also called a **proper name**) is used for the specific name of an individual person, place, or organization. The first letter in a proper noun is capitalized. "My name is *Mary*." "I work for *Walmart*."

Nouns sometimes serve as adjectives (which themselves describe nouns), such as "hockey player" and "state government."

An **abstract noun** is an idea, state, or quality. It is something that can't be touched, such as happiness, courage, evil, or humor.

A **concrete noun** is something that can be experienced through the senses (touch, taste, hear, smell, see). Examples of concrete nouns are birds, skateboard, pie, and car.

A **collective noun** refers to a collection of people, places, or things that act as one. Examples of collective nouns are as follows: team, class, jury, family, audience, and flock.

Pronouns

A word used in place of a noun is known as a **pronoun.** Pronouns are words like *I, mine, hers,* and *us*.

Pronouns can be split into different classifications (seen below) which make them easier to learn; however, it's not important to memorize the classifications.

- Personal pronouns: refer to people, places, things, etc.
  - First person: we, I, our, mine
  - Second person: you, yours
  - Third person: he, them
- Possessive pronouns: demonstrate ownership (mine, his, hers, its, ours, theirs, yours)
- Interrogative pronouns: ask questions (what, which, who, whom, whose)
- Relative pronouns: include the five interrogative pronouns and others that are relative (whoever, whomever, that, when, where)
- Demonstrative pronouns: replace something specific (this, that, those, these)
- Reciprocal pronouns: indicate something was done or given in return (each other, one another)
- Indefinite pronouns: have a nonspecific status (anybody, whoever, someone, everybody, somebody)

Indefinite pronouns such as *anybody, whoever, someone, everybody*, and *somebody* command a singular verb form, but others such as *all, none,* and *some* could require a singular or plural verb form.

Antecedents

An **antecedent** is the noun to which a pronoun refers; it needs to be written or spoken before the pronoun is used. For many pronouns, antecedents are imperative for clarity. In particular, many of the personal, possessive, and

demonstrative pronouns need antecedents. Otherwise, it would be unclear who or what someone is referring to when they use a pronoun like *he* or *this*.

Pronoun reference means that the pronoun should refer clearly to one, clear, unmistakable noun (the antecedent).

Pronoun-antecedent agreement refers to the need for the antecedent and the corresponding pronoun to agree in gender, person, and number. Here are some examples:

The *kidneys* (plural antecedent) are part of the urinary system. *They* (plural pronoun) serve several roles.

The kidneys are part of the *urinary system* (singular antecedent). *It* (singular pronoun) is also known as the renal system.

Pronoun Cases

The subjective pronouns —*I, you, he/she/it, we, they,* and *who*—are the subjects of the sentence.

Example: *They* have a new house.

The objective pronouns—*me, you* (*singular*), *him/her, us, them,* and *whom*—are used when something is being done for or given to someone; they are objects of the action.

Example: The teacher has an apple for *us*.

The possessive pronouns—*mine, my, your, yours, his, hers, its, their, theirs, our,* and *ours*—are used to denote that something (or someone) belongs to someone (or something).

Example: It's *their* chocolate cake.
Even Better Example: It's *my* chocolate cake!

One of the greatest challenges and worst abuses of pronouns concerns *who* and *whom*. Just knowing the following rule can eliminate confusion. *Who* is a subjective-case pronoun used only as a subject or subject complement. *Whom* is only objective-case and, therefore, the object of the verb or preposition.

Who is going to the concert?

You are going to the concert with *whom*?

Hint: When using *who* or *whom*, think of whether someone would say *he* or *him*. If the answer is *he*, use *who*. If the answer is *him*, use *whom*. This trick is easy to remember because *he* and *who* both end in vowels, and *him* and *whom* both end in the letter *M*.

Verbs

A **verb** is the part of speech that describes an action, state of being, or occurrence.

A verb forms the main part of a predicate of a sentence. This means that the verb explains what the noun (which will be discussed shortly) is doing. A simple example is *time <u>flies</u>*. The verb *flies* explains what the action of the noun, *time*, is doing. This example is a *main* verb.

Helping (auxiliary) verbs are words like *have, do, be, can, may, should, must,* and *will.* "I *should* go to the store." Helping verbs assist main verbs in expressing tense, ability, possibility, permission, or obligation.

Particles are minor function words like *not, in, out, up,* or *down* that become part of the verb itself. "I might *not*."

Participles are words formed from verbs that are often used to modify a noun, noun phrase, verb, or verb phrase.

The *running* teenager collided with the cyclist.

Participles can also create compound verb forms.

He is *speaking*.

Verbs have five basic forms: the **base** form, the ***-s*** form, the ***-ing*** form, the **past** form, and the **past participle** form.

The past forms are either **regular** (*love/loved; hate/hated*) or **irregular** because they don't end by adding the common past tense suffix "-ed" (*go/went; fall/fell; set/set*).

Verb Forms

Shifting verb forms entails **conjugation,** which is used to indicate tense, voice, or mood.

Verb tense is used to show when the action in the sentence took place. There are several different verb tenses, and it is important to know how and when to use them. Some verb tenses can be achieved by changing the form of the verb, while others require the use of helping verbs (e.g., *is, was,* or *has*).

Present tense shows the action is happening currently or is ongoing:

I walk to work every morning.

She is stressed about the deadline.

Past tense shows that the action happened in the past or that the state of being is in the past:

I walked to work yesterday morning.

She was stressed about the deadline.

Future tense shows that the action will happen in the future or is a future state of being:

I will walk to work tomorrow morning.

She will be stressed about the deadline.

Present perfect tense shows action that began in the past, but continues into the present:

I have walked to work all week.

She has been stressed about the deadline.

Past perfect tense shows an action was finished before another took place:

I had walked all week until I sprained my ankle.

She had been stressed about the deadline until we talked about it.

Future perfect tense shows an action that will be completed at some point in the future:

By the time the bus arrives, I will have walked to work already.

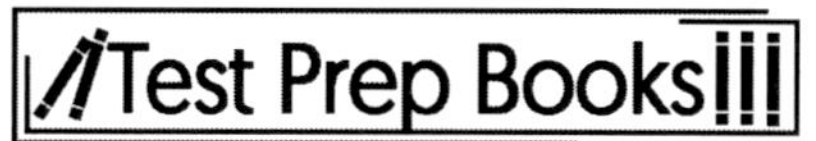

Voice

Verbs can be in the active or passive voice. When the subject completes the action, the verb is in **active voice**. When the subject receives the action of the sentence, the verb is in **passive voice**.

> Active: Jamie ate the ice cream.
>
> Passive: The ice cream was eaten by Jamie.

In active voice, the subject (*Jamie*) is the "do-er" of the action (*ate*). In passive voice, the subject *ice cream* receives the action of being eaten.

While passive voice can add variety to writing, active voice is the generally preferred sentence structure.

Mood

Mood is used to show the speaker's feelings about the subject matter. In English, there is indicative mood, imperative mood, and subjunctive mood.

Indicative mood is used to state facts, ask questions, or state opinions:

> Bob will make the trip next week.
>
> When can Bob make the trip?

Imperative mood is used to state a command or make a request:

> Wait in the lobby.
>
> Please call me next week.

Subjunctive mood is used to express a wish, an opinion, or a hope that is contrary to fact:

> If I were in charge, none of this would have happened.
>
> Allison wished she could take the exam over again when she saw her score.

Adjectives

Adjectives are words used to modify nouns and pronouns. They can be used alone or in a series and are used to further define or describe the nouns they modify.

> Mark made us a delicious, four-course meal.

The words *delicious* and *four-course* are adjectives that describe the kind of meal Mark made.

Articles are also considered adjectives because they help to describe nouns. Articles can be general or specific. The three articles in English are: *a, an*, and *the*.

Indefinite articles *(a, an)* are used to refer to nonspecific nouns. The article *a* proceeds words beginning with consonant sounds, and the article *an* proceeds words beginning with vowel sounds.

A car drove by our house.

An alligator was loose at the zoo.

He has always wanted a ukulele. (The first *u* makes a *y* sound.)

Note that *a* and *an* should only proceed nonspecific nouns that are also singular. If a nonspecific noun is plural, it does not need a preceding article.

Alligators were loose at the zoo.

The **definite article** *(the)* is used to refer to specific nouns:

The car pulled into our driveway.

Note that *the* should proceed all specific nouns regardless of whether they are singular or plural.

The cars pulled into our driveway.

Comparative adjectives are used to compare nouns. When they are used in this way, they take on positive, comparative, or superlative form.

The **positive** form is the normal form of the adjective:

Alicia is tall.

The **comparative** form shows a comparison between two things:

Alicia is taller than Maria.

Superlative form shows comparison between more than two things:

Alicia is the tallest girl in her class.

Usually, the comparative and superlative can be made by adding *–er* and *–est* to the positive form, but some verbs call for the helping verbs *more* or *most*. Other exceptions to the rule include adjectives like *bad*, which uses the comparative *worse* and the superlative *worst*.

An **adjective phrase** is not a bunch of adjectives strung together, but a group of words that describes a noun or pronoun and, thus, functions as an adjective. *Very happy* is an adjective phrase; so are *way too hungry* and *passionate about traveling*.

Adverbs

Adverbs have more functions than adjectives because they modify or qualify verbs, adjectives, or other adverbs as well as word groups that express a relation of place, time, circumstance, or cause. Therefore, adverbs answer any of the following questions: *How, when, where, why, in what way, how often, how much, in what condition,* and/or *to what degree. How good looking is he? He is <u>very</u> handsome.*

Here are some examples of adverbs for different situations:

how: quickly
when: daily
where: there
in what way: easily
how often: often
how much: much
in what condition: badly
what degree: hardly

As one can see, for some reason, many adverbs end in *-ly.*

Adverbs do things like emphasize (*really, simply,* and *so*), amplify (*heartily, completely,* and *positively*), and tone down (*almost, somewhat,* and *mildly*).

Adverbs also come in phrases.

The dog ran as though his life depended on it.

Prepositions

Prepositions are connecting words and, while there are only about 150 of them, they are used more often than any other individual groups of words. They describe relationships between other words. They are placed before a noun or pronoun, forming a phrase that modifies another word in the sentence. **Prepositional phrases** begin with a preposition and end with a noun or pronoun, the **object of the preposition.** *A pristine lake is near the store and behind the bank.*

Some commonly used prepositions are *about, after, anti, around, as, at, behind, beside, by, for, from, in, into, of, off, on, to,* and *with.*

Complex prepositions, which also come before a noun or pronoun, consist of two or three words such as *according to, in regards to,* and *because of.*

Conjunctions

Conjunctions are vital words that connect words, phrases, thoughts, and ideas. Conjunctions show relationships between components. There are two types:

Coordinating conjunctions are the primary class of conjunctions placed between words, phrases, clauses, and sentences that are of equal grammatical rank; the coordinating conjunctions are *for, and, nor, but, or, yet,* and *so.* A useful memorization trick is to remember that the first letter of these conjunctions collectively spell the word *fanboys.*

I need to go shopping, *but* I must be careful to leave enough money in the bank.
She wore a black, red, *and* white shirt.

Subordinating conjunctions are the secondary class of conjunctions. They connect two unequal parts, one **main** (or **independent**) and the other *subordinate* (or *dependent*). I must go to the store *even though* I do not have enough money in the bank.

Because I read the review, I do not want to go to the movie.

Notice that the presence of subordinating conjunctions makes clauses dependent. *I read the review* is an independent clause, but *because* makes the clause dependent. Thus, it needs an independent clause to complete the sentence.

Interjections

Interjections are words used to express emotion. Examples include *wow*, *ouch*, and *hooray*. Interjections are often separate from sentences; in those cases, the interjection is directly followed by an exclamation point. In other cases, the interjection is included in a sentence and followed by a comma. The punctuation plays a big role in the intensity of the emotion that the interjection is expressing. Using a comma or semicolon indicates less excitement than using an exclamation mark.

Capitalization Rules

Here's a non-exhaustive list of things that should be capitalized:

- The first word of every sentence
- The first word of every line of poetry
- The first letter of proper nouns (World War II)
- Holidays (Valentine's Day)
- The days of the week and months of the year (Tuesday, March)
- The first word, last word, and all major words in the titles of books, movies, songs, and other creative works (In the novel, To Kill a Mockingbird, note that a is lowercase since it's not a major word, but to is capitalized since it's the first word of the title.)
- Titles when preceding a proper noun (President Roberto Gonzales, Aunt Judy)

When simply using a word such as president or secretary, though, the word is not capitalized.

> Officers of the new business must include a *president* and *treasurer*.

Seasons—spring, fall, etc.—are not capitalized.

North, *south*, *east*, and *west* are capitalized when referring to regions but are not when being used for directions. In general, if it's preceded by *the* it should be capitalized.

> I'm from the South.
> I drove south.

End Punctuation

Periods (.) are used to end a sentence that is a statement (**declarative**) or a command (**imperative**). They should not be used in a sentence that asks a question or is an exclamation. Periods are also used in abbreviations, which are shortened versions of words.

> Declarative: The boys refused to go to sleep.
> Imperative: Walk down to the bus stop.

Abbreviations: Joan Roberts, M.D., Apple Inc., Mrs. Adamson
If a sentence ends with an abbreviation, it is inappropriate to use two periods. It should end with a single period after the abbreviation.

The chef gathered the ingredients for the pie, which included apples, flour, sugar, etc.

Question marks *(?)* are used with direct questions (**interrogative**). An **indirect question** can use a period:

Interrogative: When does the next bus arrive?

Indirect Question: I wonder when the next bus arrives.

An **exclamation point** *(!)* is used to show strong emotion or can be used as an interjection. This punctuation should be used sparingly in formal writing situations.

What an amazing shot!

Whoa!

Commas

A **comma** (,) is the punctuation mark that signifies a pause—breath—between parts of a sentence. It denotes a break of flow. Proper comma usage helps readers understand the writer's intended emphasis of ideas.

In a complex sentence—one that contains a **subordinate** (dependent) clause or clauses—the use of a comma is dictated by where the subordinate clause is located. If the subordinate clause is located before the main clause, a comma is needed between the two clauses.

I will not pay for the steak, *because I don't have that much money*.

Generally, if the subordinate clause is placed after the main clause, no punctuation is needed.

I did well on my exam because I studied two hours the night before.

Notice how the last clause is dependent because it requires the earlier independent clauses to make sense.

Use a comma on both sides of an interrupting phrase.

I will pay for the ice cream, *chocolate and vanilla*, and then will eat it all myself.

The words forming the phrase in italics are nonessential (extra) information. To determine if a phrase is nonessential, try reading the sentence without the phrase and see if it's still coherent.

A comma is not necessary in this next sentence because no interruption—nonessential or extra information—has occurred. Read sentences aloud when uncertain.

I will pay for his chocolate and vanilla ice cream and then will eat it all myself.

If the nonessential phrase comes at the beginning of a sentence, a comma should only go at the end of the phrase. If the phrase comes at the end of a sentence, a comma should only go at the beginning of the phrase.

Other types of interruptions include the following:

- interjections: Oh no, I am not going.
- abbreviations: Barry Potter, M.D., specializes in heart disorders.
- direct addresses: Yes, Claudia, I am tired and going to bed.
- parenthetical phrases: His wife, lovely as she was, was not helpful.
- transitional phrases: Also, it is not possible.

The second comma in the following sentence is called an **Oxford comma**.

I will pay for ice cream, syrup, and pop.

It is a comma used after the second-to-last item in a series of three or more items. It comes before the word *or* or *and*. Not everyone uses the Oxford comma; it is optional, but many believe it is needed. The comma functions as a tool to reduce confusion in writing. So, if omitting the Oxford comma would cause confusion, then it's best to include it.

Commas are used in math to mark the place of thousands in numerals, breaking them up so they are easier to read. Other uses for commas are in dates (*March 19, 2016*), letter greetings (*Dear Sally,*), and in between cities and states (*Louisville, KY*).

Semicolons

A **semicolon** *(;)* is used to connect ideas in a sentence in some way. There are three main ways to use semicolons.

Link two independent clauses without the use of a coordinating conjunction:

I was late for work again; I'm definitely going to get fired.

Link two independent clauses with a transitional word:

The songs were all easy to play; therefore, he didn't need to spend too much time practicing.

Between items in a series that are already separated by commas or if necessary to separate lengthy items in a list:

Starbucks has locations in Media, PA; Swarthmore, PA; and Morton, PA.

Several classroom management issues presented in the study: the advent of a poor teacher persona in the context of voice, dress, and style; teacher follow-through from the beginning of the school year to the end; and the depth of administrative support, including ISS and OSS protocol.

Colons

A **colon** (:) is used after an independent clause to present an explanation or draw attention to what comes next in the sentence. There are several uses.

Explanations of ideas:

They soon learned the hardest part about having a new baby: sleep deprivation.

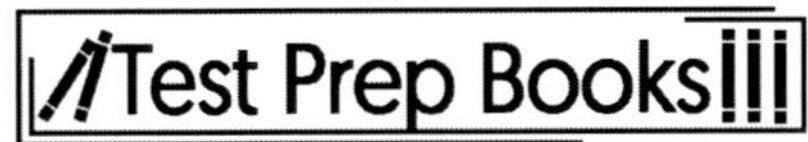

Lists of items:

> Shari picked up all the supplies she would need for the party: cups, plates, napkins, balloons, streamers, and party favors.

Time, subtitles, general salutations:

> The time is 7:15.
>
> I read a book entitled *Pluto: A Planet No More*.
>
> To whom it may concern:

Parentheses and Dashes

Parentheses are half-round brackets that look like this: *( )*. They set off a word, phrase, or sentence that is an afterthought, explanation, or side note relevant to the surrounding text but not essential. A pair of commas is often used to set off this sort of information, but parentheses are generally used for information that would not fit well within a sentence or that the writer deems not important enough to be structurally part of the sentence.

> The picture of the heart (see above) shows the major parts you should memorize.
> Mount Everest is one of three mountains in the world that are over 28,000 feet high (K2 and Kanchenjunga are the other two).

See how the sentences above are complete without the parenthetical statements? In the first example, *see above* would not have fit well within the flow of the sentence. The second parenthetical statement could have been a separate sentence, but the writer deemed the information not pertinent to the topic.

The **em-dash** (—) is a mark longer than a hyphen used as a punctuation mark in sentences and to set apart a relevant thought. Even after plucking out the line separated by the dash marks, the sentence will be intact and make sense.

> Looking out the airplane window at the landmarks—Lake Clarke, Thompson Community College, and the bridge—she couldn't help but feel excited to be home.

The dashes use is similar to that of parentheses or a pair of commas. So, what's the difference? Many believe that using dashes makes the clause within them stand out while using parentheses is subtler. It's advised to not use dashes when commas could be used instead.

Ellipses

An **ellipsi**s (...) is used to show that there is more to the quoted text than is necessary for the current discussion. Writers use them in place of words, lines, phrases, list content, or paragraphs that might just as easily have been omitted from a passage of writing. This can be done to save space or to focus only on the specifically relevant material.

> Exercise is good for some unexpected reasons. Watkins writes, "Exercise has many benefits such as...reducing cancer risk."

In the example above, the ellipsis takes the place of the other benefits of exercise that are more expected.

The ellipsis may also be used to show a pause in sentence flow.

> "I'm wondering...how this could happen," Dylan said in a soft voice.

Quotation Marks

Double quotation marks are used at the beginning and end of a direct quote. They are also used with certain titles and to indicate that a term being used is slang or referenced in the sentence. Quotation marks should not be used with an indirect quote. Single quotation marks are used to indicate a quote within a quote.

> Direct quote: "The weather is supposed to be beautiful this week," she said.
>
> Indirect quote: One of the customers asked if the sale prices were still in effect.
>
> Quote within a quote: "My little boy just said 'Mama, I want cookie,'" Maria shared.

Titles: Quotation marks should also be used to indicate titles of short works or sections of larger works, such as chapter titles. Other works that use quotation marks include poems, short stories, newspaper articles, magazine articles, web page titles, and songs.

> "The Road Not Taken" is my favorite poem by Robert Frost.
>
> "What a Wonderful World" is one of my favorite songs.

Specific or emphasized terms: Quotation marks can also be used to indicate a technical term or to set off a word that is being discussed in a sentence. Quotation marks can also indicate sarcasm.

> The new step, called "levigation," is a very difficult technique.
>
> He said he was "hungry" multiple times, but he only ate two bites.

Use with other punctuation: The use of quotation marks with other punctuation varies, depending on the role of the ending or separating punctuation.

In American English, commas and periods go inside quotation marks:

> "This is the last time you are allowed to leave early," his boss stated.
>
> The newscaster said, "We have some breaking news to report."

Question marks or exclamation points go inside the quotation marks when they are part of a direct quote:

> The doctor shouted, "Get the crash cart!"

When the question mark or exclamation point is part of the sentence, not the quote, it should be placed outside of the quotation marks:

> Was it Jackie that said, "Get some potatoes at the store"?

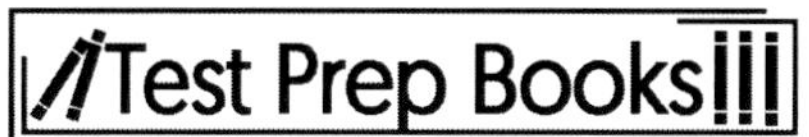

Apostrophes

This punctuation mark, the **apostrophe** (') is a versatile mark. It has several different functions:

- Quotes: Apostrophes are used when a second quote is needed within a quote.
    - In my letter to my friend, I wrote, "The girl had to get a new purse, and guess what Mary did? She said, 'I'd like to go with you to the store.' I knew Mary would buy it for her."
- Contractions: Another use for an apostrophe in the quote above is a contraction. *I'd is used for I would.*
- Possession: An apostrophe followed by the letter s shows possession (Mary's purse). If the possessive word is plural, the apostrophe generally just follows the word. Not all possessive pronouns require apostrophes.
    - The trees' leaves are all over the ground.

Hyphens

The **hyphen** (-) is a small hash mark that can be used to join words to show that they are linked.

Hyphens can connect two words that work together as a single adjective (a compound adjective).

honey-covered biscuits

Some words always require hyphens even if not serving as an adjective.

merry-go-round

Hyphens always go after certain prefixes like *anti-* & *all-*.

Hyphens should also be used when the absence of the hyphen would cause a strange vowel combination (*semi-engineer*) or confusion. For example, *re-collect* should be used to describe something being gathered twice rather than being written as *recollect*, which means to remember.

Subjects

Every sentence must include a subject and a verb. The **subject** of a sentence is who or what the sentence is about. It's often directly stated and can be determined by asking "Who?" or "What?" did the action:

Most sentences contain a **direct subject**, in which the subject is mentioned in the sentence.

Kelly mowed the lawn.

Who mowed the lawn? *Kelly*

The air-conditioner ran all night

What ran all night? *the air-conditioner*

The subject of imperative sentences is the implied *you*, because imperative subjects are commands:

Go home after the meeting.

Who should go home after the meeting? *you* (implied)

In **expletive sentences** that start with "there are" or "there is," the subject is found after the predicate. The subject cannot be "there," so it must be another word in the sentence:

There is a cup sitting on the coffee table.

What is sitting on the coffee table? *a cup*

Simple and Complete Subjects

A **complete subject** includes the simple subject and all the words modifying it, including articles and adjectives. A **simple subject** is the single noun without its modifiers.

A warm, chocolate-chip cookie sat on the kitchen table.

Complete subject: *a warm, chocolate-chip cookie*

Simple subject: *cookie*

The words *a, warm, chocolate,* and *chip* all modify the simple subject *cookie.*

There might also be a **compound subject**, which would be two or more nouns without the modifiers.

A little girl and her mother walked into the shop.

Complete subject: *A little girl and her mother*

Compound subject: *girl, mother*

In this case, *the girl and her mother* are both completing the action of walking into the shop, so this is a compound subject.

Predicates

In addition to the subject, a sentence must also have a predicate. The **predicate** contains a verb and tells something about the subject. In addition to the verb, a predicate can also contain a direct or indirect object, object of a preposition, and other phrases.

The cats napped on the front porch.

In this sentence, cats is the subject because the sentence is about cats.

The **complete predicate** is everything else in the sentence: *napped on the front porch.* This phrase is the predicate because it tells us what the cats did.

This sentence can be broken down into a simple subject and predicate:

Cats napped.

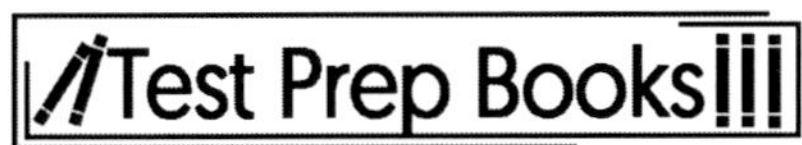

In this sentence, *cats* is the simple subject, and *napped* is the **simple predicate**.

Although the sentence is very short and doesn't offer much information, it's still considered a complete sentence because it contains a subject and predicate.

Like a compound subject, a sentence can also have a **compound predicate**. This is when the subject is or does two or more things in the sentence.

> This easy chair reclines and swivels.

In this sentence, *this easy chair* is the complete subject. *Reclines and swivels* shows two actions of the chair, so this is the compound predicate.

Subject-Verb Agreement

The subject of a sentence and its verb must agree. The cornerstone rule of subject-verb agreement is that subject and verb must agree in number. Whether the subject is singular or plural, the verb must follow suit.

> Incorrect: The houses is new.
> Correct: The houses are new.
> Also Correct: The house is new.

In other words, a singular subject requires a singular verb; a plural subject requires a plural verb.
The words or phrases that come between the subject and verb do not alter this rule.

> Incorrect: The houses built of brick is new.
> Correct: The houses built of brick are new.

> Incorrect: The houses with the sturdy porches is new.
> Correct: The houses with the sturdy porches are new.

The subject will always follow the verb when a sentence begins with *here* or *there.* Identify these with care.

> Incorrect: Here *is* the *houses* with sturdy porches.
> Correct: Here *are* the *houses* with sturdy porches.

The subject in the sentences above is not *here*, it is *houses*. Remember, *here* and *there* are never subjects. Be careful that contractions such as *here's* or *there're* do not cause confusion!

Two subjects joined by *and* require a plural verb form, except when the two combine to make one thing:

> Incorrect: Garrett and Jonathan is over there.
> Correct: Garrett and Jonathan are over there.

> Incorrect: Spaghetti and meatballs are a delicious meal!
> Correct: Spaghetti and meatballs is a delicious meal!

In the example above, *spaghetti and meatballs* is a compound noun. However, *Garrett and Jonathan* is not a compound noun.

Two singular subjects joined by *or, either/or,* or *neither/nor* call for a singular verb form.

Incorrect: Butter or syrup are acceptable.
Correct: Butter or syrup is acceptable.

Plural subjects joined by *or, either/or*, or *neither/nor* are, indeed, plural.

The chairs or the boxes are being moved next.

If one subject is singular and the other is plural, the verb should agree with the closest noun.

Correct: The chair or the boxes are being moved next.
Correct: The chairs or the box is being moved next.

Some plurals of money, distance, and time call for a singular verb.

Incorrect: Three dollars *are* enough to buy that.
Correct: Three dollars *is* enough to buy that.

For words declaring degrees of quantity such as *many of, some of,* or *most of,* let the noun that follows of be the guide:

Incorrect: Many of the books is in the shelf.
Correct: Many of the books are in the shelf.

Incorrect: Most of the pie *are* on the table.
Correct: Most of the pie *is* on the table.

For indefinite pronouns like *anybody* or *everybody*, use singular verbs.

Everybody *is* going to the store.

However, the pronouns *few, many, several, all, some,* and *both* have their own rules and use plural forms.

Some *are* ready.

Some nouns like *crowd* and *congress* are called **collective nouns** and they require a singular verb form.

Congress *is* in session.
The news *is* over.

Books and movie titles, though, including plural nouns such as *Great Expectations*, also require a singular verb. Remember that only the subject affects the verb. While writing tricky subject-verb arrangements, say them aloud. Listen to them. Once the rules have been learned, one's ear will become sensitive to them, making it easier to pick out what's right and what's wrong.

Direct Objects

The **direct object** is the part of the sentence that receives the action of the verb. It is a noun and can usually be found after the verb. To find the direct object, first find the verb, and then ask the question *who* or *what* after it.

The bear climbed the tree.

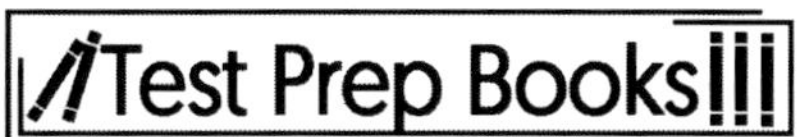

What did the bear climb? *the tree*

Indirect Objects

An **indirect object** receives the direct object. It is usually found between the verb and the direct object. A strategy for identifying the indirect object is to find the verb and ask the questions *to whom/for whom* or *to what/for what*.

Jane made her daughter a cake.

For whom did Jane make the cake? *her daughter*

Cake is the direct object because it is what Jane made, and *daughter* is the indirect object because she receives the cake.

Complements

A **complement** completes the meaning of an expression. A complement can be a pronoun, noun, or adjective. A **verb complement** refers to the direct object or indirect object in the sentence. An **object complement** gives more information about the direct object:

The magician got the kids excited.

Kids is the direct object, and *excited* is the object complement.

A **subject complement** comes after a linking verb. It is typically an adjective or noun that gives more information about the subject:

The king was noble and spared the thief's life.

Noble describes the *king* and follows the linking verb *was*.

Predicate Nouns

A **predicate noun** renames the subject:

John is a carpenter.

The subject is *John*, and the predicate noun is *carpenter*.

Predicate Adjectives

A **predicate adjective** describes the subject:

Margaret is beautiful.

The subject is *Margaret*, and the predicate adjective is *beautiful*.

Homonyms

Homonyms are words that sound the same but are spelled differently, and they have different meanings. There are several common homonyms that give writers trouble.

There, They're, and *Their*

The word *there* can be used as an adverb, adjective, or pronoun:

> *There* are ten children on the swim team this summer.
>
> I put my book over *there*, but now I can't find it.

The word *they're* is a contraction of the words *they* and *are*:

> *They're* flying in from Texas on Tuesday.

The word *their* is a possessive pronoun:

> I store *their* winter clothes in the attic.

Its and *It's*

Its is a possessive pronoun:

> The cat licked *its* injured paw.

It's is the contraction for the words *it* and *is*:

> *It's* unbelievable how many people opted not to vote in the last election.

Your and You're

Your is a possessive pronoun:

> Can I borrow *your* lawnmower this weekend?

You're is a contraction for the words *you* and *are*:

> *You're* about to embark on a fantastic journey.

To, Too, and *Two*

To is an adverb or a preposition used to show direction, relationship, or purpose:

> We are going *to* New York.
>
> They are going *to* see a show.

Too is an adverb that means more than enough, also, and very:

> You have had *too* much candy.
>
> We are on vacation that week, *too*.

Two is the written-out form of the numeral 2:

> *Two* of the shirts didn't fit, so I will have to return them.

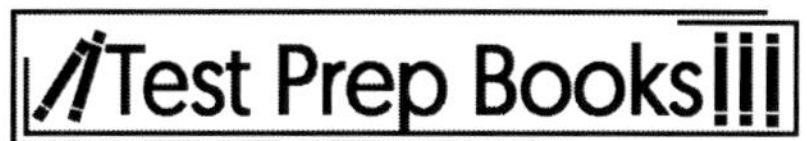

New and *Knew*

New is an adjective that means recent:

There's a *new* customer on the phone.

Knew is the past tense of the verb *know*:

I *knew* you'd have fun on this ride.

Affect and *Effect*

Affect and *effect* are complicated because they are used as both nouns and verbs, have similar meanings, and are pronounced the same.

	Affect	**Effect**
Noun Definition	emotional state	result
Noun Example	The patient's affect was flat.	The effects of smoking are well documented.
Verb Definition	to influence	to bring about
Verb Example	The pollen count affects my allergies.	The new candidate hopes to effect change.

Independent and Dependent Clauses

Independent and **dependent** clauses are strings of words that contain both a subject and a verb. An independent clause *can* stand alone as complete thought, but a dependent clause *cannot*. A dependent clause relies on other words to be a complete sentence.

Independent clause: The keys are on the counter.
Dependent clause: If the keys are on the counter

Notice that both clauses have a subject (*keys*) and a verb (*are*). The independent clause expresses a complete thought, but the word *if* at the beginning of the dependent clause makes it *dependent* on other words to be a complete thought.

Independent clause: If the keys are on the counter, please give them to me.

This example constitutes a complete sentence since it includes at least one verb and one subject and is a complete thought. In this case, the independent clause has two subjects (*keys* & an implied *you*) and two verbs (*are* & *give*).

Independent clause: I went to the store.
Dependent clause: Because we are out of milk,

Complete Sentence: Because we are out of milk, I went to the store.
Complete Sentence: I went to the store because we are out of milk.

Phrases

A **phrase** is a group of words that do not make a complete thought or a clause. They are parts of sentences or clauses. Phrases can be used as nouns, adjectives, or adverbs. A phrase does not contain both a subject and a verb.

Prepositional Phrases

A **prepositional phrase** shows the relationship between a word in the sentence and the object of the preposition. The **object of the preposition** is a noun that follows the preposition.

The orange pillows are on the couch.

On is the preposition, and *couch* is the object of the preposition.

She brought her friend with the nice car.

With is the preposition, and *car* is the object of the preposition. Here are some common prepositions:

about	as	at	after
by	for	from	in
of	on	to	with

Verbals and Verbal Phrases

Verbals are forms of verbs that act as other parts of speech. They can be used as nouns, adjectives, or adverbs. Though they are verb forms, they are not to be used as the verb in the sentence. A word group that is based on a verbal is considered a **verbal phrase**. There are three major types of verbals: participles, gerunds, and infinitives.

Participles are verbals that act as adjectives. The present participle ends in *–ing*, and the past participle ends in *–d*, -*ed*, -*n*, or-*t*.

Verb	**Present Participle**	**Past Participle**
walk	walking	walked
share	sharing	shared

Participial phrases are made up of the participle and modifiers, complements, or objects.

Crying for most of an hour, the baby didn't seem to want to nap.

Having already taken this course, the student was bored during class.

Crying for most of an hour and *Having already taken this course* are the participial phrases.

Gerunds are verbals that are used as nouns and end in *–ing*. A gerund can be the subject or object of the sentence like a noun. Note that a present participle can also end in *–ing*, so it is important to distinguish between the two. The gerund is used as a noun, while the participle is used as an adjective.

Swimming is my favorite sport.

I wish I were sleeping.

A **gerund phrase** includes the gerund and any modifiers or complements, direct objects, indirect objects, or pronouns.

Cleaning the house is my least favorite weekend activity.

Cleaning the house is the gerund phrase acting as the subject of the sentence.

The most important goal this year is raising money for charity.

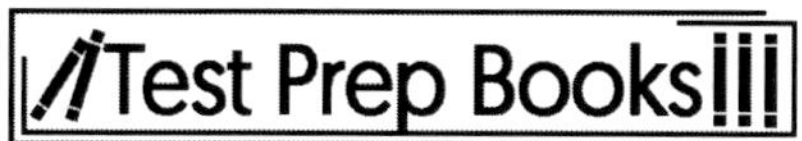

Raising money for charity is the gerund phrase acting as the direct object.

The police accused the woman of stealing the car.

The gerund phrase *stealing the car* is the object of the preposition in this sentence.

An **infinitive** is a verbal made up of the word *to* and a verb. Infinitives can be used as nouns, adjectives, or adverbs.

Examples: To eat, to jump, to swim, to lie, to call, to work

An *infinitive phrase* is made up of the infinitive plus any complements or modifiers. The infinitive phrase *to wait* is used as the subject in this sentence:

To wait was not what I had in mind.

The infinitive phrase *to sing* is used as the subject complement in this sentence:

Her dream is to sing.

The infinitive phrase *to grow* is used as an adverb in this sentence:

Children must eat to grow.

Appositive Phrases

An **appositive** is a noun or noun phrase that renames a noun that comes immediately before it in the sentence. An appositive can be a single word or several words. These phrases can be **essential** or **nonessential**. An essential appositive phrase is necessary to the meaning of the sentence and a nonessential appositive phrase is not. It is important to be able to distinguish these for purposes of comma use.

Essential: My sister Christina works at a school.

Naming which sister is essential to the meaning of the sentence, so no commas are needed.

Nonessential: My sister, who is a teacher, is coming over for dinner tonight.

Who is a teacher is not essential to the meaning of the sentence, so commas are required.

Absolute Phrases

An **absolute phrase** modifies a noun without using a conjunction. It is not the subject of the sentence and is not a complete thought on its own. Absolute phrases are set off from the independent clause with a comma.

Arms outstretched, she yelled at the sky.

All things considered, this has been a great day.

The Four Types of Sentence Structures

A **simple sentence** has one independent clause.

I am going to win.

A **compound sentence** has two independent clauses. A conjunction—*for, and, nor, but, or, yet, so*—links them together. Note that each of the independent clauses has a subject and a verb.

I am going to win, but the odds are against me.

A **complex sentence** has one independent clause and one or more dependent clauses.

I am going to win, even though I don't deserve it.

Even though I don't deserve it is a dependent clause. It does not stand on its own. Some conjunctions that link an independent and a dependent clause are *although*, *because*, *before*, *after*, *that*, *when*, *which*, and *while*.

A **compound-complex sentence** has at least three clauses, two of which are independent and at least one that is a dependent clause.

While trying to dance, I tripped over my partner's feet, but I regained my balance quickly.

The dependent clause is *While trying to dance*.

Sentence Fragments

A **sentence fragment** is an incomplete sentence. An independent clause is made up of a subject and a predicate, and both are needed to make a complete sentence.

Sentence fragments often begin with relative pronouns (when, which), subordinating conjunctions (because, although) or gerunds (trying, being, seeing). They might be missing the subject or the predicate.

The most common type of fragment is the isolated dependent clause, which can be corrected by joining it to the independent clause that appears before or after the fragment:

Fragment: While the cookies baked.

Correction: While the cookies baked, we played cards. (We played cards while the cookies baked.)

Run-on Sentences

A **run-on sentence** is created when two independent clauses (complete thoughts) are joined without correct punctuation or a conjunction. Run-on sentences can be corrected in the following ways:

Join the independent clauses with a comma and coordinating conjunction.

Run-on: We forgot to return the library books we had to pay a fine.

Correction: We forgot to return the library books, so we had to pay a fine.

Join the independent clauses with a semicolon, dash, or colon when the clauses are closely related in meaning.

Run-on: I had a salad for lunch every day this week I feel healthier already.

Correction: I had a salad for lunch every day this week; I feel healthier already.

Join the independent clauses with a semicolon and a conjunctive adverb.

Run-on: We arrived at the animal shelter on time however the dog had already been adopted.

Correction: We arrived at the animal shelter on time; however, the dog had already been adopted.

Separate the independent clauses into two sentences with a period.

Run-on: He tapes his favorite television show he never misses an episode.

Correction: He tapes his favorite television show. He never misses an episode.

Rearrange the wording of the sentence to create an independent clause and a dependent clause.

Run-on: My wedding date is coming up I am getting more excited to walk down the aisle.

Correction: As my wedding date approaches, I am getting more excited to walk down the aisle.

Dangling and Misplaced Modifiers

A **modifier** is a phrase that describes, alters, limits, or gives more information about a word in the sentence. The two most common issues are dangling and misplaced modifiers.

A **dangling modifier** is created when the phrase modifies a word that is not clearly stated in the sentence.

Dangling modifier: Having finished dinner, the dishes were cleared from the table.

Correction: Having finished dinner, Amy cleared the dishes from the table.

In the first sentence, *having finished dinner* appears to modify *the dishes*, which obviously can't finish dinner. The second sentence adds the subject *Amy*, to make it clear who has finished dinner.

Dangling modifier: Hoping to improve test scores, all new books were ordered for the school.

Correction: Hoping to improve test scores, administrators ordered all new books for the school.

Without the subject *administrators*, it appears the books are hoping to improve test scores, which doesn't make sense.

Misplaced modifiers are placed incorrectly in the sentence, which can cause confusion. Compare these examples:

Misplaced modifier: Rory purchased a new flat screen television and placed it on the wall above the fireplace, with all the bells and whistles.

Revised: Rory purchased a new flat screen television, with all the bells and whistles, and placed it on the wall above the fireplace.

The bells and whistles should modify the television, not the fireplace.

Misplaced modifier: The delivery driver arrived late with the pizza, who was usually on time.

Revised: The delivery driver, who usually was on time, arrived late with the pizza.

This suggests that the delivery driver was usually on time, instead of the pizza.

Misplaced modifier: We saw a family of ducks on the way to church.

Revised: On the way to church, we saw a family of ducks.

The misplaced modifier, here, suggests the *ducks* were on their way to church, instead of the pronoun *we*.

Split Infinitives

An **infinitive** is made up of the word *to* and a verb, such as: to run, to jump, to ask. A **split infinitive** is created when a word comes between *to* and the verb.

Split infinitive: To quickly run

Correction: To run quickly

Split infinitive: To quietly ask

Correction: To ask quietly

Double Negatives

A **double negative** is a negative statement that includes two negative elements. This is incorrect in Standard English.

Incorrect: She hasn't never come to my house to visit.

Correct: She has never come to my house to visit.

The intended meaning is that she has never come to the house, so the double negative is incorrect. However, it is possible to use two negatives to create a positive statement.

Correct: She was not unhappy with her performance on the quiz.

In this case, the double negative, *was not unhappy*, is intended to show a positive, so it is correct. This means that she was somewhat happy with her performance.

Faulty Parallelism

It is necessary to use parallel construction in sentences that have multiple similar ideas. Using parallel structure provides clarity in writing. **Faulty parallelism** is created when multiple ideas are joined using different sentence structures. Compare these examples:

Incorrect: We start each practice with stretches, a run, and fielding grounders.
Correct: We start each practice with stretching, running, and fielding grounders.

Incorrect: I watched some television, reading my book, and fell asleep.
Correct: I watched some television, read my book, and fell asleep.

Incorrect: Some of the readiness skills for kindergarten are to cut with scissors, to tie shoes, and dressing independently.
Correct: Some of the readiness skills for kindergarten are being able to cut with scissors, to tie shoes, and to dress independently.

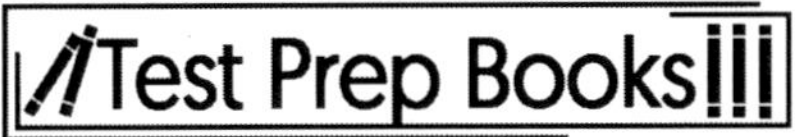

Subordination

If multiple pieces of information in a sentence are not equal, they can be joined by creating an independent clause and a dependent clause. The less important information becomes the **subordinate clause:**

> Draft: The hotel was acceptable. We wouldn't stay at the hotel again.
>
> Revised: Though the hotel was acceptable, we wouldn't stay there again.

The more important information (*we wouldn't stay there again*) becomes the main clause, and the less important information (*the hotel was acceptable*) becomes the subordinate clause.

Expression of Ideas

This section is about *how* the information is communicated rather than the subject matter itself. It's like being an editor helping the writer find the best ways to express their ideas. Things to consider include: how well a topic is developed, how accurately facts are presented, whether the writing flows logically and cohesively, and how effectively the writer uses language. This can seem like a lot to remember, but these concepts are the same ones taught way back in elementary school.

Organization

Good writing is not merely a random collection of sentences. No matter how well written, sentences must relate and coordinate appropriately to one another. If not, the writing seems random, haphazard, and disorganized. Therefore, good writing must be **organized** (where each sentence fits a larger context and relates to the sentences around it).

Transition Words

The writer should act as a guide, showing the reader how all the sentences fit together. Consider this example:

> Seat belts save more lives than any other automobile safety feature. Many studies show that airbags save lives as well. Not all cars have airbags. Many older cars don't. Air bags aren't entirely reliable. Studies show that in 15% of accidents, airbags don't deploy as designed. Seat belt malfunctions are extremely rare.

There's nothing wrong with any of these sentences individually, but together they're disjointed and difficult to follow. The best way for the writer to communicate information is through the use of **transition words**. Here are examples of transition words and phrases that tie sentences together, enabling a more natural flow:

To show causality: *as a result, therefore*, and *consequently*
To compare and contrast: *however, but,* and *on the other hand*
To introduce examples: *for instance, namely*, and *including*
To show order of importance: *foremost, primarily, secondly*, and *lastly*

The above is not a complete list of transitions. There are many more that can be used; however, most fit into these or similar categories. The important point is that the words should clearly show the relationship between sentences, supporting information, and the main idea.

Here is an update to the previous example using transition words. These changes make it easier to read and bring clarity to the writer's points:

> Seat belts save more lives than any other automobile safety feature. Many studies show that airbags save lives as well. However, not all cars have airbags. For instance, some older cars don't. Furthermore, air bags aren't entirely reliable. For example, studies show that in 15% of accidents, airbags don't deploy as designed. But, on the other hand, seat belt malfunctions are extremely rare.

Also be prepared to analyze whether the writer is using the best transition word or phrase for the situation. Take this sentence for example: "As a result, seat belt malfunctions are extremely rare." This sentence doesn't make sense in the context above because the writer is trying to show the **contrast** between seat belts and airbags, not the causality.

Logical Sequence

Even if the writer includes plenty of information to support their point, the writing is only effective when the information is in a logical order. **Logical sequencing** is really just common sense, but it's also an important writing technique. First, the writer should introduce the main idea, whether for a paragraph, a section, or the entire piece. Second, they should present evidence to support the main idea by using transitional language. This shows the reader how the information relates to the main idea and to the sentences around it. The writer should then take time to interpret the information, making sure necessary connections are obvious to the reader. Finally, the writer can summarize the information in a closing section.

Although most writing follows this pattern, it isn't a set rule. Sometimes writers change the order for effect. For example, the writer can begin with a surprising piece of supporting information to grab the reader's attention, and then transition to the main idea. Thus, if a passage doesn't follow the logical order, don't immediately assume it's wrong. However, most writing usually settles into a logical sequence after a nontraditional beginning.

Focus

Good writing stays **focused** and on topic. During the test, determine the main idea for each passage and then look for times when the writer strays from the point they're trying to make. Let's go back to the seat belt example. If the writer suddenly begins talking about how well airbags, crumple zones, or other safety features work to save lives, they might be losing focus from the topic of "safety belts."

Focus can also refer to individual sentences. Sometimes the writer does address the main topic, but in a confusing way. For example:

> Thanks to seat belt usage, survival in serious car accidents has shown a consistently steady increase since the development of the retractable seat belt in the 1950s.

This statement is definitely on topic, but it's not easy to follow. A simpler, more focused version of this sentence might look like this:

> Seat belts have consistently prevented car fatalities since the 1950s.

Providing **adequate information** is another aspect of focused writing. Statements like "seat belts are important" and "many people drive cars" are true, but they're so general that they don't contribute much to the writer's case. When reading a passage, watch for these kinds of unfocused statements.

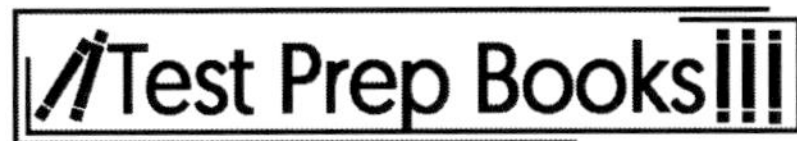

Introductions and Conclusions

Examining the writer's strategies for introductions and conclusions puts the reader in the right mindset to interpret the rest of the passage. Look for methods the writer might use for introductions such as:

- Stating the main point immediately, followed by outlining how the rest of the piece supports this claim.
- Establishing important, smaller pieces of the main idea first, and then grouping these points into a case for the main idea.
- Opening with a quotation, anecdote, question, seeming paradox, or other piece of interesting information, and then using it to lead to the main point.

Whatever method the writer chooses, the **introduction** should make their intention clear, establish their voice as a credible one, and encourage a person to continue reading.

Conclusions tend to follow a similar pattern. In them, the writer restates their main idea a final time, often after summarizing the smaller pieces of that idea. If the introduction uses a quote or anecdote to grab the reader's attention, the conclusion often makes reference to it again. Whatever way the writer chooses to arrange the conclusion, the final restatement of the main idea should be clear and simple for the reader to interpret.

Finally, conclusions shouldn't introduce any new information.

Precision

People often think of **precision** in terms of math, but precise word choice is another key to successful writing. Since language itself is imprecise, it's important for the writer to find the exact word or words to convey the full, intended meaning of a given situation. For example:

> The number of deaths has gone down since seat belt laws started.

There are several problems with this sentence. First, the word *deaths* is too general. From the context, it's assumed that the writer is referring only to *deaths* caused by car accidents. However, without clarification, the sentence lacks impact and is probably untrue. The phrase "gone down" might be accurate, but a more precise word could provide more information and greater accuracy. Did the numbers show a slow and steady decrease of highway fatalities or a sudden drop? If the latter is true, the writer is missing a chance to make their point more dramatically. Instead of "gone down" they could substitute *plummeted*, *fallen drastically*, or *rapidly diminished* to bring the information to life. Also, the phrase "seat belt laws" is unclear. Does it refer to laws requiring cars to include seat belts or to laws requiring drivers and passengers to use them? Finally, *started* is not a strong verb. Words like *enacted* or *adopted* are more direct and make the content more real. When put together, these changes create a far more powerful sentence:

> The number of highway fatalities has plummeted since laws requiring seat belt usage were enacted.

However, it's important to note that precise word choice can sometimes be taken too far. If the writer of the sentence above takes precision to an extreme, it might result in the following:

> The incidence of high-speed, automobile accident related fatalities has decreased 75% and continued to remain at historical lows since the initial set of federal legislations requiring seat belt use were enacted in 1992.

This sentence is extremely precise, but it takes so long to achieve that precision that it suffers from a lack of clarity. Precise writing is about finding the right balance between information and flow. This is also an issue of **conciseness** (discussed in the next section).

The last thing to consider with precision is a word choice that's not only unclear or uninteresting, but also confusing or misleading. For example:

> The number of highway fatalities has become hugely lower since laws requiring seat belt use were enacted.

In this case, the reader might be confused by the word *hugely*. Huge means large, but here the writer uses *hugely* to describe something small. Though most readers can decipher this, doing so disconnects them from the flow of the writing and makes the writer's point less effective.

On the test, there can be questions asking for alternatives to the writer's word choice. In answering these questions, always consider the context and look for a balance between precision and flow.

Conciseness

"Less is more" is a good rule to follow when writing a sentence. Unfortunately, writers often include extra words and phrases that seem necessary at the time, but add nothing to the main idea. This confuses the reader and creates unnecessary repetition. Writing that lacks **conciseness** is usually guilty of excessive wordiness and redundant phrases. Here's an example containing both of these issues:

> When legislators decided to begin creating legislation making it mandatory for automobile drivers and passengers to make use of seat belts while in cars, a large number of them made those laws for reasons that were political reasons.

There are several empty or "fluff" words here that take up too much space. These can be eliminated while still maintaining the writer's meaning. For example:

"decided to begin" could be shortened to "began"
"making it mandatory for" could be shortened to "requiring"
"make use of" could be shortened to "use"
"a large number" could be shortened to "many"

In addition, there are several examples of redundancy that can be eliminated:

"legislators decided to begin creating legislation" and "made those laws"
"automobile drivers and passengers" and "while in cars"
"reasons that were political reasons"

These changes are incorporated as follows:

> When legislators began requiring drivers and passengers to use seat belts, many of them did so for political reasons.

There are many examples of redundant phrases, such as "add an additional," "complete and total," "time schedule," and "transportation vehicle." If asked to identify a redundant phrase on the test, look for words that are close together with the same (or similar) meanings.

Proposition

The **proposition** (also called the **claim** since it can be true or false) is a clear statement of the point or idea the writer is trying to make. The length or format of a proposition can vary, but it often takes the form of a **topic sentence**. A good topic sentence is:

- Clear: does not weave a complicated web of words for the reader to decode or unwrap
- Concise: presents only the information needed to make the claim and doesn't clutter up the statement with unnecessary details
- Precise: clarifies the exact point the writer wants to make and doesn't use broad, overreaching statements

Look at the following example:

> The civil rights movement, from its genesis in the Emancipation Proclamation to its current struggles with de facto discrimination, has changed the face of the United States more than any other factor in its history.

Is the statement clear? Yes, the statement is fairly clear, although other words can be substituted for "genesis" and "de facto" to make it easier to understand.

Is the statement concise? No, the statement is not concise. Details about the Emancipation Proclamation and the current state of the movement are unnecessary for a topic sentence. Those details should be saved for the body of the text.

Is the statement precise? No, the statement is not precise. What exactly does the writer mean by "changed the face of the United States"? The writer should be more specific about the effects of the movement. Also, suggesting that something has a greater impact than anything else in US history is far too ambitious a statement to make.

A better version might look like this:

> The civil rights movement has greatly increased the career opportunities available for Black Americans.

The unnecessary language and details are removed, and the claim can now be measured and supported.

Support

Once the main idea or proposition is stated, the writer attempts to prove or **support** the claim with text evidence and supporting details.

Take for example the sentence, "Seat belts save lives." Though most people can't argue with this statement, its impact on the reader is much greater when supported by additional content. The writer can support this idea by:

- Providing statistics on the rate of highway fatalities alongside statistics for estimated seat belt usage.
- Explaining the science behind a car accident and what happens to a passenger who doesn't use a seat belt.
- Offering anecdotal evidence or true stories from reliable sources about how seat belts prevent fatal injuries in car crashes.

However, using only one form of supporting evidence is not nearly as effective as using a variety to support a claim. Presenting only a list of statistics can be boring to the reader, but providing a true story that's both interesting and humanizing helps. In addition, one example isn't always enough to prove the writer's larger point, so combining it with other examples is extremely effective for the writing. Thus, when reading a passage, don't just look for a single form of supporting evidence.

Another key aspect of supporting evidence is a **reliable source**. Does the writer include the source of the information? If so, is the source well known and trustworthy? Is there a potential for bias? For example, a seat belt study done by a seat belt manufacturer may have its own agenda to promote.

Effective Language Use

Language can be analyzed in a variety of ways. But one of the primary ways is its effectiveness in communicating and especially convincing others.

Rhetoric is a literary technique used to make the writing (or speaking) more effective or persuasive. Rhetoric makes use of other effective language devices such as irony, metaphors, allusion, and repetition. An example of the rhetorical use of repetition would be: "Let go, I say, let go!!!".

Figures of Speech

A **figure of speech** (sometimes called an **idiom**) is a rhetorical device. It's a phrase that's not intended to be taken literally.

When the writer uses a figure of speech, their intention must be clear if it's to be used effectively. Some phrases can be interpreted in a number of ways, causing confusion for the reader. In the SAT Writing and Language Test, questions may ask for an alternative to a problematic word or phrase. Look for clues to the writer's true intention to determine the best replacement. Likewise, some figures of speech may seem out of place in a more formal piece of writing. To show this, here is the previous seat belt example but with one slight change:

> Seat belts save more lives than any other automobile safety feature. Many studies show that airbags save lives as well. However, not all cars have airbags. For instance, some older cars don't. In addition, air bags aren't entirely reliable. For example, studies show that in 15% of accidents, airbags don't deploy as designed. But, on the other hand, seat belt malfunctions happen once in a blue moon.

Most people know that "once in a blue moon" refers to something that rarely happens. However, because the rest of the paragraph is straightforward and direct, using this figurative phrase distracts the reader. In this example, the earlier version is much more effective.

Now it's important to take a moment and review the meaning of the word *literally***.** This is because it's one of the most misunderstood and misused words in the English language. **Literally** means that something is exactly what it says it is, and there can be no interpretation or exaggeration. Unfortunately, *literally* is often used for emphasis as in the following example:

> This morning, I literally couldn't get out of bed.

This sentence meant to say that the person was extremely tired and wasn't able to get up. However, the sentence can't *literally* be true unless that person was tied down to the bed, paralyzed, or affected by a strange situation that the writer (most likely) didn't intend. Here's another example:

> I literally died laughing.

The writer tried to say that something was very funny. However, unless they're writing this from beyond the grave, it can't *literally* be true.

Rhetorical Fallacies

A **rhetorical fallacy** is an argument that doesn't make sense. It usually involves distracting the reader from the issue at hand in some way. There are many kinds of rhetorical fallacies. Here are just a few, along with examples of each:

- **Ad Hominem:** Makes an irrelevant attack against the person making the claim, rather than addressing the claim itself. For example, Senator Wilson opposed the new seat belt legislation, but should we really listen to someone who's been divorced four times?

- **Exaggeration:** Represents an idea or person in an obviously excessive manner. For example, Senator Wilson opposed the new seat belt legislation. Maybe she thinks if more people die in car accidents, it will help with overpopulation.

- **Stereotyping** (or **Categorical Claim**)**:** Claims that all people of a certain group are the same in some way. For example, Senator Wilson still opposes the new seat belt legislation. You know women can never admit when they're wrong.

When examining a possible rhetorical fallacy, carefully consider the point the writer is trying to make and if the argument directly relates to that point. If something feels wrong, there's a good chance that a fallacy is at play. The SAT Writing and Language section doesn't expect the fallacy to be named using specific terms like those above. However, questions can include identifying why something is a fallacy or suggesting a sounder argument.

Style, Tone, and Mood

Style, tone, and mood are often thought to be the same thing. Though they're closely related, there are important differences to keep in mind. The easiest way to do this is to remember that style "creates and affects" tone and mood. More specifically, **style** is *how the writer uses words* to create the desired tone and mood for their writing.

Style

Style can include any number of technical writing choices, and some may have to be analyzed on the test. A few examples of style choices include:

- Sentence Construction: When presenting facts, does the writer use shorter sentences to create a quicker sense of the supporting evidence, or do they use longer sentences to elaborate and explain the information?

- Technical Language: Does the writer use jargon to demonstrate their expertise in the subject, or do they use ordinary language to help the reader understand things in simple terms?

- Formal Language: Does the writer refrain from using contractions such as *won't* or *can't* to create a more formal tone, or do they use a colloquial, conversational style to connect to the reader?

- Formatting: Does the writer use a series of shorter paragraphs to help the reader follow a line of argument, or do they use longer paragraphs to examine an issue in great detail and demonstrate their knowledge of the topic?

On the test, examine the writer's style and how their writing choices affect the way the passage comes across.

Tone

As mentioned, **tone** refers to the writer's attitude toward the subject matter. Tone conveys how the writer feels about characters, situations, events, ideas, etc. Nonfiction writing is sometimes thought to have no tone at all, but this is incorrect.

A lot of nonfiction writing has a neutral tone, which is an extremely important tone for the writer to take. A neutral tone demonstrates that the writer is presenting a topic impartially and letting the information speak for itself. On the other hand, nonfiction writing can be just as effective and appropriate if the tone isn't neutral. For instance, take the previous examples involving seat belt use. In them, the writer mostly chooses to retain a neutral tone when presenting information. If the writer would instead include their own personal experience of losing a friend or family member in a car accident, the tone would change dramatically. The tone would no longer be neutral. Now it would show that the writer has a personal stake in the content, allowing them to interpret the information in a different way. When analyzing tone, consider what the writer is trying to achieve in the passage, and how they *create* the tone using style.

Mood

Mood refers to the feelings and atmosphere that the writer's words create for the reader. Like tone, many nonfiction pieces can have a neutral mood. To return to the previous example, if the writer would choose to include information about a person they know being killed in a car accident, the passage would suddenly carry an emotional component that is absent in the previous examples. Depending on how they present the information, the writer can create a sad, angry, or even hopeful mood. When analyzing the mood, consider what the writer wants to accomplish and whether the best choice was made to achieve that end.

Consistency

Whatever style, tone, and mood the writer uses, good writing should remain **consistent** throughout. If the writer chooses to include the tragic, personal experience above, it would affect the style, tone, and mood of the entire piece. It would seem out of place for such an example to be used in the middle of a neutral, measured, and analytical piece. To adjust the rest of the piece, the writer needs to make additional choices to remain consistent. For example, the writer might decide to use the word *tragedy* in place of the more neutral *fatality*, or they could describe a series of car-related deaths as an *epidemic*. Adverbs and adjectives such as *devastating* or *horribly* could be included to maintain this consistent attitude toward the content. When analyzing writing, look for sudden shifts in style, tone, and mood, and consider whether the writer would be wiser to maintain the prevailing strategy.

Syntax

Syntax is the order of words in a sentence. While most of the writing on the test has proper syntax, there may be questions on ways to vary the syntax for effectiveness. One of the easiest writing mistakes to spot is **repetitive sentence structure**. For example:

> Seat belts are important. They save lives. People don't like to use them. We have to pass seat belt laws. Then more people will wear seat belts. More lives will be saved.

What's the first thing that comes to mind when reading this example? The short, choppy, and repetitive sentences! In fact, most people notice this syntax issue more than the content itself. By combining some sentences and changing the syntax of others, the writer can create a more effective writing passage:

> Seat belts are important because they save lives. Since people don't like to use seat belts, though, more laws requiring their usage need to be passed. Only then will more people wear them and only then will more lives be saved.

Many rhetorical devices can be used to vary syntax (more than can possibly be named here). These often have intimidating names like anadiplosis, metastasis, and paremptosis. The test questions don't ask for definitions of these tricky techniques, but they can ask how the writer plays with the words and what effect that has on the

writing. For example, **anadiplosis** is when the last word (or phrase) from a sentence is used to begin the next sentence:

> Cars are driven by people. People cause accidents. Accidents cost taxpayers money.

The test doesn't ask for this technique by name, but be prepared to recognize what the writer is doing and why they're using the technique in this situation. In this example, the writer is probably using anadiplosis to demonstrate causation.

Practice Quiz

The next question is based on the following passage:

> Presidents' Day is a federal holiday that is celebrated in the United States on the third Monday of February. Previously, George Washington's and Abraham Lincoln's birthdays were celebrated separately. However, legislators sought to consolidate the two holidays into one. A __________ of both George Washington's and Abraham Lincoln's birthdays, Presidents' Day was officially designated as a federal holiday beginning in 1968.

1. Which choice completes the text with the most logical and precise word or phrase?
   a. opposition
   b. combination
   c. composition
   d. juxtaposition

The next question is based on the following passage from Common Sense *by Thomas Paine:*

> In the early ages of the world, according to the scripture chronology, there were no kings; the consequence of which was there were no wars; it is the pride of kings which throw mankind into confusion. Holland without a king hath enjoyed more peace for this last century than any of the monarchical governments in Europe. Antiquity favors the same remark; for the quiet and rural lives of the first patriarchs hath a happy something in them, which vanishes away when we come to the history of Jewish royalty.
>
> Government by kings was first introduced into the world by the Heathens, from whom the children of Israel copied the custom. It was the most prosperous invention the Devil ever set on foot for the promotion of idolatry. The Heathens paid divine honors to their deceased kings, and the Christian world hath improved on the plan by doing the same to their living ones. How impious is the title of sacred majesty applied to a worm, who in the midst of his splendor is crumbling into dust!

2. According to the passage, what are the Heathens responsible for?
   a. Government by kings
   b. Quiet and rural lives of patriarchs
   c. Paying divine honors to their living kings
   d. Equal rights of nature

The next question is based on the following passage:

> The Middle Ages were a time of great superstition and theological debate. Many beliefs were developed and practiced, while some died out or were listed as heresy. Boethianism is a Medieval theological philosophy that attributes sin to gratification and righteousness with virtue and God's providence. Boethianism holds that sin, greed, and corruption are means to attain temporary pleasure, but that they inherently harm the person's soul as well as other human beings.

3. What would be a potential reward for living a good life, as described in Boethianism?
   a. A long life sustained by the good deeds one has done over a lifetime
   b. Wealth and fertility for oneself and the extension of one's family line
   c. Vengeance for those who have been persecuted by others who have a capacity for committing wrongdoing
   d. God's divine favor for one's righteousness

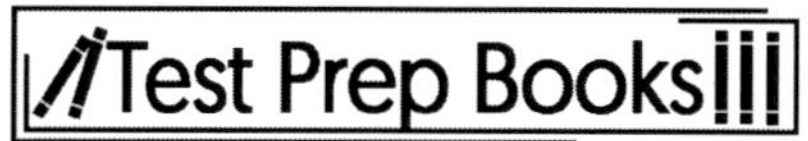

The next question is based on the following passage from Treasure Island *by Robert Louis Stevenson:*

> It had originally meant that the captain, Mr. Arrow, Hunter, Joyce, the doctor, and the squire were to occupy these six berths. Now Redruth and I were to get two of them, and Mr. Arrow and the captain were to sleep on deck in the companion, which had been enlarged on each side till you might almost have called it a round-house. Very low it was still, of course, but there was room to swing two hammocks, and even the mate seemed pleased with the _________ perhaps, had been doubtful as to the crew, but that is only a guess, for as you shall hear, we had not long the benefit of his opinion.

4. Which choice completes the text so that it conforms to the conventions of Standard English?
    a. arrangement, even he,
    b. arrangement. He
    c. arrangement: Even he
    d. arrangement. Even he,

The next question is based on the following passage:

> After the 1929 stock market crash, the standard of living for the average American dropped significantly almost overnight. This led to a large number of people attempting to withdraw their money from banks and the stock market before it lost more value, _________ causing a bank run that wiped out many people's life savings.

5. Which choice completes the text with the most logical transition?
    a. further
    b. after
    c. nevertheless
    d. consequently

See next page for answers.

Answer Explanations

1. B: Since both Washington's and Lincoln's birthdays are being celebrated on a combined holiday, *combination* fits best into the sentence. *Juxtaposition, opposition,* and *composition* do not accurately describe the previously mentioned consolidation of two holidays into Presidents' Day.

2. A: The passage states that the Heathens were the first to introduce government by kings into the world. Choice *B* is incorrect because the quiet lives of patriarchs came before the Heathens introduced this type of government and Paine puts it in opposition to government by kings. Choice *C* is incorrect because it was Christians, not Heathens, who paid divine honors to living kings. Heathens honored deceased kings. Choice *D* is incorrect because, while equal rights of nature are mentioned in the paragraph, they are not mentioned in relation to the Heathens.

3. D: The author explains that Boethianism is a Medieval theological philosophy that attributes sin to temporary pleasure and righteousness with virtue and God's providence. Other than Choice *D*, the choices listed are all physical things. While these could still be divine rewards, Boethianism holds that the true reward for being virtuous is God's favor. It is also stressed in the article that physical pleasures cannot be taken into the afterlife. Therefore, the best choice is *D*, God's favor.

4. D: Choice *D* is correct because ending the sentence with *arrangement* and a period works well grammatically, and the pronoun corresponding to the subject—*the mate*—can be identified through the last sentence's final clause, *we had not long the benefit of his opinion*. Choice *A* is incorrect because it creates a run-on sentence; a period, semicolon, or conjunction is necessary to join the independent clauses. Choice *B* is incorrect because it is missing a comma and a necessary word such as *even*. Choice *C* is incorrect because it uses a colon and does not include a comma.

5. D: Choice *D* is best as it connects the idea of a bank run to the actions that people took after the crash (withdrawing money from banks and the stock market) and illustrates their direct cause-and-effect relationship. Choice *A* is inaccurate as the bank run was not exacerbated by the actions of people after the crash but induced in the first place. Choice *B* places the timing of events out of logical order, placing the bank run before the events that caused it. Choice *C* insinuates that the bank run happened in spite of people's actions after the crash rather than as a direct result of them.

Mathematics

The Math section of the SAT focuses on a variety of math concepts and practices including real world applications of math operations and relations. The test includes a total of 44 math questions to be answered in 70 minutes. These questions are divided into two equal modules (each of which is allotted 35 minutes for 22 questions). The test contains multiple choice type questions and student-produced response questions where the test taker will be asked to enter the numeric answer rather than selecting from a number of options.

The Math section will ask the test taker to demonstrate their abilities in problem solving and modeling that reflect the types of situations that students will encounter in future college courses, careers, and everyday life. The Math section is broken down into four major content sections: Algebra, Advanced Math, Problem-Solving and Data Analysis, and Geometry and Trigonometry.

The **Algebra** section encompasses the study of algebra and the major concepts needed to solve and create linear equations and functions. Students must also use analytical and problem-solving skills to solve questions concerning linear inequalities and systems of equations. Questions in this section are presented in a variety of ways including graphical and algebraic representations of problems that require different strategies and processes to complete.

The **Advanced Math** section covers topics that will help ready students for more advanced math topics. One of the major topics in this section is knowledge of expressions and how to work with them. Also included in this section are building functions and interpreting complex equations.

The **Problem-Solving and Data Analysis** section presents questions involving units and quantities that must be manipulated and converted using ratios, rates, and proportional relationships. Test takers will also need to interpret graphs, charts, and other representations of data to identify key features of a data set such as measures of center, patterns, spread, and deviations.

The **Geometry and Trigonometry** section covers two main areas: geometric and trigonometric concepts. These include, but are not limited to, volume formulas, trigonometric ratios, and equations and theorems related to circles.

Algebra

Solving Linear Equations

A function is called **linear** if it can take the form of the equation $f(x) = ax + b$, or $y = ax + b$, for any two numbers a and b. A linear equation forms a straight line when graphed on the coordinate plane. An example of a linear function is shown below on the graph.

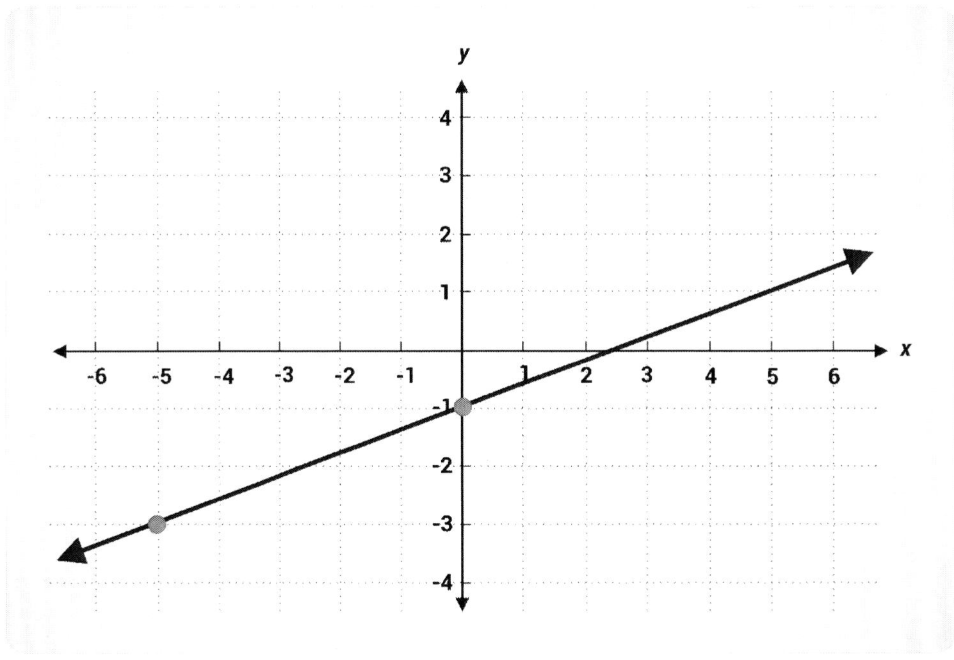

This is a graph of the following function: $y = \frac{2}{5}x - 1$. A table of values that satisfies this function is shown below.

x	y
-5	-3
0	-1
5	1
10	3

These points can be found on the graph using the form (x, y).

When graphing a linear function, note that the ratio of the change of the y-coordinate to the change in the x-coordinate is constant between any two points on the resulting line, no matter which two points are chosen. In other words, in a pair of points on a line, (x_1, y_1) and (x_2, y_2), with $x_1 \neq x_2$ so that the two points are distinct, then the ratio $\frac{y_2 - y_1}{x_2 - x_1}$ will be the same, regardless of which particular pair of points are chosen. This ratio, $\frac{y_2 - y_1}{x_2 - x_1}$, is called the **slope** of the line and is frequently denoted with the letter m. If slope m is positive, then the line goes upward when moving to the right, while if slope m is negative, then the line goes downward when moving to the right. If the

slope is 0, then the line is called **horizontal**, and the y-coordinate is constant along the entire line. In lines where the x-coordinate is constant along the entire line, y is not actually a function of x. For such lines, the slope is not defined. These lines are called **vertical** lines.

Linear functions may take forms other than $y = ax + b$. The most common forms of linear equations are explained below:

1. Standard Form: $Ax + By = C$, in which the slope is given by $m = \frac{-A}{B}$, and the y-intercept is given by $\frac{C}{B}$.

2. Slope-Intercept Form: $y = mx + b$, where the slope is m and the y-intercept is b.

3. Point-Slope Form: $y - y_1 = m(x - x_1)$, where the slope is m and (x_1, y_1) is any point on the chosen line.

4. Two-Point Form: $\frac{y-y_1}{x-x_1} = \frac{y_2-y_1}{x_2-x_1}$, where (x_1, y_1) and (x_2, y_2) are any two distinct points on the chosen line. Note that the slope is given by $m = \frac{y_2-y_1}{x_2-x_1}$.

5. Intercept Form: $\frac{x}{x_1} + \frac{y}{y_1} = 1$, in which x_1 is the x-intercept and y_1 is the y-intercept.

These five ways to write linear equations are all useful in different circumstances. Depending on the given information, it may be easier to write one of the forms over another.

If $y = mx$, y is directly proportional to x. In this case, changing x by a factor changes y by that same factor. If $y = \frac{m}{x}$, y is inversely proportional to x. For example, if x is increased by a factor of 3, then y will be decreased by the same factor, 3.

Sometimes, rather than a situation where there's an equation such as $y = ax + b$ and finding y for some value of x is requested, the result is given and finding x is requested.

The key to solving any equation is to remember that from one true equation, another true equation can be found by adding, subtracting, multiplying, or dividing both sides by the same quantity. In this case, it's necessary to manipulate the equation so that one side only contains x. Then the other side will show what x is equal to.

For example, in solving $3x - 5 = 2$, adding 5 to each side results in $3x = 7$. Next, dividing both sides by 3 results in $x = \frac{7}{3}$. To ensure the calculated results of x is correct, this calculated value can be substituted into the original equation and solved to see if it makes a true statement. For example, $3(\frac{7}{3}) - 5 = 2$ can be simplified by cancelling out the two 3s. This yields $7 - 5 = 2$, which is a true statement.

Sometimes an equation may have more than one x-term. For example, consider the following equation:

$$3x + 2 = x - 4$$

Moving all of the x-terms to one side by subtracting x from both sides results in $2x + 2 = -4$. Next, subtract 2 from both sides so that there is no constant term on the left side. This yields $2x = -6$. Finally, divide both sides by 2, which leaves $x = -3$.

Solving Linear Inequalities

Solving linear inequalities is very similar to solving equations, except for one rule: when multiplying or dividing an inequality by a negative number, the inequality symbol changes direction. Given the following inequality, solve for

x: $-2x + 5 < 13$. The first step in solving this equation is to subtract 5 from both sides. This leaves the inequality: $-2x < 8$. The last step is to divide both sides by -2. By using the rule, the answer to the inequality is $x > -4$.

Since solutions to inequalities include more than one value, number lines are often used to model the answer. For the previous example, the answer is modelled on the number line below. It shows that any number greater than -4, not including -4, satisfies the inequality.

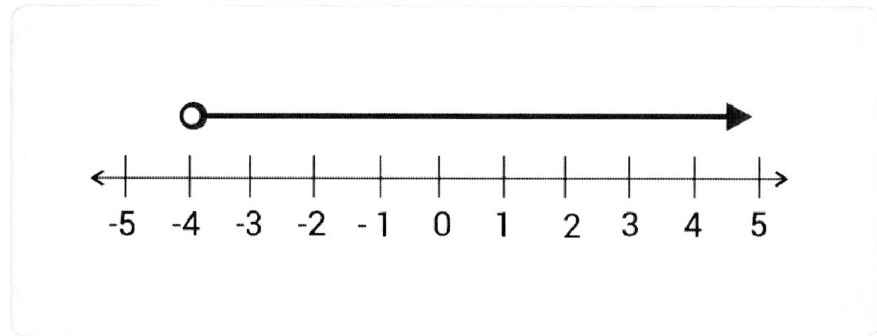

Similar to linear equations, a linear inequality may have a solution set consisting of all real numbers, or can contain no solution. When solved algebraically, a linear inequality in which the variable cancels out and results in a true statement (ex. $7 \geq 2$) has a solution set of all real numbers. A linear inequality in which the variable cancels out and results in a false statement (ex. $7 \leq 2$) has no solution.

Building Linear Functions

A **function** is a special kind of relation where, for each value of x, there is only a single value of y that satisfies the relation. So, $x^2 = y^2$ is *not* a function because in this case, if x is 1, y can be either 1 or -1: the pair $(1, 1)$ and $(1, -1)$ both satisfy the relation. More generally, for this relation, any pair of the form $(a, \pm a)$ will satisfy it. On the other hand, consider the following relation: $y = x^2 + 1$. This is a function because for each value of x, there is a unique value of y that satisfies the relation. Notice, however, there are multiple values of x that give us the same value of y. This is perfectly acceptable for a function. Therefore, y is a function of x.

To determine if a relation is a function, check to see if every x-value has a unique corresponding y-value.

A function can be viewed as an object that has x as its input and outputs a unique y-value. It is sometimes convenient to express this using **function notation**, where the function itself is given a name, often f. To emphasize that f takes x as its input, the function is written as $f(x)$. In the above example, the equation could be rewritten as:

$$f(x) = x^2 + 1$$

To write the value that a function yields for some specific value of x, that value is put in place of x in the function notation. For example, $f(3)$ means the value that the function outputs when the input value is 3. If $f(x) = x^2 + 1$, then:

$$f(3) = 3^2 + 1 = 10$$

A function can also be viewed as a table of pairs (x, y), which lists the value for y for each possible value of x.

The set of all possible values for x in $f(x)$ is called the **domain** of the function, and the set of all possible outputs is called the **range** of the function. Note that usually the domain is assumed to be all real numbers, except those for which the expression for $f(x)$ is not defined, unless the problem specifies otherwise. An example of how a function

might not be defined is in the case of $f(x) = \frac{1}{x+1}$, which is not defined when $x = -1$ (which would require dividing by zero). Therefore, in this case the domain would be all real numbers except $x = -1$.

If y is a function of x, then x is the **independent variable** and y is the **dependent variable**. This is because in many cases, the problem will start with some value of x and then see how y changes depending on this starting value.

Functions can be built out of the context of a situation. For example, the relationship between the money paid for a gym membership and the months that someone has been a member can be described through a function. If the one-time membership fee is $40 and the monthly fee is $30, then the function can be written $f(x) = 30x + 40$. The x-value represents the number of months the person has been part of the gym, while the output is the total money paid for the membership. The table below shows this relationship. It is a representation of the function because the initial cost is $40 and the cost increases each month by $30.

x (months)	y (money paid to gym)
0	40
1	70
2	100
3	130

Functions can also be built from existing functions. For example, a given function $f(x)$ can be transformed by adding a constant, multiplying by a constant, or changing the input value by a constant. The new function $g(x) = f(x) + k$ represents a vertical shift of the original function. In $f(x) = 3x - 2$, a vertical shift 4 units up would be:

$$g(x) = 3x - 2 + 4 = 3x + 2$$

Multiplying the function times a constant k represents a vertical stretch, based on whether the constant is greater than or less than 1. The function represents a stretch:

$$g(x) = kf(x) = 4(3x - 2) = 12x - 8$$

Changing the input x by a constant, forms the function:

$$g(x) = f(x + k) = 3(x + 4) - 2 = 3x + 12 - 2 = 3x + 10$$

This represents a horizontal shift to the left 4 units. If $(x - 4)$ was plugged into the function, it would represent a vertical shift.

To evaluate functions, plug in the given value everywhere the variable appears in the expression for the function. For example, find $g(-2)$ where $g(x) = 2x^2 - \frac{4}{x}$. To complete the problem, plug in -2 in the following way:

$$g(-2) = 2(-2)^2 - \frac{4}{-2} 2 \cdot 4 + 2 = 8 + 2 = 10$$

Solving Systems of Inequalities

A **linear inequality in two variables** is a statement expressing an unequal relationship between those two variables. Typically written in slope-intercept form, the variable y can be greater than, less than, greater than or equal to, or less than or equal to a linear expression that includes the variable x, such as $y > 3x$ and $y \leq \frac{1}{2}x - 3$. Questions may include instructions to model real-world scenarios, such as the following:

You work part time cutting lawns for \$15 each and cleaning houses for \$25 each. Your goal is to make more than \$90 this week. Write an inequality to represent the possible pairs of lawns and houses needed to reach your goal.

This scenario can be expressed as $15x + 25y > 90$ where x is the number of lawns cut and y is the number of houses cleaned.

The graph consists of a boundary line dividing the coordinate plane and shading on one side of the boundary. Graph the boundary line just as a linear equation would be graphed. If the inequality symbol is > or <, use a dashed line to indicate that the line is not part of the solution set. If the inequality symbol is ≥ or ≤, use a solid line to indicate that the boundary line is included in the solution set. Pick an ordered pair (x, y) on either side of the line to test in the inequality statement. If substituting the values for x and y results in a true statement $[15(3) + 25(2) > 90]$, that ordered pair and all others on that side of the boundary line are part of the solution set. To indicate this, shade that region of the graph. If substituting the ordered pair results in a false statement, the ordered pair and all others on that side are not part of the solution set. Therefore, the other region of the graph contains the solutions and should be shaded. The following is an example of the graph of $y \leq x + 2$.

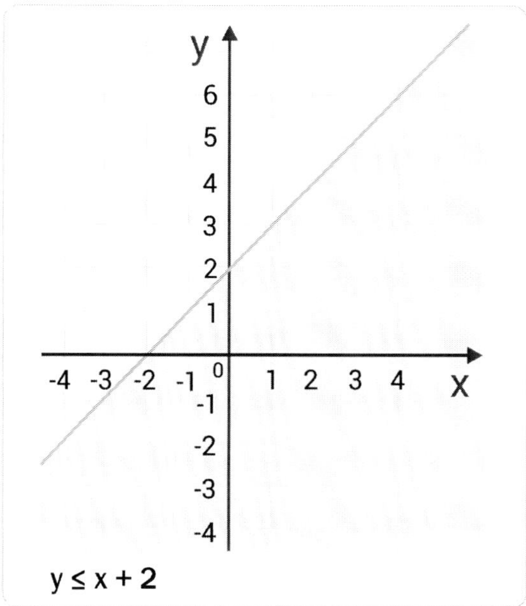

Systems of linear inequalities are like systems of equations, but the solutions are different. Since inequalities have infinitely many solutions, their systems also have infinitely many solutions. Finding the solutions of inequalities involves graphs. A system of two equations and two inequalities is linear; thus, the lines can be graphed using slope-intercept form. A system of linear inequalities consists of two linear inequalities that make comparisons between two variables. The solution set for a system of inequalities is the region of a graph consisting of ordered pairs that make BOTH inequalities true. To graph the solution set, first graph each linear inequality with appropriate shading. Identify the region of the graph where the shading for the two inequalities overlaps. This region contains the solution set for the system. In the example below, the line with the positive slope is solid, meaning the values on that line are included in the solution. The line with the negative slope is dotted, so the coordinates on that line are not included.

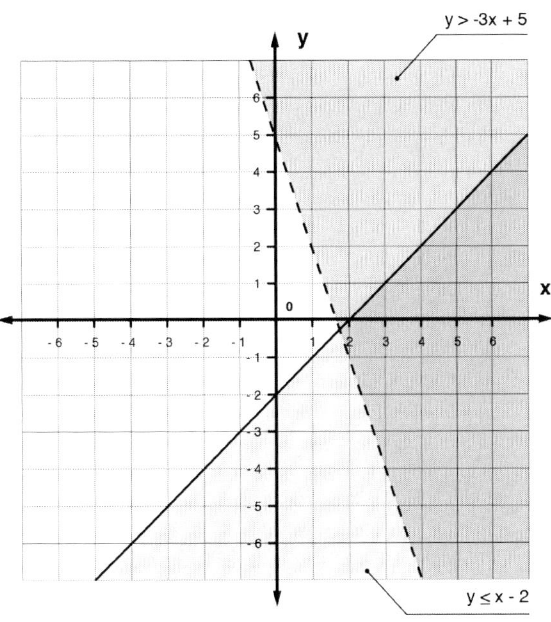

Solving Systems of Linear Equations

A **system of equations** is a group of equations that have the same variables or unknowns. These equations can be linear, but they are not always so. Finding a solution to a system of equations means finding the values of the variables that satisfy each equation. For a linear system of two equations and two variables, there could be a single solution, no solution, or infinitely many solutions.

A single solution occurs when there is one value for x and y that satisfies the system. This would be shown on the graph where the lines cross at exactly one point. When there is no solution, the lines are parallel and do not ever cross. With infinitely many solutions, the equations may look different, but they are the same line. One equation will be a multiple of the other, and on the graph, they lie on top of each other.

The process of **elimination** can be used to solve a system of equations. For example, the following equations make up a system:

$$x + 3y = 10 \text{ and } 2x - 5y = 9$$

Immediately adding these equations does not eliminate a variable, but it is possible to change the first equation by multiplying the whole equation by -2. This changes the first equation to:

$$-2x - 6y = -20$$

The equations can be then added to obtain $-11y = -11$. Solving for y yields $y = 1$. To find the rest of the solution, 1 can be substituted in for y in either original equation to find the value of $x = 7$. The solution to the system is $(7, 1)$ because it makes both equations true, and it is the point in which the lines intersect. If the system is **dependent**—having infinitely many solutions—then both variables will cancel out when the elimination method is used, resulting in an equation that is true for many values of x and y. Since the system is dependent, both equations can be simplified to the same equation or line.

A system can also be solved using **substitution**. This involves solving one equation for a variable and then plugging that solved equation into the other equation in the system. For example, $x - y = -2$ and $3x + 2y = 9$ can be solved using substitution. The first equation can be solved for x, where $x = -2 + y$. Then it can be plugged into the other equation:

$$3(-2 + y) + 2y = 9$$

Solving for y yields:

$$-6 + 3y + 2y = 9$$

That shows that $y = 3$. If $y = 3$, then $x = 1$.

This solution can be checked by plugging in these values for the variables in each equation to see if it makes a true statement.

Finally, a solution to a system of equations can be found graphically. The solution to a linear system is the point or points where the lines cross. The values of x and y represent the coordinates (x, y) where the lines intersect. Using the same system of equations as above, they can be solved for y to put them in slope-intercept form, $y = mx + b$. These equations become $y = x + 2$ and $y = -\frac{3}{2}x + 4.5$. The slope is the coefficient of x, and the y-intercept is the constant value.

This system with the solution is shown below:

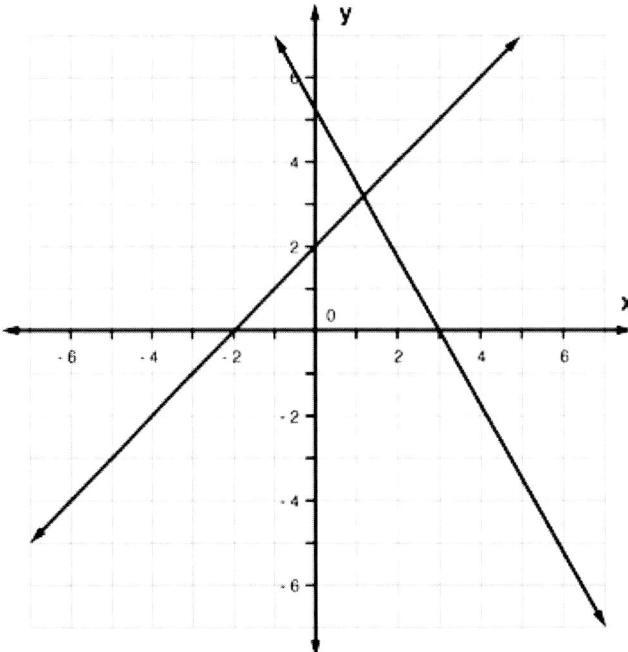

Finding solutions to systems of equations is essentially finding what values of the variables make both equations true. It is finding the input value that yields the same output value in both equations. For functions $g(x)$ and $f(x)$, the equation $g(x) = f(x)$ means the output values are being set equal to each other. Solving for the value of x

means finding the x-coordinate that gives the same output in both functions. For example, $f(x) = x + 2$ and $g(x) = -3x + 10$ is a system of equations. Setting $f(x) = g(x)$ yields the equation:

$$x + 2 = -3x + 10$$

Solving for x, gives the x-coordinate $x = 2$ where the two lines cross. This value can also be found by using a table or a graph. On a table, both equations can be given the same inputs, and the outputs can be recorded to find the point(s) where the lines cross. Any method of solving finds the same solution, but some methods are more appropriate for some systems of equations than others.

Interpreting Variables and Constants in Expressions

Algebraic expressions look similar to equations, but they do not include the equal sign. **Algebraic expressions** are comprised of numbers, variables, and mathematical operations. Some examples of algebraic expressions are $8x + 7y - 12z$, $3a^2$, and $5x^3 - 4y^4$.

Algebraic expressions and equations can be used to represent real-life situations and model the behavior of different variables. For example, $2x + 5$ could represent the cost to play games at an arcade. In this case, 5 represents the price of admission to the arcade, and 2 represents the cost of each game played. To calculate the total cost, use the number of games played for x, multiply it by 2, and add 5.

In word problems, multiple quantities are often provided with a request to find some kind of relation between them. This often will mean that one variable (the dependent variable whose value needs to be found) can be written as a function of another variable (the independent variable whose value can be figured from the given information). The usual procedure for solving these problems is to start by giving each quantity in the problem a variable, and then figuring the relationship between these variables.

For example, suppose a car gets 25 miles per gallon. How far will the car travel if it uses 2.4 gallons of fuel? In this case, *y* would be the distance the car has traveled in miles, and *x* would be the amount of fuel burned in gallons (2.4). Then the relationship between these variables can be written as an algebraic equation, $y = 25x$. In this case, the equation is $y = 25 \times 2.4 = 60$, so the car has traveled 60 miles.

Some word problems require more than just one simple equation to be written and solved. Consider the following situations and the linear equations used to model them.

Suppose Margaret is 2 miles to the east of John at noon. Margaret walks to the east at 3 miles per hour. How far apart will they be at 3 p.m.? To solve this, x would represent the time in hours past noon, and y would represent the distance between Margaret and John. Now, noon corresponds to the equation where x is 0, so the y-intercept is going to be 2. It's also known that the slope will be the rate at which the distance is changing, which is 3 miles per hour.

This means that the slope will be 3 (be careful at this point: if units were used, other than miles and hours, for x- and y-variables, a conversion of the given information to the appropriate units would be required first). The simplest way to write an equation given the y-intercept, and the slope is the Slope-Intercept form, which is $y = mx + b$. Recall that m here is the slope, and b is the y-intercept. So, $m = 3$ and $b = 2$. Therefore, the equation will be $y = 3x + 2$. The word problem asks how far to the east Margaret will be from John at 3 p.m., which means when x is 3. So, substitute $x = 3$ into this equation to obtain:

$$y = 3 \times 3 + 2 = 9 + 2 = 11$$

Therefore, she will be 11 miles to the east of him at 3 p.m.

For another example, suppose that a box with 4 cans in it weighs 6 lbs., while a box with 8 cans in it weighs 12 lbs. Find out how much a single can weighs. To do this, let *x* denote the number of cans in the box, and *y* denote the weight of the box with the cans in lbs. This line touches two pairs: $(4, 6)$ and $(8, 12)$. A formula for this relation could be written using the two-point form, with $x_1 = 4, y_1 = 6, x_2 = 8, y_2 = 12$. This would yield $\frac{y-6}{x-4} = \frac{12-6}{8-4}$, or $\frac{y-6}{x-4} = \frac{6}{4} = \frac{3}{2}$. However, only the slope is needed to solve this problem, since the slope will be the weight of a single can. From the computation, the slope is $\frac{3}{2}$. Therefore, each can weigh $\frac{3}{2}$ lb.

Understanding Connections Between Algebraic and Graphical Representations

To graph relations and functions, the **Cartesian plane** is used. This means to think of the plane as being given a grid of squares, with one direction being the x-axis and the other direction the y-axis. Generally, the independent variable is placed along the horizontal axis, and the dependent variable is placed along the vertical axis. Any point on the plane can be specified by saying how far to go along the x-axis and how far along the y-axis with a pair of numbers (x, y). Specific values for these pairs can be given names such as $C = (-1, 3)$. Negative values mean to move left or down; positive values mean to move right or up. The point where the axes cross one another is called the **origin**. The origin has coordinates $(0, 0)$ and is usually called *O* when given a specific label.

An illustration of the Cartesian plane, along with the plotted points $(2, 1)$ and $(-1, -1)$, is below.

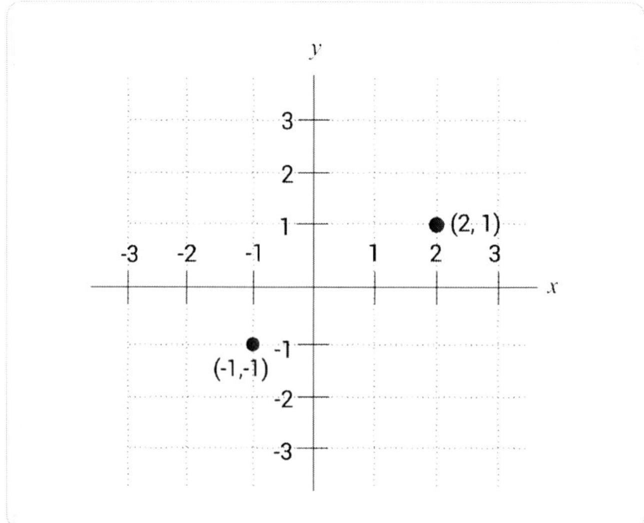

Relations also can be graphed by marking each point whose coordinates satisfy the relation. If the relation is a function, then there is only one value of *y* for any given value of x. This leads to the **vertical line test**: if a relation is graphed, then the relation is a function if any possible vertical line drawn anywhere along the graph would only touch the graph of the relation in no more than one place. Conversely, when graphing a function, then any possible vertical line drawn will not touch the graph of the function at any point or will touch the function at just one point. This test is made from the definition of a function, where each x-value must be mapped to one and only one *y*-value.

Equations and inequalities in two variables represent a relationship. Jim owns a car wash and charges $40 per car. The rent for the facility is $350 per month. An equation can be written to relate the number of cars Jim cleans to the money he makes per month. Let x represent the number of cars and y represent the profit Jim makes each month

from the car wash. The equation $y = 40x - 350$ can be used to show Jim's profit or loss. Since this equation has two variables, the coordinate plane can be used to show the relationship and predict profit or loss for Jim.

The following graph shows that Jim must wash at least nine cars to pay the rent, where $x = 9$. Anything nine cars and above yield a profit shown in the value on the y-axis.

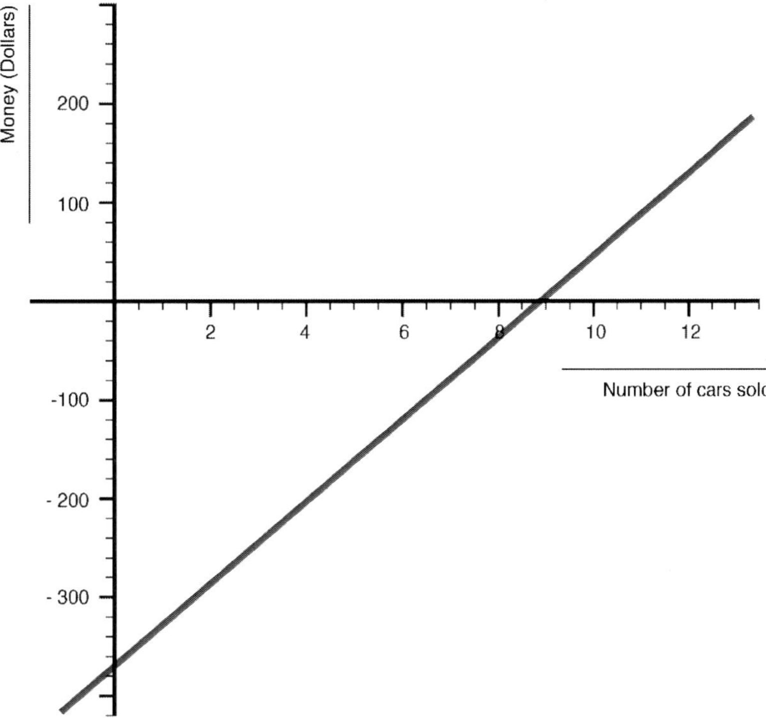

With a single equation in two variables, the solutions are limited only by the situation the equation represents. When two equations or inequalities are used, more constraints are added. For example, in a system of linear equations, there is often—although not always—only one answer. The point of intersection of two lines is the solution. For a system of inequalities, there are infinitely many answers.

Advanced Math

Creating Quadratic and Exponential Functions

A polynomial of degree 2 is called **quadratic**. Every quadratic function can be written in the form $ax^2 + bx + c$. The graph of a quadratic function, $y = ax^2 + bx + c$, is called a **parabola**. Parabolas are vaguely U-shaped.

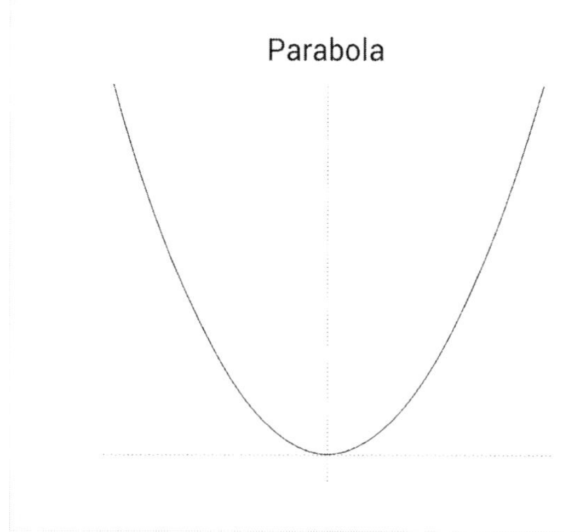

Whether the parabola opens upward or downward depends on the sign of a. If a is positive, then the parabola will open upward. If a is negative, then the parabola will open downward. The value of a will also affect how wide the parabola is. If the absolute value of a is large, then the parabola will be fairly skinny. If the absolute value of a is small, then the parabola will be quite wide.

Changes to the value of b affect the parabola in different ways, depending on the sign of a. For positive values of a, increasing b will move the parabola to the left, and decreasing b will move the parabola to the right. On the other hand, if a is negative, the effects will be the opposite: increasing b will move the parabola to the right, while decreasing b will move the parabola to the left.

Changes to the value of c move the parabola vertically. The larger that c is, the higher the parabola gets. This does not depend on the value of a.

The quantity $D = b^2 - 4ac$ is called the **discriminant** of the parabola. When the discriminant is positive, then the parabola has two real zeros, or x intercepts. However, if the discriminant is negative, then there are no real zeros, and the parabola will not cross the x-axis. The highest or lowest point of the parabola is called the **vertex.** If the discriminant is zero, then the parabola's highest or lowest point is on the x-axis, and it will have a single real zero. The x-coordinate of the vertex can be found using the equation $x = -\frac{b}{2a}$. Plug this x-value into the equation and find the y-coordinate.

A quadratic equation is often used to model the path of an object thrown into the air. The x-value can represent the time in the air, while the y-value can represent the height of the object. In this case, the maximum height of the object would be the y-value found when the x-value is $-\frac{b}{2a}$.

An **exponential function** is a function of the form $f(x) = b^x$, where b is a positive real number other than 1. In such a function, b is called the **base**.

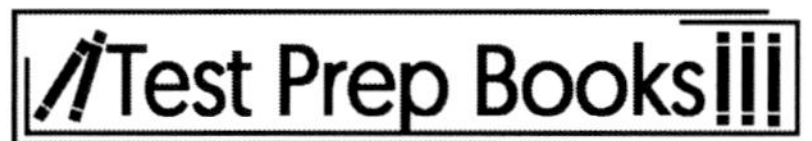

The domain of an exponential function is all real numbers, and the range is all positive real numbers. There will always be a horizontal asymptote of $y = 0$ on one side. If b is greater than 1, then the graph will be increasing moving to the right. If b is less than 1, then the graph will be decreasing moving to the right. Exponential functions are one-to-one. The basic exponential function graph will go through the point $(0, 1)$.

Example

Solve $5^{x+1} = 25$.

Get the x out of the exponent by rewriting the equation $5^{x+1} = 5^2$ so that both sides have a base of 5.

Since the bases are the same, the exponents must be equal to each other.

This leaves $x + 1 = 2$ or $x = 1$.

To check the answer, the x-value of 1 can be substituted back into the original equation.

Determining Forms of Expressions

There is a four-step process in problem-solving that can be used as a guide:

1. Understand the problem and determine the unknown information.

2. Translate the verbal problem into an algebraic equation.

3. Solve the equation by using inverse operations.

4. Check the work and answer the given question.

Example

Three times the sum of a number plus 4 equals the number plus 8. What is the number?

The first step is to determine the unknown, which is the number, or x.

The second step is to translate the problem into the equation, which is $3(x + 4) = x + 8$.

The equation can be solved as follows:

$3x + 12 = x + 8$	Apply the distributive property
$3x = x - 4$	Subtract 12 from both sides of the equation
$2x = -4$	Subtract x from both sides of the equation
$x = -2$	Divide both sides of the equation by 2

The final step is checking the solution. Plugging the value for x back into the equation yields the following problem:

$$3(-2) + 12 = -2 + 8$$

Using the order of operations shows that a true statement is made: $6 = 6$

The four-step process of problem solving can be used with geometric reasoning problems as well. There are many geometric properties and terminology included within geometric reasoning.

For example, the perimeter of a rectangle can be written in the terms of the width, or the width can be written in terms of the length.

Example

The width of a rectangle is 2 centimeters less than the length. If the perimeter of the rectangle is 44 centimeters, then what are the dimensions of a rectangle?

The first step is to determine the unknown, which is in terms of the length, l.

The second step is to translate the problem into the equation using the perimeter of a rectangle, $P = 2l + 2w$. The width is the length minus 2 centimeters. The resulting equation is:

$$2l + 2(l - 2) = 44$$

The equation can be solved as follows:

$2l + 2l - 4 = 44$	Apply the distributive property on the left side of the equation
$4l - 4 = 44$	Combine like terms on the left side of the equation
$4l = 48$	Add 4 to both sides of the equation
$l = 12$	Divide both sides of the equation by 4

The length of the rectangle is 12 centimeters. The width is the length minus 2 centimeters, which is 10 centimeters. Checking the answers for length and width forms the following equation:

$$44 = 2(12) + 2(10)$$

The equation can be solved using the order of operations to form a true statement: $44 = 44$.

Equations can also be created from complementary angles (angles that add up to 90°) and supplementary angles (angles that add up to 180°).

Example

Two angles are complementary. If one angle is four times the other angle, what is the measure of each angle?

The first step is to determine the unknown, which is the measure of the first angle. (It could be the measure of either, but we will choose to solve for the first angle.)

The second step is to translate the problem into the equation using the known statement: the sum of two complementary angles is 90°. The resulting equation is $4x + x = 90$. The equation can be solved as follows:

$5x = 90$	Combine like terms on the left side of the equation
$x = 18$	Divide both sides of the equation by 5

The first angle is 18° and the second angle is 4 times the unknown, which is 4 times 18 or 72°.

Going back to check the answer with the original question, 72 and 18 have a sum of 90, making them complementary angles. Seventy-two degrees is also four times the other angle, 18 degrees.

Creating Equivalent Expressions Involving Exponents and Radicals

An **exponent** is written as a^b. In this expression, a is called the **base** and b is called the **exponent**. It is properly stated that a is raised to the n-th power. Therefore, in the expression 2^3, the exponent is 3, while the base is 2.

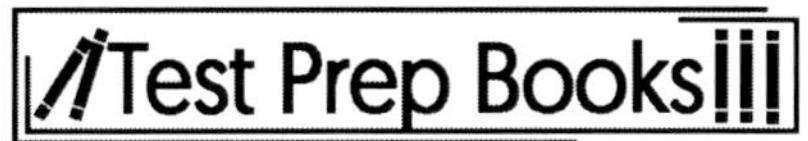

Such an expression is called an **exponential expression**. Note that when the exponent is 2, it is called **squaring** the base, and when it is 3, it is called **cubing** the base.

When the exponent is a positive integer, this indicates the base is multiplied by itself the number of times written in the exponent. So, in the expression 2^3, multiply 2 by itself with 3 copies of 2:

$$2^3 = 2 \times 2 \times 2 = 8$$

One thing to notice is that, for positive integers n and m, $a^n a^m = a^{n+m}$ is a rule. In order to make this rule be true for an integer of 0, $a^0 = 1$, so that:

$$a^n a^0 = a^{n+0} = a^n$$

And, in order to make this rule be true for negative exponents, $a^{-n} = \frac{1}{a^n}$.

Another rule for simplifying expressions with exponents is shown by the following equation: $(a^m)^n = a^{mn}$. This is true for fractional exponents as well. So, for a positive integer, define $a^{\frac{1}{n}}$ to be the number that, when raised to the n-th power, provides a. In other words, $(a^{\frac{1}{n}})^n = a$ is the desired equation. It should be noted that $a^{\frac{1}{n}}$ is the n-th root of a. This also can be written as $a^{\frac{1}{n}} = \sqrt[n]{a}$. The symbol on the right-hand side of this equation is called a **radical.** If the root is left out, assume that the 2nd root should be taken, also called the **square** root:

$$a^{\frac{1}{2}} = \sqrt[2]{a} = \sqrt{a}$$

Additionally, $\sqrt[3]{a}$ is also called the **cube** root.

Note that when multiple roots exist, $a^{\frac{1}{n}}$ is defined to be the **positive** root. So, $4^{\frac{1}{2}} = 2$. Also note that negative numbers do not have even roots in the real numbers.

This also enables finding exponents for any rational number:

$$a^{\frac{m}{n}} = (a^{\frac{1}{n}})^m = (a^m)^{\frac{1}{n}}$$

In fact, the exponent can be any real number. In general, the following rules for exponents should be used for any numbers a, b, m, and n.

$$a^1 = a$$

$$1^a = 1$$

$$a^0 = 1$$

$$a^m a^n = a^{m+n}$$

$$\frac{a^m}{a^n} = a^{m-n}$$

$$(a^m)^n = a^{m \times n}$$

$$(ab)^m = a^m b^m$$

$$(\frac{a}{b})^m = \frac{a^m}{b^m}$$

As an example of applying these rules, consider the problem of simplifying the expression:

$$(3x^2y)^3(2xy^4)$$

Start by simplifying the left term using the sixth rule listed. Applying this rule yields the following expression

$$27x^6y^3(2xy^4)$$

The exponents can now be combined with base *x* and the exponents with base *y*. Multiply the coefficients to yield $54x^7y^7$.

In mathematical expressions containing exponents and other operations, the order of operations must be followed. PEMDAS states that exponents are calculated after any parenthesis and grouping symbols but before any multiplication, division, addition, and subtraction.

Here are some of the most important properties of exponents and roots: if *n* is an integer, and if $a^n = b^n$, then $a = b$ if *n* is odd; but $a = \pm b$ if *n* is even. Similarly, if the roots of two things are equal, $\sqrt[n]{a} = \sqrt[n]{b}$, then $a = b$. This means that when starting with a true equation, both sides of that equation can be raised to a given power to obtain another true equation. Beware that when an even-powered root is taken on both sides of the equation, a $\pm$ in the result. For example, given the equation $x^2 = 16$, take the square root of both sides to solve for x. This results in the answer $x = \pm 4$ because $(-4)^2 = 16$ and $(4)^2 = 16$.

Another property is that if $a^n = a^m$, then $n = m$. This is true for any real numbers *n* and *m*.

For solving the equation $\sqrt{x+2} - 1 = 3$, start by moving the -1 over to the right-hand side. This is performed by adding 1 to both sides, which yields $\sqrt{x+2} = 4$. Now, square both sides, but remember that by squaring both sides, the signs are irrelevant. This yields $x + 2 = 16$, which simplifies to give $x = 14$.

Now consider the problem $(x+1)^4 = 16$. To solve this, take the 4th root of both sides, which means an ambiguity in the sign will be introduced because it is an even root:

$$\sqrt[4]{(x+1)^4} = \pm\sqrt[4]{16}$$

The right-hand side is 2, since $2^4 = 16$. Therefore:

$$x + 1 = \pm 2 \text{ or } x = -1 \pm 2$$

Thus, the two possible solutions are $x = -3$ and $x = 1$.

Remember that when solving equations, the answer can be checked by plugging the solution back into the problem to make a true statement.

Creating Equivalent Forms of Expressions

Algebraic expressions are made up of numbers, variables, and combinations of the two, using mathematical operations. Expressions can be rewritten based on their factors. For example, the expression $6x + 4$ can be rewritten as $2(3x + 2)$ because 2 is a factor of both $6x$ and 4. More complex expressions can also be rewritten based on their factors. The expression $x^4 - 16$ can be rewritten as $(x^2 - 4)(x^2 + 4)$. This is a different type of factoring, where a difference of squares is factored into a sum and difference of the same two terms. With some expressions, the factoring process is simple and only leads to a different way to represent the expression. With others, factoring and rewriting the expression leads to more information about the given problem.

In the following quadratic equation, factoring the binomial leads to finding the zeros of the function:

$$x^2 - 5x + 6 = y$$

This equation factors into $(x - 3)(x - 2) = y$, where 2 and 3 are found to be the zeros of the function when y is set equal to zero. The zeros of any function are the *x*-values where the graph of the function on the coordinate plane crosses the *x*-axis.

Factoring an equation is a simple way to rewrite the equation and find the zeros, but factoring is not possible for every quadratic. Completing the square is one way to find zeros when factoring is not an option. The following equation cannot be factored: $x^2 + 10x - 9 = 0$. The first step in this method is to move the constant to the right side of the equation, making it $x^2 + 10x = 9$. Then, the coefficient of x is divided by 2 and squared. This number is then added to both sides of the equation, to make the equation still true. For this example, $\left(\frac{10}{2}\right)^2 = 25$ is added to both sides of the equation to obtain:

$$x^2 + 10x + 25 = 9 + 25$$

This expression simplifies to $x^2 + 10x + 25 = 34$, which can then be factored into:

$$(x + 5)^2 = 34$$

Solving for x then involves taking the square root of both sides and subtracting 5. This leads to two zeros of the function:

$$x = \pm\sqrt{34} - 5$$

Depending on the type of answer the question seeks, a calculator may be used to find exact numbers.

Given a quadratic equation in standard form— $ax^2 + bx + c = 0$—the sign of a tells whether the function has a minimum value or a maximum value. If $a > 0$, the graph opens up and has a minimum value. If $a < 0$, the graph opens down and has a maximum value. Depending on the way the quadratic equation is written, multiplication may need to occur before a max/min value is determined.

There are also properties of numbers that are true for certain operations. The **commutative** property allows the order of the terms in an expression to change while keeping the same final answer. Both addition and multiplication can be completed in any order and still obtain the same result. However, order does matter in subtraction and division. The **associative** property allows any terms to be "associated" by parenthesis and retain the same final answer. For example:

$$(4 + 3) + 5 = 4 + (3 + 5)$$

Both addition and multiplication are associative; however, subtraction and division do not hold this property. The **distributive** property states that $a(b + c) = ab + ac$. It is a property that involves both addition and multiplication, and the a is distributed onto each term inside the parentheses.

The expression $4(3 + 2)$ is simplified using the order of operations. Simplifying inside the parenthesis first produces 4×5, which equals 20. The expression $4(3 + 2)$ can also be simplified using the distributive property:

$$4(3 + 2) = 4 \times 3 + 4 \times 2 = 12 + 8 = 20$$

Consider the following example: $4(3x - 2)$. The expression cannot be simplified inside the parenthesis because $3x$ and -2 are not like terms and therefore cannot be combined. However, the expression can be simplified by using the distributive property and multiplying each term inside of the parenthesis by the term outside of the parenthesis: $12x - 8$. The resulting equivalent expression contains no like terms, so it cannot be further simplified.

Consider the expression:

$$(3x + 2y + 1) - (5x - 3) + 2(3y + 4)$$

Again, there are no like terms, but the distributive property is used to simplify the expression. Note there is an implied one in front of the first set of parentheses and an implied -1 in front of the second set of parentheses. Distributing the 1, -1, and 2 produces:

$$1(3x) + 1(2y) + 1(1) - 1(5x) - 1(-3) + 2(3y) + 2(4)$$

$$3x + 2y + 1 - 5x + 3 + 6y + 8$$

This expression contains like terms that are combined to produce the simplified expression:

$$-2x + 8y + 12$$

Algebraic expressions are tested to be equivalent by choosing values for the variables and evaluating both expressions. For example, $4(3x - 2)$ and $12x - 8$ are tested by substituting 3 for the variable *x* and calculating to determine if equivalent values result.

Solving Quadratic Equations

A **quadratic equation** is an equation in the form:

$$ax^2 + bx + c = 0$$

There are several methods to solve such equations. The easiest method will depend on the quadratic equation in question.

Sometimes, it is possible to solve quadratic equations by manually **factoring** them. This means rewriting them in the form $(x + A)(x + B) = 0$. If this is done, then they can be solved by remembering that when $ab = 0$, either *a* or *b* must be equal to zero. Therefore, to have $(x + A)(x + B) = 0$, $(x + A) = 0$ or $(x + B) = 0$ is needed. These equations have the solutions $x = -A$ and $x = -B$, respectively.

In order to factor a quadratic equation, note that:

$$(x + A)(x + B) = x^2 + (A + B)x + AB$$

So, if an equation is in the form $x^2 + bx + c$, two numbers, *A* and *B,* need to be found that will add up to give us *b*, and multiply together to give us *c*.

As an example, consider solving the equation:

$$-3x^2 + 6x + 9 = 0$$

Start by dividing both sides by -3, leaving:

$$x^2 - 2x - 3 = 0$$

Now, notice that $1 - 3 = -2$, and also that:

$$(1)(-3) = -3$$

This means the equation can be factored into:

$$(x + 1)(x - 3) = 0$$

Now, solve $(x + 1) = 0$ and $(x - 3) = 0$ to get $x = -1$ and $x = 3$ as the solutions.

It is useful when trying to factor to remember that:

$$x^2 + 2xy + y^2 = (x + y)^2$$

$$x^2 - 2xy + y^2 = (x - y)^2$$

$$x^2 - y^2 = (x + y)(x - y)$$

However, factoring by hand is often hard to do. If there are no obvious ways to factor the quadratic equation, solutions can still be found by using the **quadratic formula**.

The quadratic formula is:

$$x = \frac{-b \pm \sqrt{b^2 - 4ac}}{2a}$$

This method will always work, although it sometimes can take longer than factoring by hand, if the factors are easy to guess. Using the standard form $ax^2 + bx + c = 0$, plug the values of *a*, *b*, and *c* from the equation into the formula and solve for *x*. There will either be two answers, one answer, or no real answer. No real answer comes when the value of the discriminant, the number under the square root, is a negative number. Since there are no real numbers that square to get a negative, the answer will be no real roots.

Here is an example of solving a quadratic equation using the quadratic formula. Suppose the equation to solve is:

$$-2x^2 + 3x + 1 = 0$$

There is no obvious way to factor this, so the quadratic formula is used, with $a = -2, b = 3, c = 1$. After substituting these values into the quadratic formula, it yields this:

$$x = \frac{-3 \pm \sqrt{3^2 - 4(-2)(1)}}{2(-2)}$$

This can be simplified to obtain:

$$\frac{3 \pm \sqrt{9 + 8}}{4}$$

or

$$\frac{3 \pm \sqrt{17}}{4}$$

Challenges can be encountered when asked to find a quadratic equation with specific roots. Given roots A and B, a quadratic function can be constructed with those roots by taking $(x - A)(x - B)$. So, in constructing a quadratic equation with roots $x = -2, 3$, it would result in:

$$(x + 2)(x - 3) = x^2 - x - 6$$

Multiplying this by a constant also could be done without changing the roots.

Adding, Subtracting, and Multiplying Polynomial Expressions

An expression of the form ax^n, where n is a non-negative integer, is called a **monomial** because it contains one term. A sum of monomials is called a **polynomial.** For example, $-4x^3 + x$ is a polynomial, while $5x^7$ is a monomial. A function equal to a polynomial is called a **polynomial function**.

The monomials in a polynomial are also called the **terms** of the polynomial.

The constants that precede the variables are called **coefficients**.

The highest value of the exponent of x in a polynomial is called the **degree** of the polynomial. So, $-4x^3 + x$ has a degree of 3, while $-2x^5 + x^3 + 4x + 1$ has a degree of 5. When multiplying polynomials, the degree of the result will be the sum of the degrees of the two polynomials being multiplied.

To add polynomials, add the coefficients of like powers of x. For example:

$$(-2x^5 + x^3 + 4x + 1) + (-4x^3 + x)$$

$$-2x^5 + (1 - 4)x^3 + (4 + 1)x + 1$$

$$-2x^5 - 3x^3 + 5x + 1$$

Likewise, subtraction of polynomials is performed by subtracting coefficients of like powers of x. So:

$$(-2x^5 + x^3 + 4x + 1) - (-4x^3 + x)$$

$$-2x^5 + (1 + 4)x^3 + (4 - 1)x + 1$$

$$-2x^5 + 5x^3 + 3x + 1$$

To multiply two polynomials, multiply each term of the first polynomial by each term of the second polynomial and add the results. For example:

$$(4x^2 + x)(-x^3 + x)$$

$$4x^2(-x^3) + 4x^2(x) + x(-x^3) + x(x)$$

$$-4x^5 + 4x^3 - x^4 + x^2$$

In the case where each polynomial has two terms, like in this example, some students find it helpful to remember this as multiplying the First terms, then the Outer terms, then the Inner terms, and finally the Last terms, with the mnemonic FOIL. For longer polynomials, the multiplication process is the same, but there will be, of course, more terms, and there is no common mnemonic to remember each combination.

Solving Equations with Radicals or Variables in the Denominator

When solving radical and rational equations, extraneous solutions must be accounted for when finding the answers. For example, the equation $\frac{x}{x-5} = \frac{3x}{x+3}$ has two values that create a 0 denominator: $x \neq 5, -3$. When solving for x, these values must be considered because they cannot be solutions. In the given equation, solving for x can be done using cross-multiplication, yielding the equation:

$$x(x+3) = 3x(x-5)$$

Distributing results in the quadratic equation $x^2 + 3x = 3x^2 - 15x$; therefore, all terms must be moved to one side of the equals sign. This results in $2x^2 - 18x = 0$, which in factored form is $2x(x-9) = 0$. Setting each factor equal to zero, the apparent solutions are $x = 0$ and $x = 9$. These two solutions are neither 5 nor -3, so they are viable solutions. Neither 0 nor 9 create a 0 denominator in the original equation.

A similar process exists when solving radical equations. One must check to make sure the solutions are defined in the original equations. Solving an equation containing a square root involves isolating the root and then squaring both sides of the equals sign. Solving a cube root equation involves isolating the radical and then cubing both sides. In either case, the variable can then be solved for because there are no longer radicals in the equation.

For example, the following expression is a radical that can be simplified: $\sqrt{24x^2}$. First, the number must be factored out to the highest perfect square. Any perfect square can be taken out of a radical. Twenty-four can be factored into 4 and 6, and 4 can be taken out of the radical. $\sqrt{4} = 2$ can be taken out, and 6 stays underneath. If $x > 0$, x can be taken out of the radical because it is a perfect square. The simplified radical is $2x\sqrt{6}$. An approximation can be found using a calculator.

Solving a System with One Linear Equation and One Quadratic Equation

A system of equations may also be made up of a linear and a quadratic equation. These systems may have one solution, two solutions, or no solutions. The graph of these systems involves one straight line and one parabola. Algebraically, these systems can be solved by solving the linear equation for one variable and plugging that answer in to the quadratic equation. If possible, the equation can then be solved to find part of the answer. The graphing method is commonly used for these types of systems. On a graph, these two lines can be found to intersect at one point, at two points across the parabola, or at no points.

Solving a system of one linear equation and one quadratic equation algebraically involves using the substitution method. Consider the following system: $y = x^2 + 9x + 11$; $y = 2x - 1$. Substitute the equivalent value of y from the linear equation $(2x - 1)$ into the quadratic equation. The resulting equation would be:

$$2x - 1 = x^2 + 9x + 11$$

Next, solve the resulting quadratic equation using the appropriate method—factoring, taking square roots, or using the quadratic formula. This equation can be solved by factoring:

$$0 = x^2 + 7x + 120$$

$$(x+3)(x+4)$$

$$x + 3 = 0 \text{ or } x + 4 = 0$$

$$x = -3 \text{ or } x = -4$$

Next, find the corresponding y-values by substituting the x-values into the original linear equation:

$$y = 2(-4) - 1 = -9$$

$$y = 2(-3) - 1 = -7$$

Write the solutions as ordered pairs: $(-4, -9)$ and $(-3, -7)$. Finally, check the possible solutions by substituting each into both original equations. (In this case, both solutions "check out.")

Rewriting Simple Rational Expressions

A fraction, or ratio, wherein each part is a polynomial, defines **rational expressions**. Some examples include $\frac{2x+6}{x}$, $\frac{1}{x^2-4x+8}$, and $\frac{z^2}{x+5}$. Exponents on the variables are restricted to whole numbers, which means roots and negative exponents are not included in rational expressions.

Rational expressions can be transformed by factoring. For example, the expression $\frac{x^2-5x+6}{(x-3)}$ can be rewritten by factoring the numerator to obtain:

$$\frac{(x-3)(x-2)}{(x-3)}$$

Therefore, the common binomial $(x - 3)$ can cancel so that the simplified expression is:

$$\frac{(x-2)}{1} = (x-2)$$

Additionally, other rational expressions can be rewritten to take on different forms. Some may be factorable in themselves, while others can be transformed through arithmetic operations. Rational expressions are closed under addition, subtraction, multiplication, and division by a nonzero expression. **Closed** means that if any one of these operations is performed on a rational expression, the result will still be a rational expression. The set of all real numbers is another example of a set closed under all four operations.

Adding and subtracting rational expressions is based on the same concepts as adding and subtracting simple fractions. For both concepts, the denominators must be the same for the operation to take place. For example, here are two rational expressions:

$$\frac{x^3-4}{(x-3)} + \frac{x+8}{(x-3)}$$

Since the denominators are both $(x - 3)$, the numerators can be combined by collecting like terms to form:

$$\frac{x^3+x+4}{(x-3)}$$

If the denominators are different, they need to be made common (the same) by using the **Least Common Denominator** (LCD). Each denominator needs to be factored, and the LCD contains each factor that appears in any one denominator the greatest number of times it appears in any denominator. The original expressions need to be multiplied times a form of 1, which will turn each denominator into the LCD. This process is like adding fractions with unlike denominators. It is also important when working with rational expressions to define what value of the variable makes the denominator zero. For this particular value, the expression is undefined.

Multiplication of rational expressions is performed like multiplication of fractions. The numerators are multiplied; then, the denominators are multiplied. The final fraction is then simplified. The expressions are simplified by factoring and cancelling out common terms. In the following example, the numerator of the second expression can be factored first to simplify the expression before multiplying:

$$\frac{x^2}{(x-4)} \times \frac{x^2 - x - 12}{2}$$

$$\frac{x^2}{(x-4)} \times \frac{(x-4)(x+3)}{2}$$

The $(x - 4)$ on the top and bottom cancel out:

$$\frac{x^2}{1} \times \frac{(x+3)}{2}$$

Then multiplication is performed, resulting in:

$$\frac{x^3 + 3x^2}{2}$$

Dividing rational expressions is similar to the division of fractions, where division turns into multiplying by a reciprocal. So, the following expression can be rewritten as a multiplication problem:

$$\frac{x^2 - 3x + 7}{x - 4} \div \frac{x^2 - 5x + 3}{x - 4}$$

$$\frac{x^2 - 3x + 7}{x - 4} \times \frac{x - 4}{x^2 - 5x + 3}$$

The $x - 4$ cancels out, leaving:

$$\frac{x^2 - 3x + 7}{x^2 - 5x + 3}$$

The final answers should always be completely simplified. If a function is composed of a rational expression, the zeros of the graph can be found from setting the polynomial in the numerator as equal to zero and solving. The values that make the denominator equal to zero will either exist on the graph as a hole or a vertical asymptote.

Interpreting Parts of Nonlinear Expressions

When a nonlinear function is used to model a real-life scenario, some aspects of the function may be relevant, while others may not. The context of each scenario will dictate what should be used. In general, x- and y-intercepts will be points of interest. A y-intercept is the value of y when $x = 0$, and an x-intercept is the value of x when $y = 0$. Suppose a nonlinear function models the value of an investment (y) over the course of time (x). It would be relevant to determine the initial value. This initial value would be the y-intercept of the function (where time equals 0). It would also be useful to note any point in time in which the value of the investment would be 0. These would be the x-intercepts of the function.

Another aspect of a function that is typically desired is the **rate of change**. This tells how fast the outputs are growing or decaying with respect to given inputs. The rate of change for a quadratic function in standard form, $y = ax^2 + bx + c$, is determined by the value of a. A positive value indicates growth, and a negative value indicates decay. The rate of change for an exponential function in standard form, $y = (a)(b^x)$, is determined by the value of b. If b is greater than 1, the function describes exponential growth, and if b is less than 1, the function describes exponential decay.

For polynomial functions, the rate of change can be estimated by the highest power of the function. Polynomial functions also include absolute and/or relative minimums and maximums. Consider functions modeling production or expenses. Maximum and minimum values would be relevant aspects of these models.

Finally, the domain and range for a function should be considered for relevance. The domain consists of all input values, and the range consists of all output values. Suppose a function models the volume of a container to be produced in relation to its height. Although the function that models the scenario may include negative values for inputs and outputs, these parts of the function would obviously not be relevant.

Understanding the Relationship Between Zeros and Factors of Polynomials

Finding the zeros of polynomial functions is the same process as finding the solutions of polynomial equations. These are the points at which the graph of the function crosses the x-axis. As stated previously, factors can be used to find the zeros of a polynomial function. The degree of the function shows the number of possible zeros. If the highest exponent on the independent variable is 4, then the degree is 4, and the number of possible zeros is 4. If there are complex solutions, the number of roots is less than the degree.

Given the function $y = x^2 + 7x + 6$, y can be set equal to zero, and the polynomial can be factored. The equation turns into $0 = (x + 1)(x + 6)$, where $x = -1$ and $x = -6$ are the zeros. Since this is a quadratic equation, the shape of the graph will be a parabola. Knowing that zeros represent the points where the parabola crosses the x-axis, the maximum or minimum point is the only other piece needed to sketch a rough graph of the function. By looking at the function in standard form, the coefficient of x is positive; therefore, the parabola opens *up*.

Using the zeros and the minimum, the following rough sketch of the graph can be constructed:

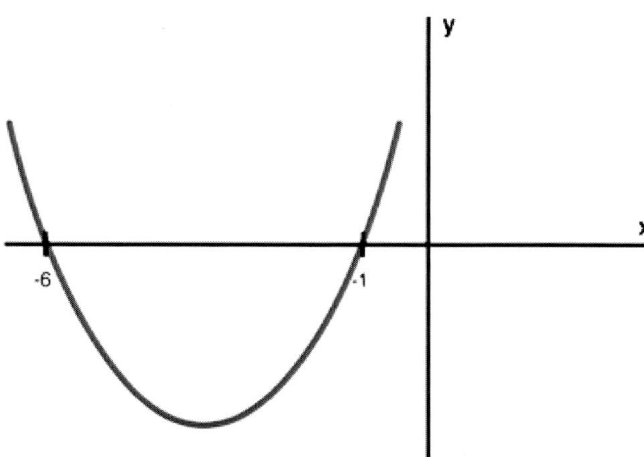

Factors for polynomials are similar to factors for integers—they are numbers, variables, or polynomials that, when multiplied together, give a product equal to the polynomial in question. One polynomial is a factor of a second polynomial if the second polynomial can be obtained from the first by multiplying by a third polynomial.

$6x^6 + 13x^4 + 6x^2$ can be obtained by multiplying together $(3x^4 + 2x^2)(2x^2 + 3)$. This means $2x^2 + 3$ and $3x^4 + 2x^2$ are factors of $6x^6 + 13x^4 + 6x^2$.

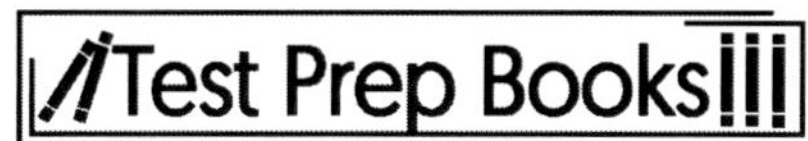

In general, finding the factors of a polynomial can be tricky. However, there are a few types of polynomials that can be factored in a straightforward way.

If a certain monomial is in each term of a polynomial, it can be factored out. There are several common forms polynomials take, which if you recognize, you can solve. The first example is a perfect square trinomial. To factor this polynomial, first expand the middle term of the expression:

$$x^2 + 2xy + y^2$$

$$x^2 + xy + xy + y^2$$

Factor out a common term in each half of the expression (in this case x from the left and y from the right):

$$x(x + y) + y(x + y)$$

Then the same can be done again, treating $(x + y)$ as the common factor:

$$(x + y)(x + y) = (x + y)^2$$

Therefore, the formula for this polynomial is:

$$x^2 + 2xy + y^2 = (x + y)^2$$

Next is another example of a perfect square trinomial. The process is the similar, but notice the difference in sign:

$$x^2 - 2xy + y^2$$

$$x^2 - xy - xy + y^2$$

Factor out the common term on each side:

$$x(x - y) - y(x - y)$$

Factoring out the common term again:

$$(x - y)(x - y) = (x - y)^2$$

Thus:

$$x^2 - 2xy + y^2 = (x - y)^2$$

The next is known as a difference of squares. This process is effectively the reverse of binomial multiplication:

$$x^2 - y^2$$

$$x^2 - xy + xy - y^2$$

$$x(x - y) + y(x - y)$$

$$(x + y)(x - y)$$

Therefore:

$$x^2 - y^2 = (x + y)(x - y)$$

The following two polynomials are known as the sum or difference of cubes. These are special polynomials that take the form of $x^3 + y^3$ or $x^3 - y^3$. The following formula factors the sum of cubes:

$$x^3 + y^3 = (x + y)(x^2 - xy + y^2)$$

Next is the difference of cubes, but note the change in sign. The formulas for both are similar, but the order of signs for factoring the sum or difference of cubes can be remembered by using the acronym SOAP, which stands for "same, opposite, always positive." The first sign is the same as the sign in the first expression, the second is opposite, and the third is always positive. The next formula factors the difference of cubes:

$$x^3 - y^3 = (x - y)(x^2 + xy + y^2)$$

The following two examples are expansions of cubed binomials. Similarly, these polynomials always follow a pattern:

$$x^3 + 3x^2y + 3xy^2 + y^3 = (x + y)^3$$

$$x^3 - 3x^2y + 3xy^2 - y^3 = (x - y)^3$$

These rules can be used in many combinations with one another. For example, the expression $3x^3 - 24$ has a common factor of 3, which becomes:

$$3(x^3 - 8)$$

A difference of cubes still remains which can then be factored out:

$$3(x - 2)(x^2 + 2x + 4)$$

There are no other terms to be pulled out, so this expression is completely factored.

When factoring polynomials, a good strategy is to multiply the factors to check the result. Let's try another example:

$$4x^3 + 16x^2$$

Both sides of the expression can be divided by 4, and both contain x^2, because $4x^3$ can be thought of as $4x^2(x)$, so the common term can simply be factored out:

$$4x^2(x + 4)$$

It sometimes can be necessary to rewrite the polynomial in some clever way before applying the above rules. Consider the problem of factoring $x^4 - 1$. This does not immediately look like any of the previous polynomials. However, it's possible to think of this polynomial as $x^4 - 1 = (x^2)^2 - (1^2)^2$, and now it can be treated as a difference of squares to simplify this:

$$(x^2)^2 - (1^2)^2$$

$$(x^2)^2 - x^2 1^2 + x^2 1^2 - (1^2)^2$$

$$x^2(x^2 - 1^2) + 1^2(x^2 - 1^2)$$

$$(x^2 + 1^2)(x^2 - 1^2)$$

$$(x^2 + 1)(x^2 - 1)$$

Understanding Nonlinear Relationships

A polynomial function consists of a monomial or sum of monomials arranged in descending exponential order. The graph of a polynomial function is a smooth continuous curve that extends infinitely on both ends.

The end behavior of the graph of a polynomial function can be determined by the **degree of the function** (largest exponent) and the **leading coefficient** (coefficient of the term with the largest exponent). If the degree is odd and the coefficient is positive, the graph falls to the left and rises to the right. If the degree is odd and the coefficient is negative, the graph rises to the left and falls to the right. If the degree is even and the coefficient is positive, the graph rises to the left and rises to the right. If the degree is even and the coefficient is negative, the graph falls to the left and falls to the right.

The y-intercept for any function is the point at which the graph crosses the y-axis. At this point, $x = 0$; therefore, to determine the y-intercept, substitute $x = 0$ into the function, and solve for y. Likewise, the x-intercepts, also called **zeros**, can be found by substituting $y = 0$ into the function and finding all solutions for x. For a given zero of a function, the graph can either pass through that point or simply touch that point (the graph turns at that zero). This is determined by the multiplicity of that zero. The multiplicity of a zero is the number of times its corresponding factor is multiplied to obtain the function in standard form. For example, $y = x^3 - 4x^2 - 3x + 18$ can be written in factored form as:

$$y = (x + 2)(x - 3)(x - 3) \text{ or } y = (x + 2)(x - 3)^2$$

The zeros of the function would be -2 and 3. The zero at -2 would have a multiplicity of 1, and the zero at 3 would have a multiplicity of 2. If a zero has an even multiplicity, then the graph touches the x-axis at that zero and turns around. If a zero has an odd multiplicity, then the graph crosses the x-axis at that zero.

The graph of a polynomial function can have several **turning points** (where the curve changes from rising to falling or vice versa) equal to one less than the degree of the function. For example, the function $y = 3x^5 + 2x^2 - 3x$ could have no more than four turning points.

Using Function Notation

A **function** is defined as a relationship between inputs and outputs where there is only one output value for a given input. As an example, the following function is in **function notation**:

$$f(x) = 3x - 4$$

The $f(x)$ represents the output value for an input of x. If $x = 2$, the equation becomes:

$$f(2) = 3(2) - 4 = 6 - 4 = 2$$

The input of 2 yields an output of 2, forming the ordered pair $(2, 2)$. The following set of ordered pairs corresponds to the given function: $(2, 2)$, $(0, -4)$, $(-2, -10)$. The set of all possible inputs of a function is its **domain**, and all possible outputs is called the **range**. By definition, each member of the domain is paired with only one member of the range.

Functions can also be defined recursively. In this form, they are not defined explicitly in terms of variables. Instead, they are defined using previously-evaluated function outputs, starting with either $f(0)$ or $f(1)$. An example of a recursively-defined function is:

$$f(1) = 2, f(n) = 2f(n - 1) + 2n, n > 1$$

The domain of this function is the set of all integers.

In many cases, a function can be defined by giving an equation. For instance, $f(x) = x^2$ indicates that given a value for x, the output of f is found by squaring x.

Not all equations in x and y can be written in the form $y = f(x)$. An equation can be written in such a form if it satisfies the **vertical line test**: no vertical line meets the graph of the equation at more than a single point. In this case, y is said to be a **function of x**. If a vertical line meets the graph in two places, then this equation cannot be written in the form $y = f(x)$.

The graph of a function $f(x)$ is the graph of the equation $y = f(x)$. Thus, it is the set of all pairs (x, y) where $y = f(x)$. In other words, it is all pairs $\left(x, f(x)\right)$. The x-intercepts are called the **zeros** of the function. The y-intercept is given by $f(0)$.

If, for a given function f, the only way to get $f(a) = f(b)$ is for $a = b$, then f is **one-to-one**. Often, even if a function is not one-to-one on its entire domain, it is one-to-one by considering a restricted portion of the domain.

A function $f(x) = k$ for some number k is called a **constant function**. The graph of a constant function is a horizontal line.

The function $f(x) = x$ is called the **identity function**. The graph of the identity function is the diagonal line pointing to the upper right at 45 degrees, $y = x$.

Given two functions, $f(x)$ and $g(x)$, new functions can be formed by adding, subtracting, multiplying, or dividing the functions. Any algebraic combination of the two functions can be performed, including one function being the exponent of the other. If there are expressions for f and g, then the result can be found by performing the desired operation between the expressions. So, if $f(x) = x^2$ and $g(x) = 3x$, then:

$$f \cdot g(x) = x^2 \cdot 3x = 3x^3$$

Given two functions, $f(x)$ and $g(x)$, where the domain of g contains the range of f, the two functions can be combined together in a process called **composition**. The function — "g composed of f" — is written:

$$(g \circ f)(x) = g(f(x))$$

This requires the input of x into f, then taking that result and plugging it in to the function g.

If f is one-to-one, then there is also the option to find the function $f^{-1}(x)$, called the **inverse** of f. Algebraically, the inverse function can be found by writing y in place of $f(x)$, and then solving for x. The inverse function also makes this statement true:

$$f^{-1}\left(f(x)\right) = x$$

Computing the inverse of a function f entails the following procedure:

Given $f(x) = x^2$, with a domain of $x \geq 0$.

$x = y^2$is written down o find the inverse.

The square root of both sides is determined to solve for y.

Normally, this would mean $\pm\sqrt{x} = y$. However, the domain of f does not include the negative numbers, so the negative option needs to be eliminated.

The result is $y = \sqrt{x}$, so $f^{-1}(x) = \sqrt{x}$, with a domain of $x \geq 0$.

A function is called **monotone** if it is either always increasing or always decreasing. For example, the functions $f(x) = 3x$ and $f(x) = -x^5$ are monotone.

An **even function** looks the same when flipped over the y-axis:

$$f(x) = f(-x)$$

The following image shows a graphic representation of an even function.

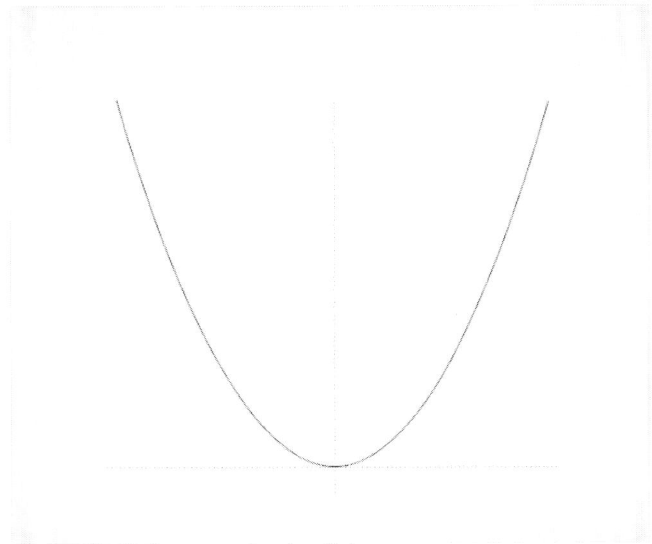

An **odd function** looks the same when flipped over the y-axis and then flipped over the x-axis:

$$f(x) = -f(-x)$$

The following image shows an example of an odd function.

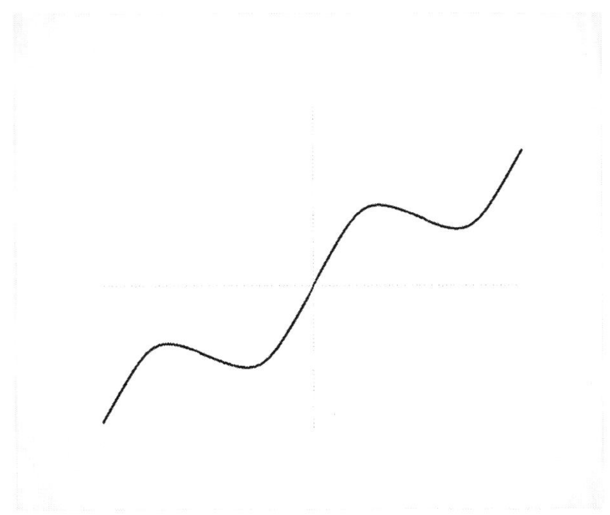

Using Structure to Isolate a Quantity of Interest

Solving equations with one variable is the process of isolating a variable on one side of the equation. For example, in $3x - 7 = 20$, the variable x needs to be isolated. Using opposite operations, the -7 is moved to the right side of the equation by adding seven to both sides:

$$3x - 7 + 7 = 20 + 7$$

$$3x = 27$$

Dividing by three on each side, $\frac{3x}{3} = \frac{27}{3}$, results in isolation of the variable. It is important to note that if an operation is performed on one side of the equals sign, it has to be performed on the other side to maintain equality. The solution is found to be $x = 9$. This solution can be checked for accuracy by plugging $x = 9$ in the original equation. After simplifying the equation, $20 = 20$ is found, which is a true statement.

Formulas are mathematical expressions that define the value of one quantity given the value of one or more different quantities. A formula or equation expressed in terms of one variable can be manipulated to express the relationship in terms of any other variable. The equation $y = 3x + 2$ is expressed in terms of the variable y. By manipulating the equation, it can be written as $x = \frac{y-2}{3}$, which is expressed in terms of the variable x. To manipulate an equation or formula to solve for a variable of interest, consider how the equation would be solved if all other variables were numbers. Follow the same steps for solving, leaving operations in terms of the variables instead of calculating numerical values.

The formula $P = 2l + 2w$ expresses how to calculate the perimeter of a rectangle given its length and width. To write a formula to calculate the width of a rectangle given its length and perimeter, use the previous formula relating the three variables, and solve for the variable w. If P and l were numerical values, this would be a two-step linear equation solved by subtraction and division. To solve the equation $P = 2l + 2w$ for w, first subtract $2l$ from both sides:

$$P - 2l = 2w$$

Then, divide both sides by 2:

$$\frac{P-2l}{2} = w \text{ or } \frac{P}{2} - l = w$$

Problem-Solving and Data Analysis

Ratios, Rates, and Proportions

Ratios are used to show the relationship between two quantities. The ratio of oranges to apples in the grocery store may be 3 to 2. That means that for every 3 oranges, there are 2 apples. This comparison can be expanded to represent the actual number of oranges and apples, such as 36 oranges to 24 apples. Another example may be the number of boys to girls in a math class. If the ratio of boys to girls is given as 2 to 5, that means there are 2 boys to every 5 girls in the class. Ratios can also be compared if the units in each ratio are the same. The ratio of boys to girls in the math class can be compared to the ratio of boys to girls in a science class by stating which ratio is higher and which is lower.

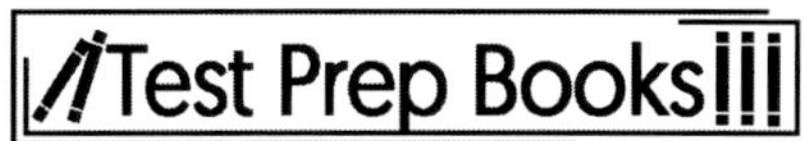

Rates are used to compare two quantities with different units. **Unit rates** are the simplest form of rate. With unit rates, the denominator in the comparison of two units is one. For example, if someone can type at a rate of 1,000 words in 5 minutes, then their unit rate for typing is $\frac{1,000}{5} = 200$ words in one minute or 200 words per minute. Any rate can be converted into a unit rate by dividing to make the denominator one. 1,000 words in 5 minutes has been converted into the unit rate of 200 words per minute.

Ratios and rates can be used together to convert rates into different units. For example, if someone is driving 50 kilometers per hour, that rate can be converted into miles per hour by using a ratio known as the **conversion factor**. Since the given value contains kilometers and the final answer needs to be in miles, the ratio relating miles to kilometers needs to be used. There are 0.62 miles in 1 kilometer. This, written as a ratio and in fraction form, is

$$\frac{0.62 \text{ miles}}{1 \text{ km}}$$

To convert 50 km/hour into miles per hour, the following conversion needs to be set up:

$$\frac{50 \text{ km}}{\text{hour}} \times \frac{0.62 \text{ miles}}{1 \text{ km}} = 31 \text{ miles per hour}$$

The ratio between two similar geometric figures is called the **scale factor**. For example, a problem may depict two similar triangles, A and B. The scale factor from the smaller triangle A to the larger triangle B is given as 2 because the length of the corresponding side of the larger triangle, 16, is twice the corresponding side on the smaller triangle, 8. This scale factor can also be used to find the value of a missing side, x, in triangle A. Since the scale factor from the smaller triangle (A) to larger one (B) is 2, the larger corresponding side in triangle B (given as 25), can be divided by 2 to find the missing side in A ($x = 12.5$). The scale factor can also be represented in the equation $2A = B$ because two times the lengths of A gives the corresponding lengths of B. This is the idea behind similar triangles.

Much like a scale factor can be written using an equation like $2A = B$, a **relationship** is represented by the equation $Y = kX$. X and Y are proportional because as values of X increase, the values of Y also increase. A relationship that is inversely proportional can be represented by the equation $Y = \frac{k}{X}$, where the value of Y decreases as the value of X increases and vice versa.

Proportional reasoning can be used to solve problems involving ratios, percentages, and averages. Ratios can be used in setting up proportions and solving them to find unknowns. For example, if a student completes an average of 10 pages of math homework in 3 nights, how long would it take the student to complete 22 pages? Both ratios can be written as fractions. The second ratio would contain the unknown.

The following proportion represents this problem, where x is the unknown number of nights:

$$\frac{10 \text{ pages}}{3 \text{ nights}} = \frac{22 \text{ pages}}{x \text{ nights}}$$

Solving this proportion entails cross-multiplying and results in the following equation: $10x = 22 \times 3$. Simplifying and solving for x results in the exact solution: $x = 6.6$ nights. The result would be rounded up to 7 because the homework would actually be completed on the seventh night.

The following problem uses ratios involving percentages:

> If 20% of the class is girls and 30 students are in the class, how many girls are in the class?

To set up this problem, it is helpful to use the common proportion:

$$\frac{\%}{100} = \frac{is}{of}$$

Within the proportion, % is the percentage of girls, 100 is the total percentage of the class, *is* is the number of girls, and *of* is the total number of students in the class. Most percentage problems can be written using this language. To solve this problem, the proportion should be set up as $\frac{20}{100} = \frac{x}{30}$ and then solved for x. Cross-multiplying results in the equation $20 \times 30 = 100x$, which results in the solution $x = 6$. There are 6 girls in the class.

Ratios can be used to solve problems that concern length, volume, and other units. A problem may ask for the volume of a cone that has a radius, $r = 7m$ and a height, $h = 16m$. Referring to the formulas provided on the test, the volume of a cone is given as:

$$V = \pi r^2 \frac{h}{3}$$

r is the radius, and h is the height. Plugging $r = 7$ and $h = 16$ into the formula, the following is obtained:

$$V = \pi(7^2)\frac{16}{3}$$

Therefore, the volume of the cone is found to be approximately 821m^3. Sometimes, answers in different units are sought. If this problem wanted the answer in liters, 821m^3 would need to be converted.

Using the equivalence statement $1 \text{ m}^3 = 1{,}000 \text{ L}$, the following ratio would be used to solve for liters:

$$821 \text{ m}^3 \times \frac{1{,}000 \text{ L}}{1 \text{ m}^3}$$

Cubic meters in the numerator and denominator cancel each other out, and the answer is converted to 821,000 liters, or 8.21×10^5 L.

Other conversions can also be made between different given and final units. If the temperature in a pool is 30 °C, what is the temperature of the pool in degrees Fahrenheit? To convert these units, an equation is used relating Celsius to Fahrenheit. The following equation is used:

$$T_{°F} = 1.8T_{°C} + 32$$

Plugging in the given temperature and solving the equation for T yields the result:

$$T_{°F} = 1.8(30) + 32 = 86 \text{ °F}$$

Units in both the metric system and US customary system are widely used.

Percentages

The word **percent** comes from the Latin phrase for "per one hundred." A percent is a way of writing out a fraction. It is a fraction with a denominator of 100. Thus, $65\% = \frac{65}{100}$.

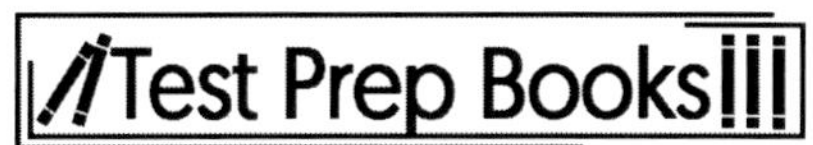

To convert a fraction to a percent, the denominator is written as 100. For example:

$$\frac{3}{5} = \frac{60}{100} = 60\%$$

In converting a percent to a fraction, the percent is written with a denominator of 100, and the result is simplified. For example:

$$30\% = \frac{30}{100} = \frac{3}{10}$$

The basic percent equation is the following:

$$\frac{is}{of} = \frac{\%}{100}$$

The placement of numbers in the equation depends on what the question asks.

Example 1
Find 40% of 80.

Basically, the problem is asking, "What is 40% of 80?" The 40% is the percent, and 80 is the number to find the percent "of." The equation is:

$$\frac{x}{80} = \frac{40}{100}$$

After cross-multiplying, the problem becomes 100x = 80(40). Solving for *x* produces the answer: *x* = 32.

Example 2
What percent of 100 is 20?

20 fills in the "is" portion, while 100 fills in the "of." The question asks for the percent, so that will be *x*, the unknown. The following equation is set up:

$$\frac{20}{100} = \frac{x}{100}$$

Cross-multiplying yields the equation $100x = 20(100)$. Solving for x gives the answer: 20%.

Example 3
30% of what number is 30?

The following equation uses the clues and numbers in the problem:

$$\frac{30}{x} = \frac{30}{100}$$

Cross-multiplying results in the equation $30(100) = 30x$. Solving for x gives the answer: $x = 100$.

Unit Rates and Conversions

When rates are expressed as a quantity of one, they are considered **unit rates**. To determine a unit rate, the first quantity is divided by the second. Knowing a unit rate makes calculations easier than simply having a rate. For example, suppose a 3-pound bag of onions costs $1.77. To calculate the price of 5 pounds of onions, a proportion could show:

$$\frac{3}{1.77} = \frac{5}{x}$$

However, by knowing the unit rate, the value of pounds of onions is multiplied by the unit price. The unit price is calculated:

$$\frac{\$1.77}{3 \text{ lb}} = \$0.59/\text{lb}$$

Multiplying the weight of the onions by the unit price yields:

$$5 \text{ lb} \times \frac{\$0.59}{\text{lb}} = \$2.95$$

The lb units cancel out.

Similar to unit-rate problems, unit conversions appear in real-world scenarios including cooking, measurement, construction, and currency. Given the conversion rate, unit conversions are written as a fraction (ratio) and multiplied by a quantity in one unit to convert it to the corresponding unit. To determine how many minutes are in $3\frac{1}{2}$ hours, the conversion rate of 60 minutes to 1 hour is written as $\frac{60 \text{ min}}{1 \text{ h}}$. Multiplying the quantity by the conversion rate results in:

$$3\frac{1}{2}\text{h} \times \frac{60 \text{ min}}{1\text{h}} = 210 \text{ min}$$

(The h unit is canceled)

To convert a quantity in minutes to hours, the fraction for the conversion rate is flipped to cancel the *min* unit. To convert 195 minutes to hours, $195 \text{ min} \times \frac{1 \text{ h}}{60 \text{ min}}$ is multiplied. The result is $\frac{195 \text{ h}}{60}$ which reduces to $3\frac{1}{4}$ h.

Converting units may require more than one multiplication. The key is to set up conversion rates so that units cancel each other out and the desired unit is left. To convert 3.25 yards to inches, given that 1yd = 3ft and 12in = 1ft, the calculation is performed by multiplying:

$$3.25 \text{ yd} \times \frac{3 \text{ ft}}{1 \text{ yd}} \times \frac{12 \text{ in}}{1 \text{ ft}}$$

The yd and ft units will cancel, resulting in 117 in.

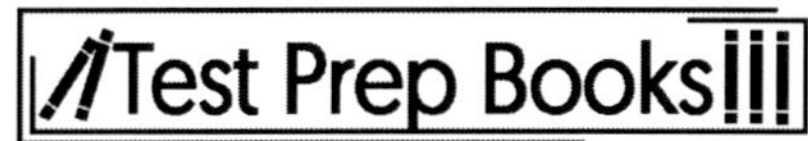

When working with different systems of measurement, conversion from one unit to another may be necessary. The conversion rate must be known to convert units. One method for converting units is to write and solve a proportion. The arrangement of values in a proportion is extremely important. Suppose that a problem requires converting 20 fluid ounces to cups. To do so, a proportion can be written using the conversion rate of $8 \text{ fl oz} = 1 \text{ c}$ with x representing the missing value. The proportion can be written in any of the following ways:

$$\frac{1}{8} = \frac{x}{20} \left(\frac{c\ for\ conversion}{fl\ oz\ for\ conversion} = \frac{unknown\ c}{fl\ oz\ given} \right)$$

$$\frac{8}{1} = \frac{20}{x} \left(\frac{fl\ oz\ for\ conversion}{c\ for\ conversion} = \frac{fl\ oz\ given}{unknown\ c} \right)$$

$$\frac{1}{x} = \frac{8}{20} \left(\frac{c\ for\ conversion}{unknown\ c} = \frac{fl\ oz\ for\ conversion}{fl\ oz\ given} \right)$$

$$\frac{x}{1} = \frac{20}{8} \left(\frac{unknown\ c}{c\ for\ conversion} = \frac{fl\ oz\ given}{fl\ oz\ for\ conversion} \right)$$

To solve a proportion, the ratios are cross-multiplied and the resulting equation is solved. When cross-multiplying, all four proportions above will produce the same equation:

$$(8)(x) = (20)(1) \rightarrow 8x = 20$$

Divide by 8 to isolate the variable x, which yields $x = 2.5$. The variable x represented the unknown number of cups. Therefore, the conclusion is that 20 fluid ounces converts (is equal) to 2.5 cups.

Sometimes converting units requires writing and solving more than one proportion. Suppose an exam question asks to determine how many hours are in 2 weeks. Without knowing the conversion rate between hours and weeks, this can be determined knowing the conversion rates between weeks and days, and between days and hours. First, weeks are converted to days, then days are converted to hours. To convert from weeks to days, the following proportion can be written:

$$\frac{7}{1} = \frac{x}{2} \left(\frac{days\ conversion}{weeks\ conversion} = \frac{days\ unknown}{weeks\ given} \right)$$

Cross-multiplying produces:

$$(7)(2) = (x)(1) \rightarrow 14 = x$$

Therefore, 2 weeks is equal to 14 days. Next, a proportion is written to convert 14 days to hours:

$$\frac{24}{1} = \frac{x}{14} \left(\frac{conversion\ hours}{conversion\ days} = \frac{unknown\ hours}{given\ days} \right)$$

Cross-multiplying produces:

$$(24)(14) = (x)(1) \rightarrow 336 = x$$

Therefore, the answer is that there are 336 hours in 2 weeks.

Scatterplots

A **scatter plot** is a way to visually represent the relationship between two variables. Each variable has its own axis, and usually the independent variable is plotted on the horizontal axis while the dependent variable is plotted on the vertical axis. Data points are plotted in a process that's similar to how ordered pairs are plotted on an xy-plane. Once all points from the data set are plotted, the scatter plot is finished. Below is an example of a scatter plot that's plotting the quality and price of an item. Note that price is the independent variable and quality is the dependent variable:

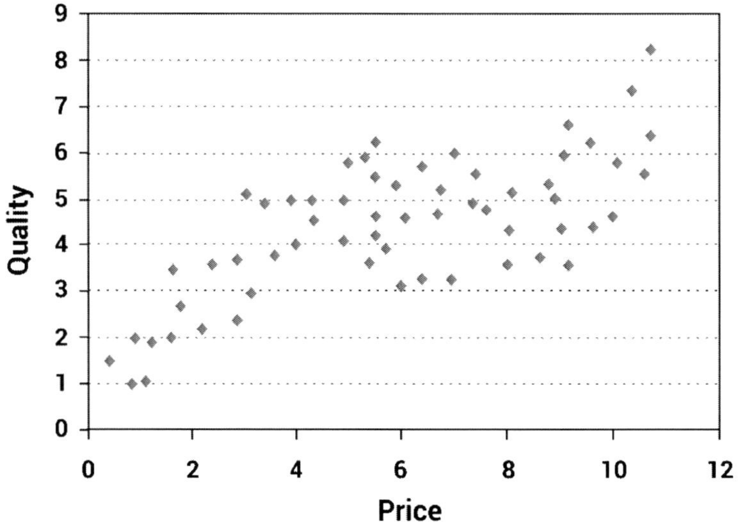

In this example, the quality of the item increases as the price increases.

Regression lines are a way to calculate a relationship between the independent variable and the dependent variable. A straight line means that there's a linear trend in the data. Technology can be used to find the equation of this line (e.g., a graphing calculator or Microsoft Excel®). In either case, all of the data points are entered, and a line is "fit" that best represents the shape of the data. If the line of best-fit has a positive slope (rises from left to right), then the variables have a positive correlation. If the line of best-fit has a negative slope (falls from left to right), then the variables have a negative correlation. If a line of best-fit cannot be drawn, then no correlation exists. A positive or negative correlation can be categorized as strong or weak, depending on how closely the points are graphed around the line of best-fit. Other functions used to model data sets include quadratic and exponential models.

Regression lines can be used to estimate data points not already given. Consider a data set with the average daily temperature at the beach and number of beach visitors. If an equation of a line is found that fits this data set, its input is the average daily temperature and its output is the projected number of visitors. Thus, the number of beach visitors on a 100-degree day can be estimated. The output is a data point on the regression line, and the number of daily visitors is expected to be greater than on a 96-degree day because the regression line has a positive slope.

The formula for a regression line is $y = mx + b$, where m is the slope and b is the y-intercept. Both the slope and y-intercept are found in the **Method of Least Squares**, which is the process of finding the equation of the line through minimizing residuals. The slope represents the rate of change in y as x gets larger. Therefore, because y is the dependent variable, the slope actually provides the predicted values given the independent variable. The y-intercept is the predicted value for when the independent variable equals zero. In the temperature example, the y-intercept is the expected number of beach visitors for a very cold average daily temperature of zero degrees.

Investigating Key Features of a Graph

When a linear equation is written in standard form, $Ax + By = C$, it is easy to identify the x- and y-intercepts for the graph of the line. Just as the y-intercept is the point at which the line intercepts the y-axis, the x-intercept is the point at which the line intercepts the x-axis. At the y-intercept, $x = 0$, and at the x-intercept, $y = 0$. Given an equation in standard form, substitute $x = 0$ to find the y-intercept, and substitute $y = 0$ to find the x-intercept. For example, to graph $3x + 2y = 6$, substituting 0 for y results in $3x + 2(0) = 6$. Solving for x yields $x = 2$; therefore, an ordered pair for the line is $(2, 0)$. Substituting 0 for x results in $3(0) + 2y = 6$. Solving for y yields $y = 3$; therefore, an ordered pair for the line is $(0, 3)$. Plot the two ordered pairs (the x- and y-intercepts), and construct a straight line through them.

T - chart

x	y
0	3
2	0

Intercepts

x - intercept : (2,0)

y - intercept : (0,3)

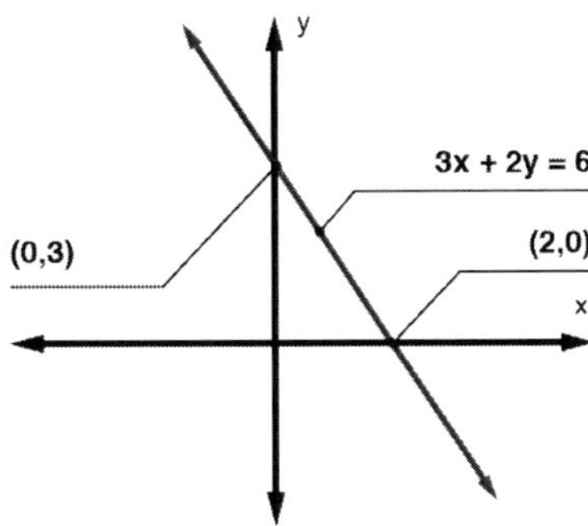

The standard form of a quadratic function is:

$$y = ax^2 + bx + c$$

The graph of a quadratic function is a U-shaped (or upside-down U) curve, called a **parabola**, which is symmetric about a vertical line (axis of symmetry). To graph a parabola, determine its vertex (high or low point for the curve) and at least two points on each side of the axis of symmetry.

Given a quadratic function in standard form, the axis of symmetry for its graph is the line $x = -\frac{b}{2a}$. The vertex for the parabola has an x-coordinate of $-\frac{b}{2a}$. To find the y-coordinate for the vertex, substitute the calculated x-coordinate. To complete the graph, select two different x-values, and substitute them into the quadratic function to obtain the corresponding y-values. This will give two points on the parabola. Use these two points and the axis of symmetry to determine the two points corresponding to these. The corresponding points are the same distance from the axis of symmetry (on the other side) and contain the same y-coordinate.

Plotting the vertex and four other points on the parabola allows for construction of the curve.

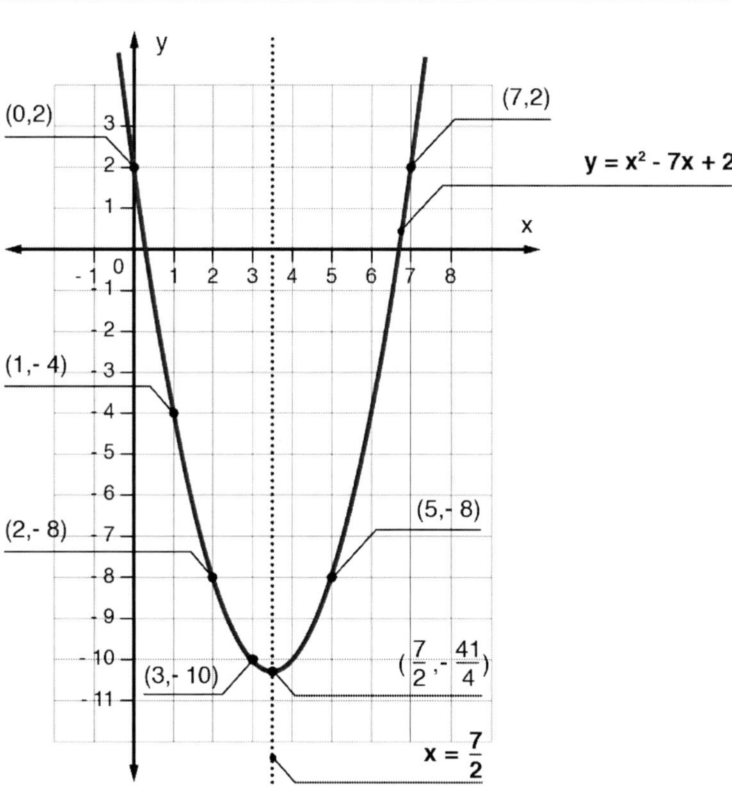

Exponential functions have a general form of $y = (a)(b^x)$. The graph of an exponential function is a curve that slopes upward or downward from left to right. The graph approaches a line, called an **asymptote**, as x or y increases or decreases. To graph the curve for an exponential function, select x-values, and substitute them into the function to obtain the corresponding y-values. A general rule of thumb is to select three negative values, zero, and three positive values.

Plotting the seven points on the graph for an exponential function should allow for the construction of a smooth curve through them.

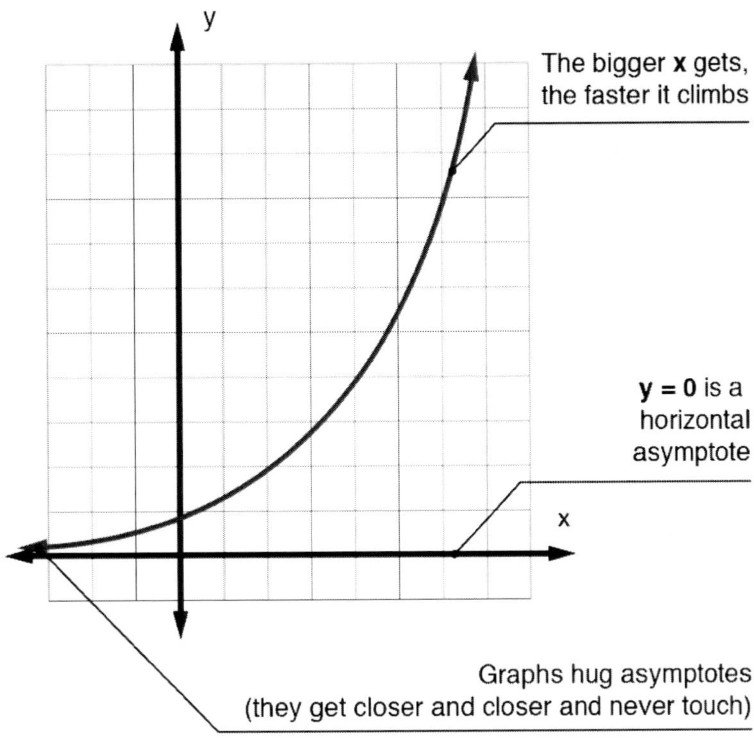

Comparing Linear and Exponential Growth

Linear functions are simpler than exponential functions, and the independent variable x has an exponent of 1. Written in the most common form, $y = mx + b$, the coefficient of x indicates how fast the function grows at a constant rate, and the b-value denotes the starting point. An exponential function has an independent variable in the exponent $y = ab^x$. The graph of these types of functions is described as **growth** or **decay**, based on whether the base, b, is greater than or less than 1. These functions are different from quadratic functions because the base stays constant. A common base is base e.

The following two functions model a linear and exponential function respectively: $y = 2x$ and $y = 2^x$. Their graphs are shown below. The first graph, modeling the linear function, shows that the growth is constant over each interval. With a horizontal change of 1, the vertical change is 2. It models constant positive growth. The second graph models the exponential function, where the horizontal change of 1 yields a vertical change that increases more and more with each iteration of horizontal change. The exponential graph gets very close to the x-axis, but never touches it, meaning there is an asymptote there. The y-value can never be zero because the base of 2 can never be raised to an input value that yields an output of zero.

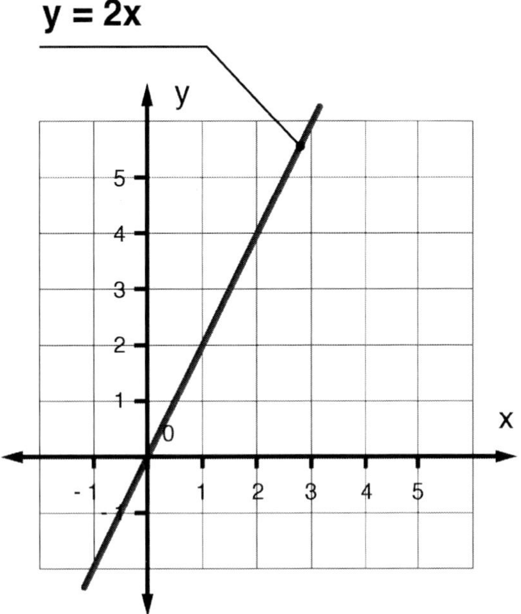

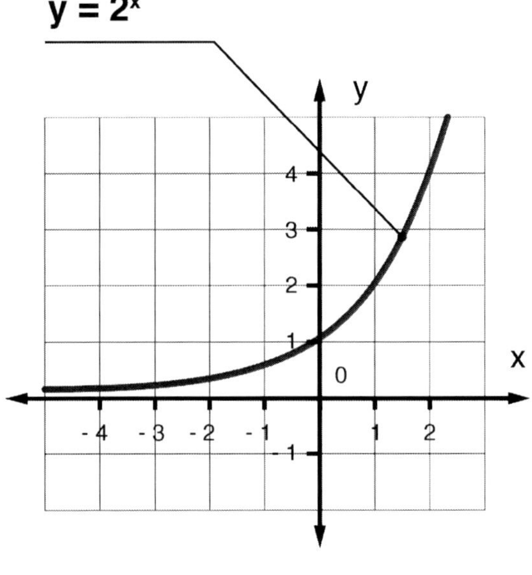

Given a table of values, the type of function can be determined by observing the change in y over equal intervals. For example, the tables below model two functions. The changes in interval for the x-values is 1 for both tables. For the first table, the y-values increase by 5 for each interval. Since the change is constant, the situation can be described as a linear function. The equation would be:

$$y = 5x + 3$$

For the second table, the change for y is 20, 100, and 500, respectively. The increases are multiples of 5, meaning the situation can be modeled by an exponential function. The equation below models this situation:

$$y = 5^x + 3$$

$y = 5x + 3$	
x	y
1	8
2	13
3	18
4	23

$y = 5^x + 3$	
x	y
1	8
2	28
3	128
4	628

Two-Way Tables

Data that isn't described using numbers is known as **categorical data.** For example, age is numerical data but hair color is categorical data. Categorical data is summarized using two-way frequency tables. A **two-way frequency table** counts the relationship between two sets of categorical data. There are rows and columns for each category, and each cell represents frequency information that shows the actual data count between each combination.

For example, the graphic on the left-side below is a two-way frequency table showing the number of girls and boys taking language classes in school. Entries in the middle of the table are known as the **joint frequencies**. For example, the number of girls taking French class is 12, which is a joint frequency. The totals are the **marginal frequencies**. For example, the total number of boys is 20, which is a marginal frequency. If the frequencies are changed into percentages based on totals, the table is known as a **two-way relative frequency table.** Percentages can be calculated using the table total, the row totals, or the column totals.

Here's the process of obtaining the two-way relative frequency table using the table total:

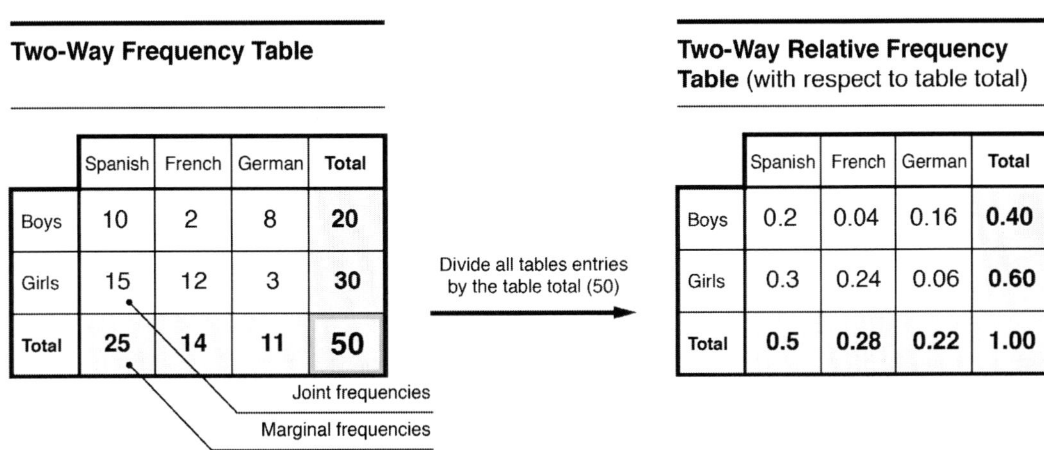

Two-Way Frequency Table

	Spanish	French	German	Total
Boys	10	2	8	**20**
Girls	15	12	3	**30**
Total	**25**	**14**	**11**	**50**

Two-Way Relative Frequency Table (with respect to table total)

	Spanish	French	German	Total
Boys	0.2	0.04	0.16	**0.40**
Girls	0.3	0.24	0.06	**0.60**
Total	**0.5**	**0.28**	**0.22**	**1.00**

The middle entries are known as **joint probabilities** and the totals are **marginal probabilities**. In this data set, it appears that more girls than boys take Spanish class. However, that might not be the case because more girls than boys were surveyed, and the results might be misleading. To avoid such errors, **conditional relative frequencies** are used. The relative frequencies are calculated based on a row or column.

Here are the conditional relative frequencies using column totals:

Two-Way Frequency Table

	Spanish	French	German	Total
Boys	10	2	8	**20**
Girls	15	12	3	**30**
Total	**25**	**14**	**11**	**50**

Divide each column entry by that column's total

Two-Way Relative Frequency Table (with respect to table total)

	Spanish	French	German	Total
Boys	0.4	0.14	0.73	**0.4**
Girls	0.6	0.86	0.27	**0.6**
Total	**1.00**	**1.00**	**1.00**	**1.00**

Two-way frequency tables can help in making many conclusions about the data. If either the row or column of conditional relative frequencies differs between each row or column of the table, then an association exists between the two categories. For example, in the above tables, the majority of boys are taking German while the majority of girls are taking French. If the frequencies are equal across the rows, there is no association, and the variables are labelled as independent. It's important to note that the association does exist in the above scenario, though these results may not occur the next semester when students are surveyed.

When measuring event probabilities, two-way frequency tables can be used to report the raw data and then used to calculate probabilities. If the frequency tables are translated into relative frequency tables, the probabilities presented in the table can be plugged directly into the formulas for conditional probabilities. By plugging in the correct frequencies, the data from the table can be used to determine if events are independent or dependent.

Conditional probability is the probability that event A will happen given that event B has already occurred. An example of this is calculating the probability that a person will eat dessert once they have eaten dinner. This is different than calculating the probability of a person just eating dessert.

The formula for the conditional probability of event A occurring given B is:

$$P(A|B) = \frac{P\ (A \text{ and } B)}{P(B)}$$

It's defined as the probability of both A and B occurring divided by the probability of event B occurring. If A and B are independent, then the probability of both A and B occurring is equal to $P(A)P(B)$, so $P(A|B)$ reduces to just $P(A)$. This means that A and B have no relationship, and the probability of A occurring is the same as the conditional probability of A occurring given B. Similarly, $P(B|A) = \frac{P\ (B \text{ and A })}{P(A)} = P(B)$, if A and B are independent.

Two events aren't always independent. For example, having glasses and having brown hair aren't independent characteristics. There definitely can be overlap because people with brown hair can wear glasses. Also, two events that exist at the same time don't have to have a relationship. For example, even if everyone in a given sample is wearing glasses, the characteristics aren't related. In this case, the probability of a brunette wearing glasses is equal to the probability of a female being a brunette multiplied by the probability of a female wearing glasses. This mathematical test of $P(A \cap B) = P(A)P(B)$ verifies that two events are independent.

Conditional probability is the probability that an event occurs given that another event has happened. If the two events are related, the probability that the second event will occur changes if the other event has happened. However, if the two events aren't related and are therefore independent, the first event to occur won't impact the probability of the second event occurring.

Making Inferences About Population Parameters

Inferential statistics attempts to use data about a subset of some population to make inferences about the rest of the population. An example of this would be taking a collection of students who received tutoring and comparing their results to a collection of students who did not receive tutoring, then using that comparison to try to predict whether the tutoring program in question is beneficial.

To be sure that inferences have a high probability of being true for the whole population, the subset that is analyzed needs to resemble a miniature version of the population as closely as possible. For this reason, statisticians like to choose random samples from the population to study, rather than picking a specific group of people based on some similarity. For example, studying the incomes of people who live in Portland does not tell anything useful about the incomes of people who live in Tallahassee.

A **population** is the entire set of people or things of interest. Suppose a study is intended to determine the number of hours of sleep per night for college females in the United States. The population would consist of EVERY college female in the country. A **sample** is a subset of the population that may be used for the study. It would not be practical to survey every female college student, so a sample might consist of one hundred students per school from twenty different colleges in the country. From the results of the survey, a sample statistic can be calculated. A sample statistic is a numerical characteristic of the sample data, including mean and variance. A sample statistic can be used to estimate a corresponding population parameter. A **population parameter** is a numerical characteristic of the entire population. Suppose our sample data had a mean (average) of 5.5. This sample statistic can be used as an estimate of the population parameter (average hours of sleep for every college female in the United States).

A population parameter is usually unknown and therefore estimated using a sample statistic. This estimate may be very accurate or relatively inaccurate based on errors in sampling. A **confidence interval** indicates a range of values likely to include the true population parameter. These are constructed at a given confidence level, such as 95 percent. This means that if the same population is sampled repeatedly, the true population parameter would occur within the interval for 95 percent of the samples.

The accuracy of a population parameter based on a sample statistic may also be affected by **measurement error**. Measurement error is the difference between a quantity's true value and its measured value. Measurement error can be divided into random error and systematic error. An example of random error for the previous scenario would be a student reporting 8 hours of sleep when she sleeps 7 hours per night. Systematic errors are those attributed to the measurement system. Suppose the sleep survey gave response options of 2, 4, 6, 8, or 10 hours. This would lead to systematic measurement error.

Statistics

The field of **statistics** describes relationships between quantities that are related, but not necessarily in a deterministic manner. For example, a graduating student's salary will often be higher when the student graduates with a higher GPA, but this is not always the case. Likewise, people who smoke tobacco are more likely to develop lung cancer, but, in fact, it is possible for non-smokers to develop the disease as well. Statistics describes these kinds of situations, where the likelihood of some outcome depends on the starting data.

Comparing data sets within statistics can mean many things. The first way to compare data sets is by looking at the center and spread of each set. The center of a data set is measured by mean, median, and mode.

Suppose that X is a set of data points $(x_1, x_2, x_3, \ldots x_n)$ and some description of the general properties of this data need to be found.

The first property that can be defined for this set of data is the **mean**. To find the mean, add up all the data points, then divide by the total number of data points. This can be expressed using **summation notation** as:

$$\bar{X} = \frac{x_1 + x_2 + x_3 + \ldots + x_n}{n} = \frac{1}{n}\sum_{i=1}^{n} x_i$$

For example, suppose that in a class of 10 students, the scores on a test were 50, 60, 65, 65, 75, 80, 85, 85, 90, 100. Therefore, the average test score will be:

$$\frac{1}{10}(50 + 60 + 65 + 65 + 75 + 80 + 85 + 85 + 90 + 100) = 75.5$$

The mean is a useful number if the distribution of data is normal (more on this later), which roughly means that the frequency of different outcomes has a single peak and is roughly equally distributed on both sides of that peak.

However, it is less useful in some cases where the data might be split or where there are some **outliers**. Outliers are data points that are far from the rest of the data. For example, suppose there are 90 employees and 10 executives at a company. The executives make \$1,000 per hour, and the employees make \$10 per hour. Therefore, the average pay rate will be $\frac{1{,}000\cdot 10+10\cdot 90}{100} = 109$, or \$109 per hour. In this case, this average is not very descriptive.

Another useful measurement is the **median**. In a data set X consisting of data points $x_1, x_2, x_3, \ldots x_n$, the median is the point in the middle. The middle refers to the point where half the data comes before it and half comes after, when the data is recorded in numerical order. If *n* is odd, then the median is $x_{\frac{n+1}{2}}$. If *n* is even, it is defined as $\frac{1}{2}\left(x_{\frac{n}{2}} + x_{\frac{n}{2}+1}\right)$, the mean of the two data points closest to the middle of the data points. In the previous example of test scores, the two middle points are 75 and 80. Since there is no single point, the average of these two scores needs to be found. The average is:

$$\frac{75+80}{2} = 77.5$$

The median is generally a good value to use if there are a few outliers in the data. It prevents those outliers from affecting the "middle" value as much as when using the mean.

Since an outlier is a data point that is far from most of the other data points in a data set, this means an outlier also is any point that is far from the median of the data set. The outliers can have a substantial effect on the mean of a data set, but they usually do not change the median or mode, or do not change them by a large quantity. For example, consider the data set (3, 5, 6, 6, 6, 8). This has a median of 6 and a mode of 6, with a mean of $\frac{34}{6} \approx 5.67$. Now, suppose a new data point of 1,000 is added so that the data set is now (3, 5, 6, 6, 6, 8, 1,000). The median and mode, which are both still 6, remain unchanged. However, the average is now $\frac{1{,}034}{7}$, which is approximately 147.7. In this case, the median and mode will be better descriptions for most of the data points.

Outliers in a given data set are sometimes the result of an error by the experimenter, but oftentimes, they are perfectly valid data points that must be taken into consideration.

One additional measure to define for X is the **mode**. This is the data point that appears more frequently. If two or more data points all tie for the most frequent appearance, then each of them is considered a mode. In the case of the test scores, where the numbers were 50, 60, 65, 65, 75, 80, 85, 85, 90, 100, there are two modes: 65 and 85.

The **spread** of a data set refers to how far the data points are from the center (mean or median). The spread can be measured by the range or the quartiles and interquartile range. A data set with all its data points clustered around the center will have a small spread. A data set covering a wide range of values will have a large spread. The **interquartile range** *(IQR)* is the range of the middle 50 percent of the data set. This range can be seen in the large rectangle on a box plot. The **standard deviation** *(σ)* quantifies the amount of variation with respect to the mean. A lower standard deviation shows that the data set doesn't differ greatly from the mean. A larger standard deviation shows that the data set is spread out farther from the mean. The formula used for standard deviation depends on whether it's being used for a population or a sample (a subset of a population). The formula for sample standard deviation is:

$$s = \sqrt{\frac{\sum(x-\bar{x})^2}{n-1}}$$

In this formula, s represents the standard deviation value, x is each value in the data set, $\bar{x}$ is the sample mean, and n is the total number of data points in the set. Note that sample standard deviations use *one less than the total* in the denominator. The population standard deviation formula is similar:

$$\sigma = \sqrt{\frac{\sum(x - \mu)^2}{N}}$$

For population standard deviations, sigma (σ) represents the standard deviation, x represents each value in the data set, mu (μ) is the population mean, and N is the total number of data points for the population.

The shape of a data set is another way to compare two or more sets of data. If a data set isn't symmetric around its mean, it's said to be **skewed.** If the tail to the left of the mean is longer, it's said to be **skewed to the left**. In this case, the mean is less than the median. Conversely, if the tail to the right of the mean is longer, it's said to be **skewed to the right** and the mean is greater than the median. When classifying a data set according to its shape, its overall **skewness** is being discussed. If the mean and median are equal, the data set isn't skewed; it is **symmetric**, and is considered normally distributed.

Evaluating Reports

The presentation of statistics can be manipulated to produce a desired outcome. Consider the statement, "Four out of five dentists recommend our toothpaste." This is a vague statement that is obviously biased. (Who are the five dentists this statement references?) This statement is very different from the statement, "Four out of every five dentists recommend our toothpaste." Whether intentional or unintentional, statistics can be misleading. Statistical reports should be examined to verify the validity and significance of the results. The context of the numerical values allows for deciphering the meaning, intent, and significance of the survey or study. Questions on this material will require students to use critical-thinking skills to justify or reject results and conclusions.

When analyzing a report, consider who conducted the study and their intent. Was it performed by a neutral party or by a person or group with a vested interest? A study on health risks of smoking performed by a health insurance company would have a much different intent than one performed by a cigarette company. Consider the sampling method and the data collection method. Was it a true random sample of the population, or was one subgroup overrepresented or underrepresented?

The three most common types of data gathering techniques are sample surveys, experiments, and observational studies. **Sample surveys** involve collecting data from a random sample of people from a desired population. The measurement of the variable is only performed on this set of people. To have accurate data, the sampling must be unbiased and random. For example, surveying students in an advanced calculus class on how much they enjoy math classes is not a useful sample if the population should be all college students based on the research question. An **experiment** is the method in which a hypothesis is tested using a controlled process called the scientific method.

A cause and the effect of that cause are measured, and the hypothesis is accepted or rejected. Experiments are usually completed in a controlled environment where the results of a control population are compared to the results of a test population. The groups are selected using a randomization process in which each group has a representative mix of the population being tested. Finally, an **observational study** is similar to an experiment. However, this design is used when circumstances prevent or do not allow for a designated control group and experimental group (e.g., lack of funding or unrealistic expectations). Instead, existing control and test populations must be used, so this method has a lack of randomization.

Consider the sleep study scenario from the previous section. If all twenty schools included in the study were state colleges, the results may be biased due to a lack of private-school participants. Consider the measurement system used to obtain the data. Was the system accurate and precise, or was it a flawed system? If, for the sleep study, the possible responses were limited to 2, 4, 6, 8, or 10 hours, it could be argued that the measurement system was flawed. Would odd numbers be rounded up or down? Without clarity of the system, the results could vary greatly. What about students who sleep 12 hours per night? The closest option for them would be 10 hours, which is significantly less.

Every scenario involving statistical reports will be different. The key is to examine all aspects of the study before determining whether to accept or reject the results and corresponding conclusions.

Geometry and Trigonometry

Solving Problems Using Volume Formulas

Geometry in three dimensions is similar to geometry in two dimensions. The main new feature is that three points now define a unique **plane** that passes through each of them. Below, some of the possible three-dimensional figures will be provided, along with formulas for their volumes.

A **rectangular prism** is a box whose sides are all rectangles meeting at 90° angles. Such a box has three dimensions: length, width, and height. If the length is x, the width is y, and the height is z, then the volume is given by $V = xyz$.

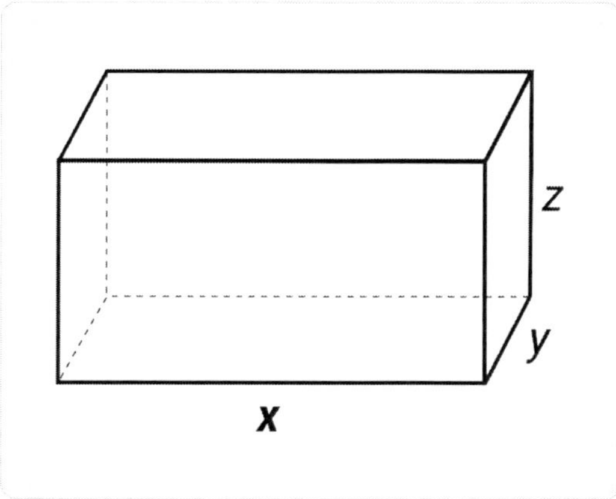

A **rectangular pyramid** is a figure with a rectangular base and four triangular sides that meet at a single vertex. If the rectangle has sides of length x and y, then the volume will be given by:

$$V = \frac{1}{3}xyh$$

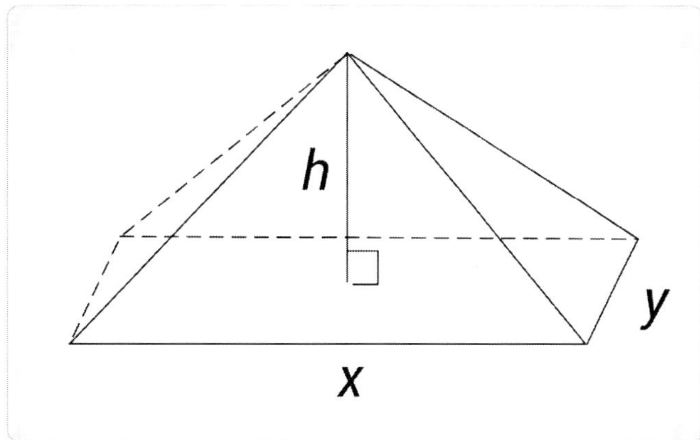

A **sphere** is a set of points all of which are equidistant from some central point. It is like a circle, but in three dimensions. The volume of a sphere of radius r is given by:

$$V = \frac{4}{3}\pi r^3$$

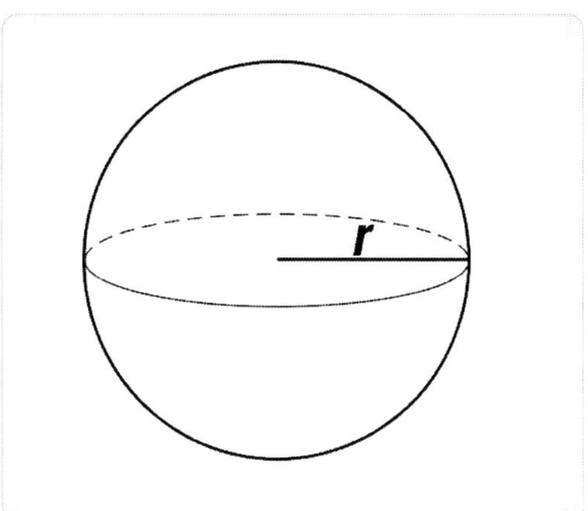

The volume of a **cylinder** is calculated by multiplying the area of the base (which is a circle) by the height of the cylinder. Doing so results in the equation:

$$V = \pi r^2 h$$

The volume of a cone is $\frac{1}{3}$ of the volume of a cylinder. Therefore, the formula for the volume of a cone is:

$$\frac{1}{3}\pi r^2 h$$

Using Trigonometric Ratios and the Pythagorean Theorem

The **Pythagorean theorem** is an important relationship between the three sides of a right triangle. It states that the square of the side opposite the right triangle, known as the **hypotenuse** (denoted as c^2), is equal to the sum of the squares of the other two sides ($a^2 + b^2$). Thus, $a^2 + b^2 = c^2$. Any three integers that work together in the formula can be referred to as Pythagorean triples. There are many Pythagorean triples, and it may be helpful to memorize some of the most common ones:

- 3, 4, 5
- 5, 12, 13
- 7, 24, 25
- 8, 15, 17
- 11, 60, 61

Looking at the first set of triples in the list, a would be 3, b would 4, c would be 5. Any set of triples can be multiplied by a common integer and still work out correctly. For instance, if each integer in the set 7, 24, and 25 is multiplied by 3, the new set of Pythagorean triples is 21, 72, and 75. When plugged into the Pythagorean formula, it works out as follows:

$$21^2 + 72^2 = 75^2$$

$$441 + 5{,}184 = 5{,}625$$

Both the trigonometric functions and the Pythagorean theorem can be used in problems that involve finding either a missing side or a missing angle of a right triangle. To do so, one must look to see what sides and angles are given and select the correct relationship that will help find the missing value. These relationships can also be used to solve application problems involving right triangles. Often, it's helpful to draw a figure to represent the problem to see what's missing.

To prove theorems about triangles, basic definitions involving triangles (e.g., equilateral, isosceles, etc.) need to be realized. Proven theorems concerning lines and angles can be applied to prove theorems about triangles. Common theorems to be proved include: the sum of all angles in a triangle equals 180 degrees; the sum of the lengths of two sides of a triangle is greater than the length of the third side; the base angles of an isosceles triangle are congruent; the line segment connecting the midpoint of two sides of a triangle is parallel to the third side and its length is half the length of the third side; and the medians of a triangle all meet at a single point.

An **isosceles triangle** contains at least two equal sides. Therefore, it must also contain two equal angles and, subsequently, contain two medians of the same length. An isosceles triangle can also be labelled as an **equilateral triangle** (which contains three equal sides and three equal angles) when it meets these conditions. In an equilateral triangle, the measure of each angle is always 60 degrees. Also, within an equilateral triangle, the medians are of the same length. A **scalene triangle** can never be an equilateral or an isosceles triangle because it contains no equal sides and no equal angles. Also, medians in a scalene triangle can't have the same length. However, a **right triangle**, which is a triangle containing a 90-degree angle, can be a scalene triangle.

There are two types of special right triangles. The **30-60-90 right triangle** has angle measurements of 30 degrees, 60 degrees, and 90 degrees. Because of the nature of this triangle, and through the use of the Pythagorean theorem, the side lengths have a special relationship. If x is the length opposite the 30-degree angle, the length opposite the

60-degree angle is $\sqrt{3}x$, and the hypotenuse has length $2x$. The **45-45-90 right triangle** is also special as it contains two angle measurements of 45 degrees. It can be proven that, if x is the length of the two equal sides, the hypotenuse is $x\sqrt{2}$. The properties of all of these special triangles are extremely useful in determining both side lengths and angle measurements in problems where some of these quantities are given and some are not.

Trigonometric functions are also used to describe behavior in mathematics. **Trigonometry** is the relationship between the angles and sides of a triangle. **Trigonometric functions** include sine, cosine, tangent, secant, cosecant, and cotangent. The functions are defined through ratios in a right triangle. SOHCAHTOA is a common acronym used to remember these ratios, which are defined by the relationships of the sides and angles relative to the right angle. **Sine** is opposite over hypotenuse, **cosine** is adjacent over hypotenuse, and **tangent** is opposite over adjacent. These ratios are the reciprocals of secant, cosecant, and cotangent, respectively. Angles can be measured in degrees or radians. Here is a diagram of SOHCAHTOA:

SOH $\sin\theta = \frac{\text{opposite}}{\text{hypotenuse}}$

CAH $\cos\theta = \frac{\text{adjacent}}{\text{hypotenuse}}$

TOA $\tan\theta = \frac{\text{opposite}}{\text{adjacent}}$

hypotenuse

opposite side

adjacent side

Consider the right triangle shown in this figure:

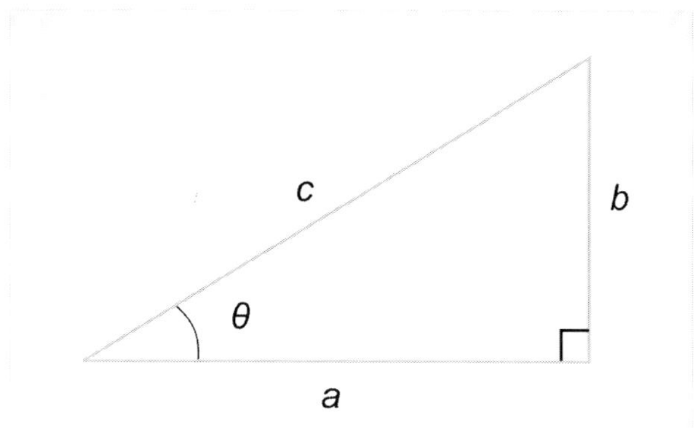

The following hold true:

- $c \sin\theta = b$
- $c \cos\theta = a$
- $\tan\theta = \frac{b}{a}$
- $b \csc\theta = c$
- $a \sec\theta = c$

- $\cot\theta = \frac{a}{b}$

A triangle that isn't a right triangle is known as an **oblique triangle**. It should be noted that even if the triangle consists of three acute angles, it is still referred to as an oblique triangle. *Oblique*, in this case, does not refer to an angle measurement. Consider the following oblique triangle:

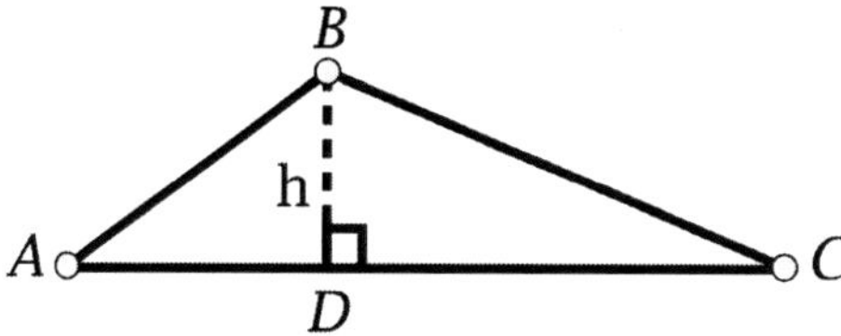

For this triangle:

$$Area = \frac{1}{2} \times base \times height = \frac{1}{2} \times AC \times BD$$

The auxiliary line drawn from the vertex B perpendicular to the opposite side AC represents the height of the triangle. This line splits the larger triangle into two smaller right triangles, which allows for the use of the trigonometric functions (specifically that $\sin A = \frac{h}{AB}$). Therefore:

$$Area = \frac{1}{2} \times AC \times AB \times \sin A$$

Typically, the sides are labelled as the lowercase letter of the vertex that's opposite. Therefore, the formula can be written as $Area = \frac{1}{2}ab \sin A$. This area formula can be used to find areas of triangles when given side lengths and angle measurements, or it can be used to find side lengths or angle measurements based on a specific area and other characteristics of the triangle.

The **law of sines** and **law of cosines** are two more relationships that exist within oblique triangles. Consider a triangle with sides a, b, and c, and angles *A*, *B*, and *C* opposite the corresponding sides.

The law of cosines states that:

$$c^2 = a^2 + b^2 - 2ab\ \cos C$$

The law of sines states that:

$$\frac{\sin A}{a} = \frac{\sin B}{b} = \frac{\sin C}{c}$$

In addition to the area formula, these two relationships can help find unknown angle and side measurements in oblique triangles.

Complex Numbers

Complex numbers are made up of the sum of a real number and an imaginary number. **Imaginary numbers** are the result of taking the square root of -1, and $\sqrt{-1} = i$.

Some examples of complex numbers include $6 + 2i$, $5 - 7i$, and $-3 + 12i$. Adding and subtracting complex numbers is similar to collecting like terms. The real numbers are added together, and the imaginary numbers are added together. For example, if the problem asks to simplify the expression $6 + 2i - 3 + 7i$, the 6 and (-3) are combined to make 3, and the $2i$ and $7i$ combine to make $9i$. Multiplying and dividing complex numbers is similar to working with exponents. One rule to remember when multiplying is that $i \times i = -1$.

For example, if a problem asks to simplify the expression $4i(3 + 7i)$, the $4i$ should be distributed throughout the 3 and the $7i$. This leaves the final expression $12i - 28$. The 28 is negative because $i * i$ results in a negative number. The last type of operation to consider with complex numbers is the conjugate. The **conjugate** of a complex number is a technique used to change the complex number into a real number. For example, the conjugate of $4 - 3i$ is $4 + 3i$. Multiplying $(4 - 3i)(4 + 3i)$ results in $16 + 12i - 12i + 9$, which has a final answer of:

$$16 + 9 = 25$$

Complex numbers may result from solving polynomial equations using the quadratic equation. Since complex numbers result from taking the square root of a negative number, the number found under the radical in the quadratic formula—called the **determinant**—tells whether or not the answer will be real or complex. If the determinant is negative, the roots are complex. Even though the coefficients of the polynomial may be real numbers, the roots are complex.

Solving polynomials by factoring is an alternative to using the quadratic formula. For example, in order to solve $x^2 - b^2 = 0$ for x, it needs to be factored. It factors into:

$$(x + b)(x - b) = 0$$

The solution set can be found by setting each factor equal to zero, resulting in $x = \pm b$. When b^2 is negative, the factors are complex numbers. For example, $x^2 + 64 = 0$ can be factored into:

$$(x + 8i)(x - 8i) = 0$$

The two roots are then found to be $x = \pm 8i$.

When dealing with polynomials and solving polynomial equations, it is important to remember the **fundamental theorem of algebra**. When given a polynomial with a degree of n, the theorem states that there will be n roots. These roots may or may not be complex. For example, the following polynomial equation of degree 2 has two complex roots: $x^2 + 1 = 0$. The factors of this polynomial are $(x + i)$ and $(x - i)$, resulting in the roots $x = i, -i$. As seen on the graph below, imaginary roots occur when the graph does not touch the x-axis.

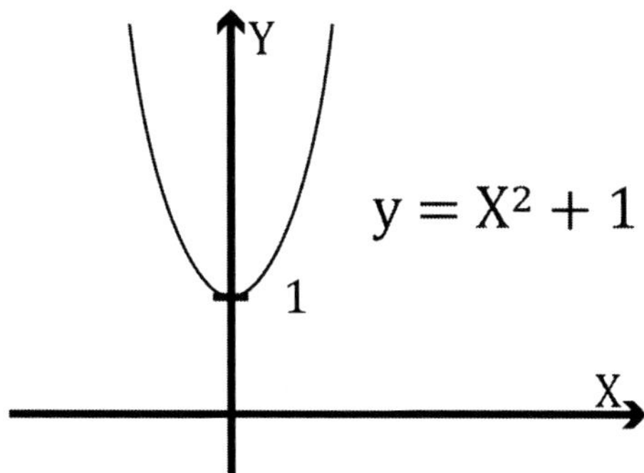

When a graphing calculator is permitted, the graph can always confirm the number and types of roots of the polynomial.

A polynomial identity is a true equation involving polynomials. For example:

$$x^2 - 5x + 6 = (x - 3)(x - 2)$$

This can be proved through multiplication by the FOIL method and factoring. This idea can be extended to involve complex numbers. For example:

$$i^2 = -1$$

$$x^3 + 9x = x(x^2 + 9) = x(x + \sqrt{3}i)(x - \sqrt{3}i)$$

This identity can also be proven through FOIL and factoring.

Converting Between Degrees and Radians

A **radian** is equal to the angle that subtends the arc with the same length as the radius of the circle. It is another unit for measuring angles, in addition to degrees. The unit circle is used to describe different radian measurements and the trigonometric ratios for special angles. The circle has a center at the origin, $(0, 0)$, and a radius of 1, which can be seen below. The points where the circle crosses an axis are labeled.

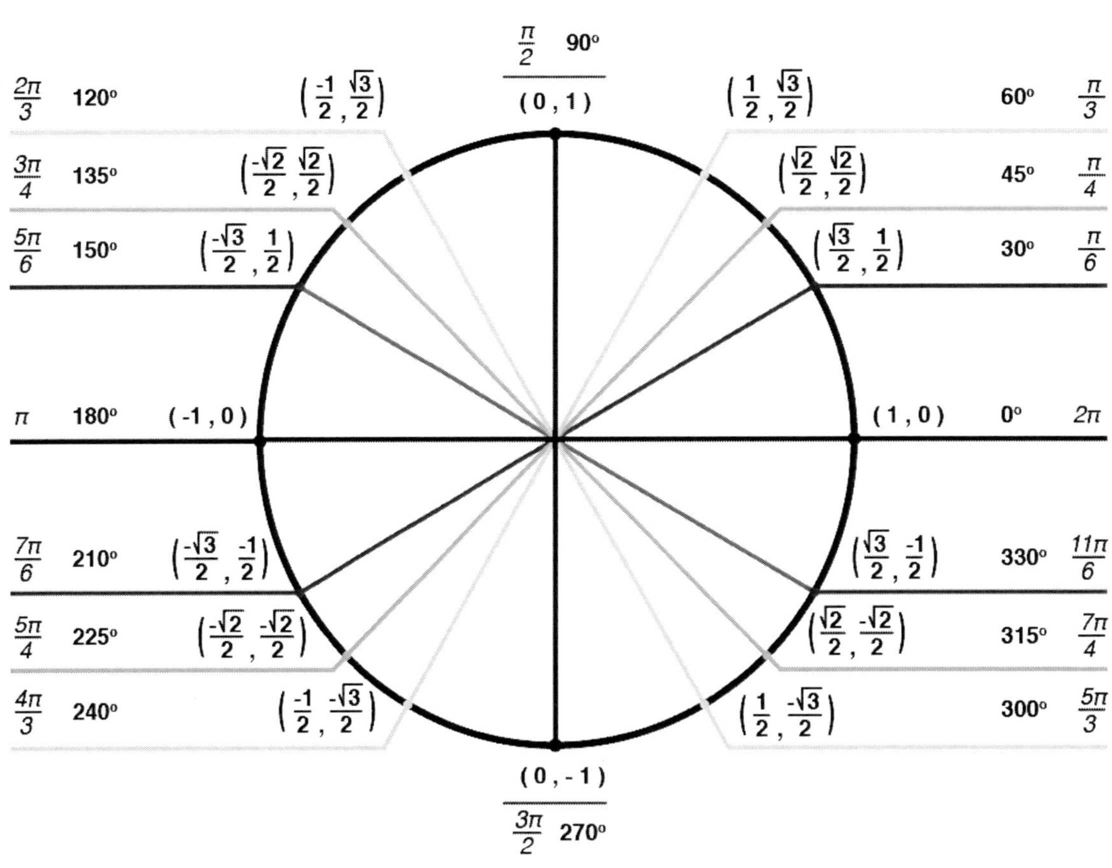

The circle begins on the right-hand side of the x-axis at 0 radians. Since the circumference of a circle is $2\pi r$ and the radius $r = 1$, the circumference is 2π. Zero and 2π are labeled as radian measurements at the point $(1, 0)$ on the

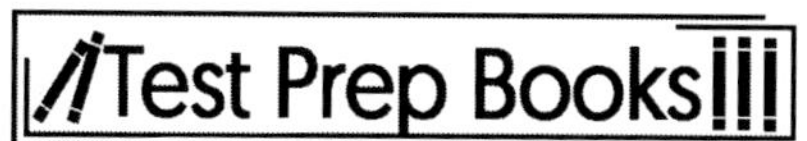

graph. The radian measures around the rest of the circle are labeled also in relation to π; π is at the point $(-1, 0)$, also known as 180 degrees. Since these two measurements are equal, $\pi = 180$ degrees written as a ratio can be used to convert degrees to radians or vice versa. For example, to convert 30 degrees to radians, $30 \text{ degrees} \times \frac{\pi}{180 \text{ degrees}}$ can be used to obtain $\frac{1}{6}\pi$ or $\frac{\pi}{6}$. This radian measure is a point the unit circle

The coordinates labeled on the unit circle are found based on two common right triangles. The ratios formed in the coordinates can be found using these triangles. Each of these triangles can be inserted into the circle to correspond 30, 45, and 60 degrees or $\frac{\pi}{6}, \frac{\pi}{4}$, and $\frac{\pi}{3}$ radians.

By letting the hypotenuse length of these triangles equal 1, these triangles can be placed inside the unit circle. These coordinates can be used to find the trigonometric ratio for any of the radian measurements on the circle.

Given any (x, y) on the unit circle, $\sin(\theta) = y$, $\cos(\theta) = x$, and $\tan(\theta) = \frac{y}{x}$. The value θ is the angle that spans the arc around the unit circle. For example, finding $\sin\left(\frac{\pi}{4}\right)$ means finding the y-value corresponding to the angle $\theta = \frac{\pi}{4}$. The answer is $\frac{\sqrt{2}}{2}$.

Finding $\cos\left(\frac{\pi}{3}\right)$ means finding the x-value corresponding to the angle $\theta = \frac{\pi}{3}$. The answer is $\frac{1}{2}$ or 0.5. Both angles lie in the first quadrant of the unit circle. Trigonometric ratios can also be calculated for radian measures past $\frac{\pi}{2}$, or 90 degrees. Since the same special angles can be moved around the circle, the results only differ with a change in sign. This can be seen at two points labeled in the second and third quadrant.

Trigonometric functions are periodic. Both sine and cosine have period 2π. For each input angle value, the output value follows around the unit circle. Once it reaches the starting point, it continues around and around the circle. It is true that:

$$\sin(0) = \sin(2\pi) = \sin(4\pi), \text{ etc.}$$

and

$$\cos(0) = \cos(2\pi) = \cos(4\pi)$$

Tangent has period π, and its output values repeat themselves every half of the unit circle. The domain of sine and cosine are all real numbers, and the domain of tangent is all real numbers, except the points where cosine equals zero. It is also true that

$$\sin(-x) = -\sin x$$

$$\cos(-x) = \cos(x)$$

$$\tan(-x) = -\tan(\text{x})$$

So, sine and tangent are odd functions, while cosine is an even function. Sine and tangent are symmetric with respect the origin, and cosine is symmetric with respect to the y-axis.

Applying Theorems About Circles

The distance from the middle of a circle to any other point on the circle is known as the **radius**. A **chord** of a circle is a straight line formed when its endpoints are allowed to be any two points on the circle. Many angles exist within a circle. A **central angle** is formed by using two radii as its rays and the center of the circle as its vertex. An **inscribed**

angle is formed by using two chords as its rays, and its vertex is a point on the circle itself. Finally, a **circumscribed angle** has a vertex that is a point outside the circle and rays that intersect with the circle.

Some relationships exist between these types of angles, and, in order to define these relationships, arc measure must be understood. An **arc** of a circle is a portion of the circumference. Finding the **arc measure** is the same as finding the degree measure of the central angle that intersects the circle to form the arc. The measure of an inscribed angle is half the measure of its intercepted arc. It's also true that the measure of a circumscribed angle is equal to 180 degrees minus the measure of the central angle that forms the arc in the angle.

A **tangent line** is a line that touches a curve at a single point without going through it. A **compass** and a **straight edge** are the tools necessary to construct a tangent line from a point *P* outside the circle to the circle. A tangent line is constructed by drawing a line segment from the center of the circle *O* to the point *P*, and then finding its midpoint *M* by bisecting the line segment. By using *M* as the center, a compass is used to draw a circle through points *O* and *P*. *N* is defined as the intersection of the two circles. Finally, a line segment is drawn through *P* and *N*. This is the tangent line. Each point on a circle has only one tangent line, which is perpendicular to the radius at that point. A line similar to a tangent line is a **secant line.** Instead of intersecting the circle at one point, a secant line intersects the circle at two points. A **chord** is a smaller portion of a secant line.

Here's an example:

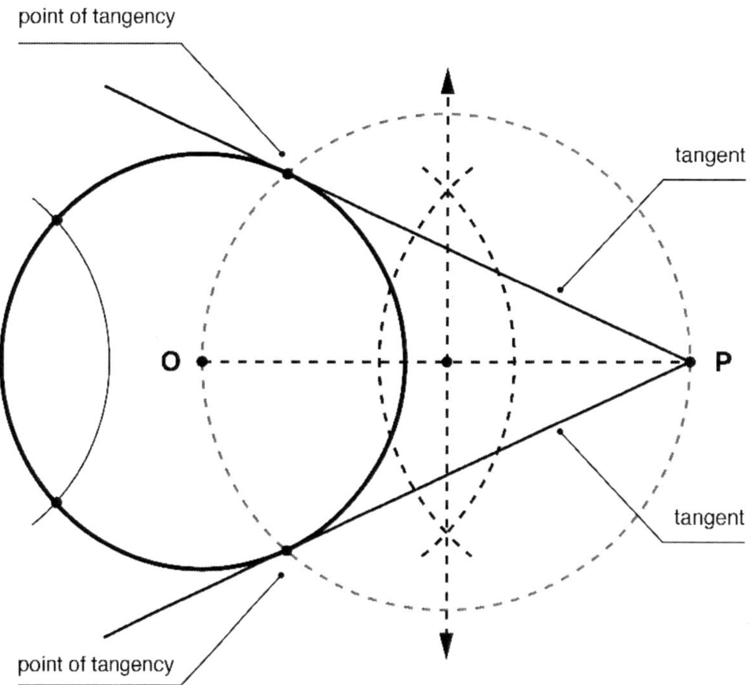

As previously mentioned, angles can be measured in radians, and 180 degrees equals π radians. Therefore, the measure of a complete circle is 2π radians. In addition to arc measure, **arc length** can also be found because the length of an arc is a portion of the circle's circumference. The following proportion is true:

$$\frac{Arc\ measure}{360°} = \frac{arc\ length}{arc\ circumference}$$

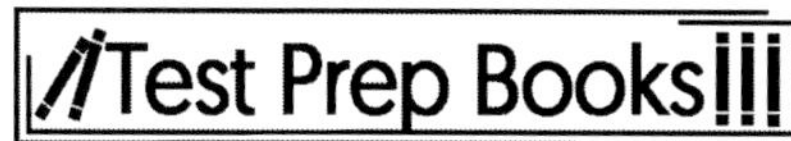

Arc measure is the same as the measure of the central angle, and this proportion can be rewritten as:

$$arc\ length = \frac{central\ angle}{360°} \times circumference$$

In addition, the degree measure can be replaced with radians to allow the use of both units. The arc length of a circle in radians is:

$$arc\ length = central\ angle\ \times\ radius$$

Note that arc length is a fractional part of circumference because $\frac{central\ angle}{360°} < 1$.

A **sector** of a circle is a portion of the circle that's enclosed by two radii and an arc. It resembles a piece of a pie, and the area of a sector can be derived using known definitions. The area of a circle can be calculated using the formula $A = \pi r^2$, where r is the radius of the circle. The area of a sector of a circle is a fraction of that calculation. For example, if the central angle θ is known in radians, the area of a sector is defined as:

$$A_s = \pi r^2 \frac{\theta}{2\pi} = \frac{\theta r^2}{2}$$

If the angle θ in degrees is known, the area of the sector is:

$$A_s = \frac{\theta \pi r^2}{360}$$

Finally, if the arc length L is known, the area of the sector can be reduced to:

$$A_s = \frac{rL}{2}$$

A chord is a line segment that contains endpoints on a circle. Given the radius of the circle and the central angle that inscribes the chord, the length of the chord can be determined.

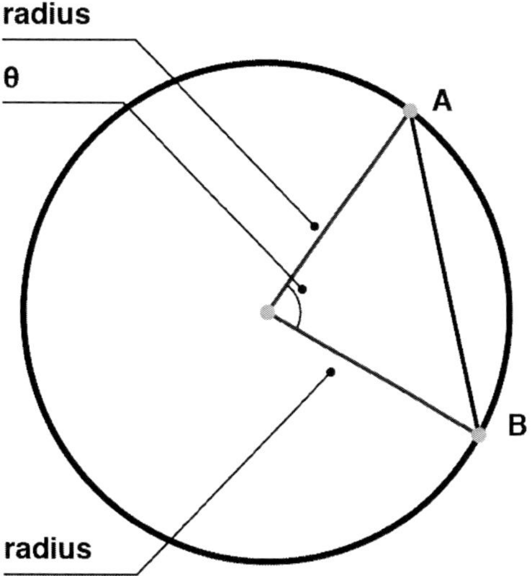

In the above figure, $\overline{AB}$ is a chord inscribed by $\angle\,\theta$. By constructing an angle bisector, the chord is also bisected at a 90-degree angle.

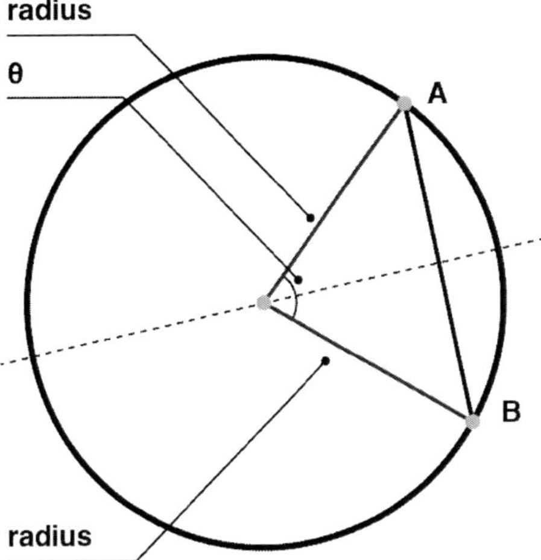

A right triangle is formed consisting of the radius as the hypotenuse, an angle equal to half the measure of θ, and a side opposite to that angle with a length half the length of the chord. Given an angle and the hypotenuse, the sin function can be used to determine the length of the side opposite the angle. Therefore, the formula $n\frac{\theta}{2} = \frac{c}{r}$, where c is the side of the triangle equal to half of the chord, can be used. Manipulating this formula results in:

$$c = r \times \sin\frac{\theta}{2}$$

(Remember that in this formula, c represents half the length of the chord, so double this length to determine the length of the chord.)

Congruence and Similarity

Sometimes, two figures are **similar**, meaning they have the same basic shape and the same interior angles, but they have different dimensions. If the ratio of two corresponding sides is known, then that ratio, or **scale factor**, holds true for all of the dimensions of the new figure.

Here is an example of applying this principle. Suppose that Lara is 5 feet tall and is standing 30 feet from the base of a light pole, and her shadow is 6 feet long. How high is the light on the pole? To figure this, it helps to make a sketch of the situation:

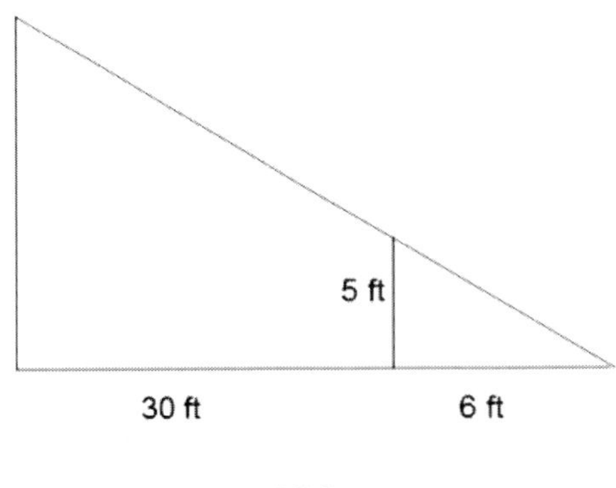

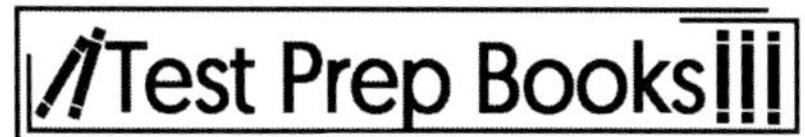

The light pole is the left side of the triangle. Lara is the 5-foot vertical line. Notice that there are two right triangles here, and that they have all the same angles as one another. Therefore, they form similar triangles. So, the ratio of proportionality between them must be determined.

The bases of these triangles are known. The small triangle, formed by Lara and her shadow, has a base of 6 feet. The large triangle formed by the light pole along with the line from the base of the pole out to the end of Lara's shadow is $30 + 6 = 36$ feet long. So, the ratio of the big triangle to the little triangle will be $\frac{36}{6} = 6$. The height of the little triangle is 5 feet. Therefore, the height of the big triangle will be $6 \times 5 = 30$ feet, meaning that the light is 30 feet up the pole.

Notice that the perimeter of a figure changes by the ratio of proportionality between two similar figures, but the area changes by the square of the ratio. This is because if the length of one side is doubled, the area is quadrupled.

As an example, suppose two rectangles are similar, but the edges of the second rectangle are three times longer than the edges of the first rectangle. The area of the first rectangle is 10 square inches. How much more area does the second rectangle have than the first?

To answer this, note that the area of the second rectangle is $3^2 = 9$ times the area of the first rectangle, which is 10 square inches. Therefore, the area of the second rectangle is going to be $9 \times 10 = 90$ square inches. This means it has $90 - 10 = 80$ square inches more area than the first rectangle.

As a second example, suppose X and Y are similar right triangles. The hypotenuse of X is 4 inches. The area of Y is $\frac{1}{4}$ the area of X. What is the hypotenuse of Y?

First, realize the area has changed by a factor of $\frac{1}{4}$. The area changes by a factor that is the square of the ratio of changes in lengths, so the ratio of the lengths is the square root of the ratio of areas. That means that the ratio of lengths must be is $\sqrt{\frac{1}{4}} = \frac{1}{2}$, and the hypotenuse of Y must be $\frac{1}{2} \times 4 = 2$ inches.

Volumes between similar solids change like the cube of the change in the lengths of their edges. Likewise, if the ratio of the volumes between similar solids is known, the ratio between their lengths is known by finding the cube root of the ratio of their volumes.

For example, suppose there are two similar rectangular pyramids X and Y. The base of X is 1 inch by 2 inches, and the volume of X is 8 inches. The volume of Y is 64 inches. What are the dimensions of the base of Y?

To answer this, first find the ratio of the volume of Y to the volume of X. This will be given by $\frac{64}{8} = 8$. Now the ratio of lengths is the cube root of the ratio of volumes, or $\sqrt[3]{8} = 2$. So, the dimensions of the base of Y must be 2 inches by 4 inches.

A **rigid motion** is a transformation that preserves distance and length. Every line segment in the resulting image is congruent to the corresponding line segment in the pre-image. **Congruence** between two figures means a series of transformations (or a rigid motion) can be defined that maps one of the figures onto the other. Basically, two figures are congruent if they have the same shape and size.

A shape is dilated, or a **dilation** occurs, when each side of the original image is multiplied by a given scale factor. If the scale factor is less than 1 and greater than 0, the dilation contracts the shape, and the resulting shape is smaller. If the scale factor equals 1, the resulting shape is the same size, and the dilation is a rigid motion. Finally, if the scale factor is greater than 1, the resulting shape is larger and the dilation expands the shape. The **center of dilation** is the point where the distance from it to any point on the new shape equals the scale factor times the distance from the center to the corresponding point in the pre-image. Dilation isn't an isometric transformation because distance isn't preserved. However, angle measure, parallel lines, and points on a line all remain unchanged.

Two figures are congruent if there is a rigid motion that can map one figure onto the other. Therefore, all pairs of sides and angles within the image and pre-image must be congruent. For example, in triangles, each pair of the three sides and three angles must be congruent. Similarly, in two four-sided figures, each pair of the four sides and four angles must be congruent.

Two figures are **similar** if there is a combination of translations, reflections, rotations, and dilations, which maps one figure onto the other. The difference between congruence and similarity is that dilation can be used in similarity. Therefore, side lengths between each shape can differ. However, angle measure must be preserved within this definition. If two polygons differ in size so that the lengths of corresponding line segments differ by the same factor, but corresponding angles have the same measurement, they are similar.

There are five theorems to show that triangles are congruent when it's unknown whether each pair of angles and sides are congruent. Each theorem is a shortcut that involves different combinations of sides and angles that must be true for the two triangles to be congruent. For example, **side-side-side (SSS)** states that if all sides are equal, the triangles are congruent. **Side-angle-side (SAS)** states that if two pairs of sides are equal and the included angles are congruent, then the triangles are congruent. Similarly, **angle-side-angle (ASA)** states that if two pairs of angles are congruent and the included side lengths are equal, the triangles are similar.

Angle-angle-side (AAS) states that two triangles are congruent if they have two pairs of congruent angles and a pair of corresponding equal side lengths that aren't included. Finally, **hypotenuse-leg (HL)** states that if two right triangles have equal hypotenuses and an equal pair of shorter sides, then the triangles are congruent. An important item to note is that angle-angle-angle *(AAA)* is not enough information to have congruence. It's important to understand why these rules work by using rigid motions to show congruence between the triangles with the given properties. For example, three reflections are needed to show why *SAS* follows from the definition of congruence.

If two angles of one triangle are congruent with two angles of a second triangle, the triangles are similar. This is because, within any triangle, the sum of the angle measurements is 180 degrees. Therefore, if two are congruent, the third angle must also be congruent because their measurements are equal. Three congruent pairs of angles mean that the triangles are similar.

The criteria needed to prove triangles are congruent involves both angle and side congruence. Both pairs of related angles and sides need to be of the same measurement to use congruence in a proof. The criteria to prove similarity in triangles involves proportionality of side lengths. Angles must be congruent in similar triangles; however, corresponding side lengths only need to be a constant multiple of each other. Once similarity is established, it can be used in proofs as well. Relationships in geometric figures other than triangles can be proven using triangle congruence and similarity. If a similar or congruent triangle can be found within another type of geometric figure, their criteria can be used to prove a relationship about a given formula. For instance, a rectangle can be broken up into two congruent triangles.

Similarity, Triangles, and Trigonometric Ratios

Within similar triangles, corresponding sides are proportional, and angles are congruent. In addition, within similar triangles, the ratio of the side lengths is the same. This property is true even if side lengths are different. Within right triangles, trigonometric ratios can be defined for the acute angle within the triangle. The functions are defined through ratios in a right triangle. Sine of acute angle, A, is opposite over hypotenuse, cosine is adjacent over hypotenuse, and tangent is opposite over adjacent. Note that expanding or shrinking the triangle won't change the ratios. However, changing the angle measurements will alter the calculations.

Angles that add up to 90 degrees are **complementary**. Within a right triangle, two complementary angles exist because the third angle is always 90 degrees. In this scenario, the **sine** of one of the complementary angles is equal to the **cosine** of the other angle. The opposite is also true. This relationship exists because sine and cosine will be calculated as the ratios of the same side lengths.

Two lines can be parallel, perpendicular, or neither. If two lines are **parallel**, they have the same slope. This is proven using the idea of similar triangles. Consider the following diagram with two parallel lines, L1 and L2:

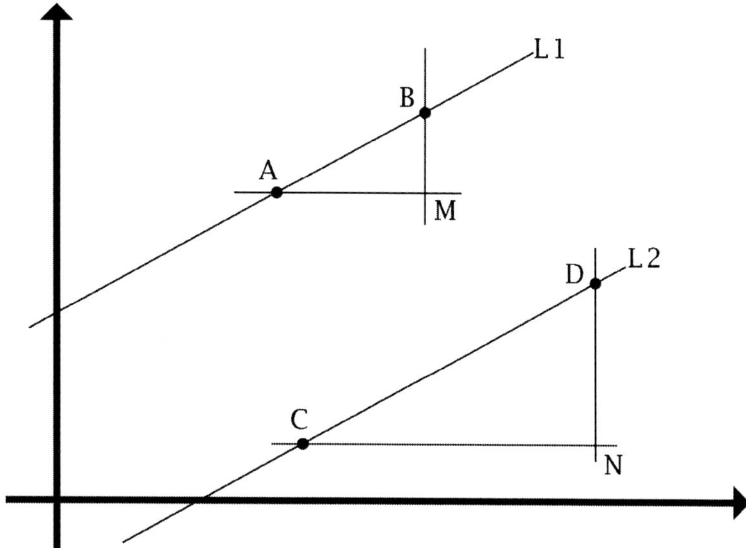

A and B are points on L1, and C and D are points on L2. Right triangles are formed with vertex M and N where lines BM and DN are parallel to the y-axis and AM and CN are parallel to the x-axis. Because all three sets of lines are parallel, the triangles are similar. Therefore, $\frac{\text{BM}}{\text{DN}} = \frac{\text{MA}}{\text{NC}}$. This shows that the rise/run is equal for lines L1 and L2. Hence, their slopes are equal.

Another similar theorem states that if there is a line parallel to one side of a triangle, and it intersects the other sides of the triangle, then the sides that are intersected are divided proportionally.

Secondly, if two lines are perpendicular, the product of their slopes equals -1. This means that their slopes are negative reciprocals of each other. Consider two perpendicular lines, *l* and *n*:

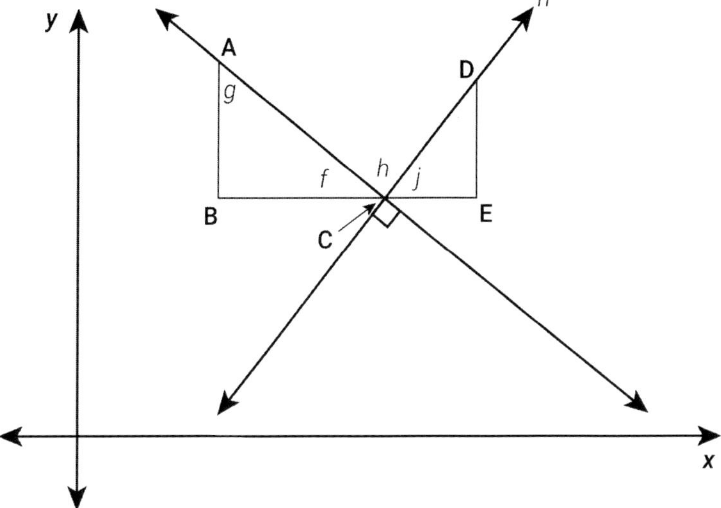

Right triangles ABC and CDE are formed so that lines BC and CE are parallel to the x-axis, and AB and DE are parallel to the y-axis. Because line BE is a straight line, angles $f + h + i = 180$ degrees. However, angle h is a right angle, so $f + j = 90$ degrees. By construction, $f + g = 90$, which means that $g = j$. Therefore, because angles $B = E$ and $g = j$, the triangles are similar and $\frac{\text{AB}}{\text{BC}} = \frac{\text{CE}}{\text{DE}}$. Because slope is equal to rise/run, the slope of line l is $-\frac{AB}{BC}$ and the slope of line *n* is $\frac{DE}{CE}$. Multiplying the slopes together gives:

$$-\frac{AB}{BC} \times \frac{DE}{CE} = -\frac{CE}{DE} \times \frac{DE}{CE} = -1$$

This proves that the product of the slopes of two perpendicular lines equals -1. Both parallel and perpendicular lines can be integral in many geometric proofs, so knowing and understanding their properties is crucial for problem-solving.

Creating Equations to Solve Problems Involving Circles

A **circle** can be defined as the set of all points that are the same distance (known as the radius, r) from a single point *C* (known as the center of the circle). The center has coordinates (h, k), and any point on the circle can be labelled with coordinates (x, y).

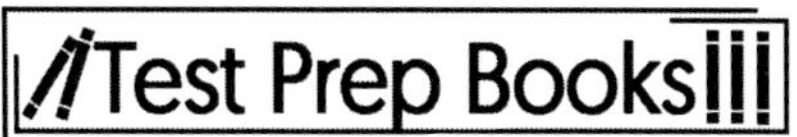

As shown below, a **right triangle** is formed with these two points:

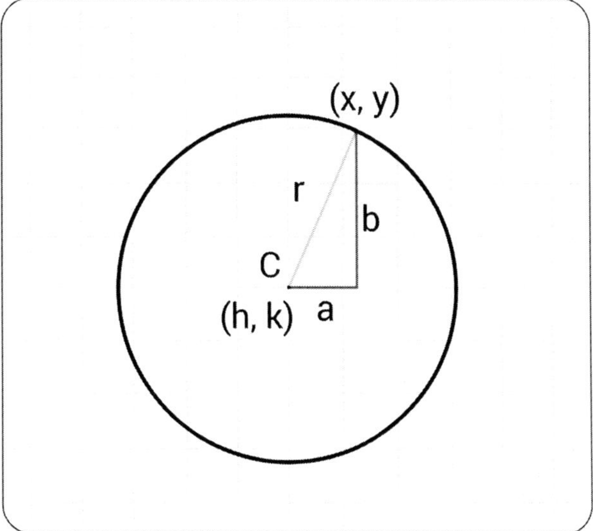

The Pythagorean theorem states that:

$$a^2 + b^2 = r^2$$

However, a can be replaced by $|x - h|$ and b can be replaced by $|y - k|$ by using the **distance formula** which is:

$$d = \sqrt{(x_2 - x_1)^2 + (y_2 - y_1)^2}$$

That substitution results in:

$$(x - h)^2 + (y - k)^2 = r^2$$

This is the formula for finding the equation of any circle with a center (h, k) and a radius r. Note that sometimes c is used instead of r.

Circles aren't always given in the form of the circle equation where the center and radius can be seen so easily. Oftentimes, they're given in the more general format of:

$$ax^2 + by^2 + cx + dy + e = 0$$

This can be converted to the center-radius form using the algebra technique of completing the square in both variables. First, the constant term is moved over to the other side of the equals sign, and then the x- and y-variable terms are grouped together. Then the equation is divided through by a and, because this is the equation of a circle, $a = b$. At this point, the x-term coefficient is divided by 2, squared, and then added to both sides of the equation. This value is grouped with the x terms. The same steps then need to be completed with the y-term coefficient. The trinomial in both x and y can now be factored into a square of a binomial, which gives both $(x - h)^2$ and $(y - k)^2$.

Practice Quiz

1. Solve for *x*, if $x^2 - 2x - 8 = 0$.
   a. $2 \pm \frac{\sqrt{30}}{2}$
   b. $2 \pm 4\sqrt{2}$
   c. 1 ± 3
   d. $4 \pm \sqrt{2}$

2. Write the expression for three times the sum of twice a number and one minus 6.
   a. $2x + 1 - 6$
   b. $3x + 1 - 6$
   c. $3(x + 1) - 6$
   d. $3(2x + 1) - 6$

3. What is the definition of a factor of the number 36?
   a. A number that can be divided by 36 and have no remainder
   b. A number that 36 can be divided by and have no remainder
   c. A prime number that is multiplied by 36
   d. An even number that is multiplied by 36

4. The total perimeter of a rectangle is 36 cm. If the length is 12 cm, what is the width?

5. What are the coordinates of the focus of the parabola $y = -9x^2$?
   a. $(-3, 0)$
   b. $\left(-\frac{1}{36}, 0\right)$
   c. $(0, -3)$
   d. $\left(0, -\frac{1}{36}\right)$

See next page for answers.

Answer Explanations

1. C: The quadratic formula can be used to solve this problem. Given the equation, use the values $a = 1$, $b = -2$, and $c = -8$.

$$x = \frac{-b \pm \sqrt{b^2 - 4ac}}{2a} = \frac{-(-2) \pm \sqrt{(-2)^2 - 4(1)(-8)}}{2(1)}$$

From here, simplify to solve for x.

$$x = \frac{2 \pm \sqrt{4 + 32}}{2} = \frac{2 \pm \sqrt{36}}{2} = \frac{2 \pm 6}{2} = 1 \pm 3$$

2. D: "Sum" means the result of adding, so "the sum of twice a number and one" can be written as $2x + 1$. Next, "three times the sum of twice a number and one" would be $3(2x + 1)$. Finally, "six less than three times the sum of twice a number and one" would be $3(2x + 1) - 6$.

3. B: A factor of 36 is any number that can be divided into 36 and have no remainder.

$$36 = 36 \times 1, 18 \times 2, 9 \times 4, \text{and } 6 \times 6$$

Therefore, it has 7 unique factors: 36, 18, 9, 6, 4, 2, and 1.

4. 6: The formula for the perimeter of a rectangle is $P = 2L + 2W$, where P is the perimeter, L is the length, and W is the width. The first step is to substitute all of the data into the formula:

$$36 = 2(12) + 2W$$

Simplify by multiplying 2×12:

$$36 = 24 + 2W$$

Simplify this further by subtracting 24 on each side, then divide by 2:

$$36 - 24 = 24 - 24 + 2W$$

$$12 = 2W$$

$$6 = W$$

The width is 6 cm. Remember to test this answer by substituting this value into the original formula:

$$36 = 2(12) + 2(6)$$

5. D: A parabola of the form $y = \frac{1}{4f}x^2$ has a focus $(0, f)$.

Because $y = -9x^2$, set $-9 = \frac{1}{4f}$.

Solving this equation for f results in $f = -\frac{1}{36}$. Therefore, the coordinates of the focus are $\left(0, -\frac{1}{36}\right)$.

SAT Practice Test #1

Reading and Writing: Module 1

The next question is based on the following passage:

Tonight, after more days and trials than we can count, we finished building a strange thing, from the remains of the Unmentionable Times, a box of glass, devised to give forth the power of the sky of greater strength than we had ever achieved before. And when we put our wires to this box, when we closed the current—the wire glowed! It came to life, it turned red, and a circle of light lay on the stone before us.

We stood, and we held our head in our hands. We could not conceive of that which we had created. We had touched no flint, made no fire. Yet here was light, light that came from nowhere, light from the heart of metal.

We blew out the candle. Darkness swallowed us. There was nothing left around us, nothing save night and a thin thread of flame in it, as a crack in the wall of a prison. We stretched our hands to the wire, and we saw our fingers in the red glow. We could not see our body nor feel it, and in that moment nothing existed save our two hands over a wire glowing in a black abyss.

Excerpt from *Anthem* by Ayn Rand

1. Which literary device is used in the following sentence from the last paragraph?

Darkness swallowed us.

a. Metaphor
b. Synecdoche
c. Flashback
d. Personification

The next question is based on the following passage:

What you see too often in Washington and elsewhere around the country is a system of government that seems incapable of action. You see a Congress twisted and pulled in every direction by hundreds of well-financed and powerful special interests. You see every extreme position defended to the last vote, almost to the last breath by one unyielding group or another. You often see a balanced and a fair approach that demands sacrifice, a little sacrifice from everyone, abandoned like an orphan without support and without friends.

Often you see paralysis and stagnation and drift. You don't like it, and neither do I. What can we do?

First of all, we must face the truth, and then we can change our course. We simply must have faith in each other, faith in our ability to govern ourselves, and faith in the future of this Nation. Restoring that faith and that confidence to America is now the most important task we face. It is a true challenge of this generation of Americans.

Excerpt from "The Crisis of Confidence" by Jimmy Carter

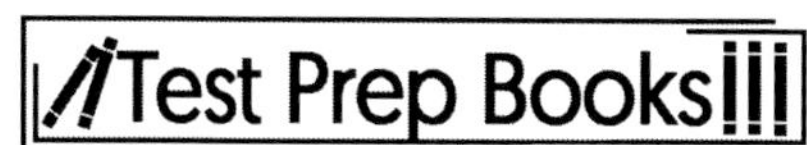

2. What is the underlying message of Jimmy Carter's speech?
    a. There is no hope for the future of the United States.
    b. The American people have lost faith in their government.
    c. Finding the way again as a nation will be hard and will require facing difficult facts.
    d. America was once as great as other Western countries, but it no longer is.

The next question is based on the following passage:

> At the present moment in world history nearly every nation must choose between alternative ways of life. The choice is too often not a free one.
>
> One way of life is based upon the will of the majority, and is distinguished by free institutions, representative government, free elections, guarantees of individual liberty, freedom of speech and religion, and freedom from political oppression.
>
> The second way of life is based upon the will of a minority forcibly imposed upon the majority. It relies upon terror and oppression, a controlled press and radio, fixed elections, and the suppression of personal freedoms.

Excerpt from "The Truman Doctrine" by Harry S. Truman

3. President Truman describes two ways of life. Which statement corresponds to his description?
    a. The first way of life is distinguished by free institutions; the second is marked by freedom of religion.
    b. The first way of life relies on terror and oppression; the second controls the press and radio.
    c. The first way of life guarantees individual liberties; the second suppresses personal freedoms.
    d. The first way of life suppresses individual liberties; the second guarantees personal freedoms.

4. What does the underlined word mean in the following sentence?

> "We cannot allow changes in the status quo in violation of the Charter of the United Nations by such methods as coercion, or by such <u>subterfuges</u> as political infiltration."

    a. Helpful pieces of intel
    b. Tricky deceptions
    c. Time-consuming activities
    d. Underground routes

5. Which of the following would be the best choice for the underlined portion of the following interrogative sentence?

> <u>How if earlier perceptions of technology</u> continued to influence people's understanding of the development of modern civilization?

    a. NO CHANGE
    b. How perceptions of technology
    c. How, have, earlier perceptions of technology
    d. How have earlier perceptions of technology

The next question is based on the following passage:

> Insects are the flower's auxiliaries. Flies, wasps, honey bees, bumble bees, beetles, butterflies, all vie with one another in rendering aid by carrying the pollen of the stamens to the stigmas. They

dive into the flower, enticed by a honeyed drop expressly prepared at the bottom of the corolla. In their efforts to obtain it they shake the stamens and daub themselves with pollen, which they carry from one flower to another. Who has not seen bumble bees coming out of the bosom of the flowers all covered with pollen? Their hairy stomachs, powdered with pollen, have only to touch a stigma in passing to communicate life to it. When in the spring you see on a blooming pear-tree, a whole swarm of flies, bees, and butterflies, hurrying, humming, and fluttering, it is a triple feast, my friends: a feast for the insect that pilfers in the depth of the flowers; a feast for the tree whose ovaries are quickened by all these merry little people; and a feast for man, to whom abundant harvest is promised. The insect is the best distributor of pollen. All the flowers it visits receive their share of quickening dust.

Excerpt from *The Storybook of Science* by Jean-Henri Fabre

6. The diction Jean-Henri Fabre uses in the passage is:
   a. Pedantic
   b. Emotional
   c. Whimsical
   d. Ambiguous

7. What does the underlined word mean in the following sentence?

   After the bee has traversed a few flowers along the spike and has become well supplied with free pollen, it begins to collect it from its body, head, and forward appendages and to transfer it to the <u>posterior</u> pair of legs.

   a. Strongest
   b. Anterior
   c. Ambulatory
   d. Rear

The next question is based on the following passage:

Experiment 80. Fill a test tube one-fourth full of cold water. Slowly stir in salt until no more will dissolve. Add half a teaspoonful more of salt than will dissolve. Dry the outside of the test tube and heat the salty water over the Bunsen burner. Will hot water dissolve things more readily or less readily than cold? Why do you wash dishes in hot water?

Excerpt from "Common Science" by Carleton W. Washburne

8. What is the most likely result of Experiment 80?
   a. The heat is unable to dissolve the additional salt.
   b. Once heated, the additional salt dissolves completely.
   c. The additional salt prevents the water from heating up higher than room temperature.
   d. The heated salt and water solution can be used to wash dishes.

The next question is based on the following texts:

Text 1: Aspiring fiction writers ought to practice writing short, precise sentences. Control your diction. Each word must be strong. Use "scorching," not "very hot." Vocabulary is the bricks with which you build the story.

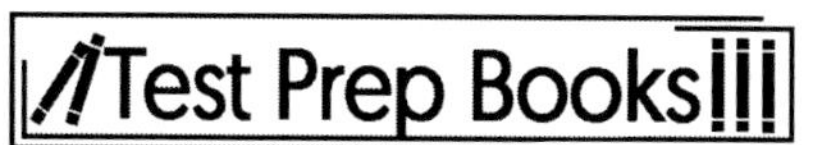

Text 2: You can spot an amateur author most quickly through their word choice. Newbies try to flaunt their skill, rather than letting their written "voice" flow naturally. It's not really their fault—our universities' praise for dense books (like Melville's *Moby-Dick*) brainwashes pretty much everyone into trying to write fancy.

9. Based on the texts above, which statement would BOTH authors agree with?
   a. New writers don't devote enough attention to crafting good sentences.
   b. There is always a best word to use when describing a particular situation.
   c. Literature courses should focus less on classic works and more on contemporary fiction.
   d. Simple words are less effective because they don't inspire strong emotions.

The next question is based on the following texts:

Text 1: The problem with modern painting is a lack of technical expertise. Modern work can be wonderfully inventive and expressive, but it still doesn't compare with classic masters like da Vinci. This isn't just prejudice! Compared to the old, new paintings don't depict the same level of anatomical realism. The artists just haven't put in the work.

Text 2: Each painter ought to ask themselves, "What's the point of painting?" Should art be made for a purpose, with a message? Or, is the highest value of art simply to reproduce nature? If so, well, photography's always going to be a better artist than a painter.

10. Based on these two texts, which of the following goals is always important when creating a painting?
   a. Message
   b. Creativity
   c. Realism
   d. Subject

11. Which of the following would be the best choice for the underlined portion of the following sentence?

While all dogs <u>descend through gray wolves</u>, it's easy to notice that dog breeds come in a variety of shapes and sizes.

   a. NO CHANGE
   b. descend by gray wolves
   c. descend from gray wolves
   d. descended through gray wolves

12. Which of the following would be the best choice for the underlined portion of the following sentences?

Modern livestock is larger and more productive than previous generations. <u>This was done through a process called selective breeding.</u>

   a. NO CHANGE
   b. This was done, through a process called selective breeding.
   c. This was done, through a process, called selective breeding.
   d. This was done through selective breeding, a process.

13. Which of the following would be the best choice for the underlined portion of the following sentence?

> I want to talk about that profound moment when curiosity is sparked in another person drawing them to pay attention to what is before them and expand their knowledge.

a. NO CHANGE
b. in another person, drawing them to pay attention to what is before them
c. in another person; drawing them to pay attention to what is before them
d. in another person, drawing them to pay attention to what is before them.

14. Which of the following would be the best choice for the underlined portion of the following sentence?

> Some scientists believe the sail serves to regulate the Spinosaurus' body temperature and yet others believe its used to attract mates.

a. NO CHANGE
b. the sail serves to regulate the Spinosaurus' body temperature, yet others believe it's used to attract mates.
c. the sail serves to regulate the Spinosaurus' body temperature and yet others believe it's used to attract mates.
d. the sail serves to regulate the Spinosaurus' body temperature however others believe it's used to attract mates.

15. Which of the following would be the best choice for the underlined portion of the following sentence?

> To do an evil act in order to gain a result that's supposedly good would ultimately warp the final act.

a. NO CHANGE
b. for an outcome that's for a greater good would ultimately warp the final act.
c. to gain a final act would warp its goodness.
d. to achieve something that's supposedly good would ultimately warp the final result.

16. Which of the following would be the best choice for the underlined portion of the following sentences?

> Today's news reaches a wider audience than ever, and it's presented in a wide and growing variety of ways. What's clear is that the broader the media the more ways there are to tell a story.

a. NO CHANGE
b. What's clear, is that the broader the media
c. What's clear about the news today is that the broader the media,
d. What's clear is that the broader the media,

The next question is based on the following passage:

> The final expression of the opinion of the people with us is through free and honest elections, with valid choices on basic issues and candidates. The secret ballot is an essential to free elections but you must have a choice before you. I have heard my husband say many times that a people need never lose their freedom if they kept their right to a secret ballot and if they used that secret ballot to the full. Basic decisions of our society are made through the expressed will of the people. That is why when we see these liberties threatened, instead of falling apart, our nation becomes unified and our democracies come together as a unified group in spite of our varied backgrounds and many racial strains.

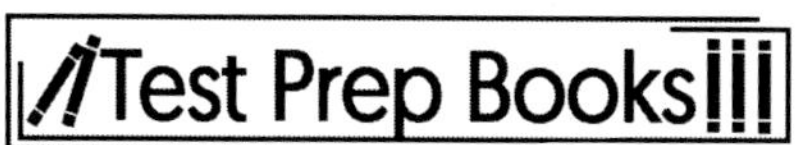

Excerpt from Eleanor Roosevelt's "The Struggle for Human Rights," September 28, 1948

17. Why does Roosevelt assert that a "secret" ballot is important?
    a. Public votes were too raucous an event.
    b. It decreases the chance for bribery.
    c. Privacy secures freedom of choice.
    d. It ensures physical safety.

The next question is based on the following passage:

> At times history and fate meet at a single time in a single place to shape a turning point in man's unending search for freedom. So it was at Lexington and Concord. So it was a century ago at Appomattox. So it was last week in Selma, Alabama. There, long-suffering men and women peacefully protested the denial of their rights as Americans. Many were brutally assaulted. One good man, a man of God, was killed.

Excerpt from Lyndon Johnson's "Address to Joint Session of Congress," March 15, 1965

18. What was being protested in Selma?
    a. The closing of a bridge
    b. Denial of rights
    c. A murder
    d. Loss of wealth

19. Which of the following would be the best choice for the underlined portion of the sentence below?

> Besides the novel's engaging <u>writing style the story's central theme</u> remains highly relevant in a world of constant discovery and moral dilemmas.

    a. NO CHANGE
    b. writing style the central theme of the story
    c. writing style, the story's central theme
    d. the story's central theme's writing style

The next question is based on the following graph:

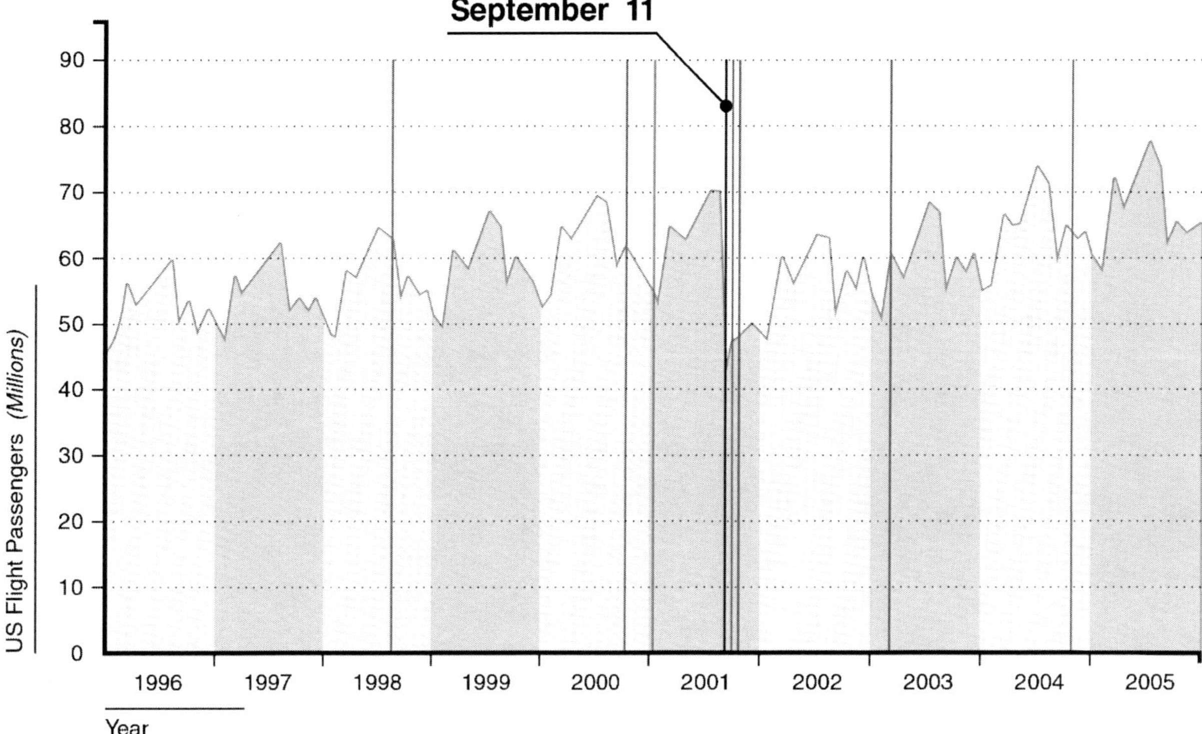

20. Which statement about September 11 is best supported by the graph above?
    a. As canceled flights were rescheduled, air travel became backed up and chaotic for quite some time.
    b. Over 500 flights had to turn back or be redirected to other countries.
    c. Canada alone received 226 flights and thousands of stranded passengers.
    d. In the first few months following the attacks, there was a significant decrease in passengers boarding flights.

The next question is based on the following passage:

> As I take my rest there, the idea of the old patriarchal life is awakened around me. I see them, our old ancestors, how they formed their friendships and contracted alliances at the fountain-side; and I feel how fountains and streams were guarded by beneficent spirits. He who is a stranger to these sensations has never really enjoyed cool repose at the side of a fountain after the fatigue of a weary summer day.

Excerpt from *The Sorrows of Young Werther* by Johann Wolfgang von Goethe

21. Given the final analogy, which word best describes the sensation that von Goethe describes?
    a. Strain
    b. Warmth
    c. Excitement
    d. Relaxation

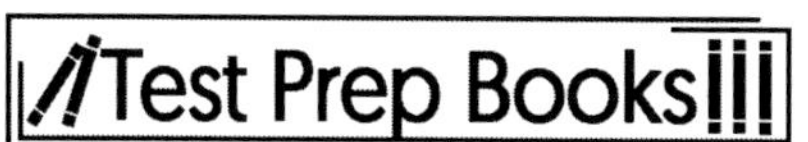

The next question is based on the following passage:

> I took a taxi and drove straight to the Foreign Office. Sir Walter did not keep me waiting long. But when his secretary took me to his room I would not have recognized the man I had known eighteen months before. His big frame seemed to have dropped flesh and there was a stoop in the square shoulders. His face had lost its rosiness and was red in patches, like that of a man who gets too little fresh air. His hair was much greyer and very thin about the temples, and there were lines of overwork below the eyes. But the eyes were the same as before, keen and kindly and shrewd, and there was no change in the firm set of the jaw.

Excerpt from *Greenmantle* by John Buchan

22. Which of the following inferences can reasonably be made from this text?
    a. The narrator and Sir Walter have never met in the Foreign Office before.
    b. Sir Walter has undergone a great change in health since the narrator last saw him.
    c. Sir Walter has just accepted a position at the Foreign Office.
    d. The narrator is upset that Sir Walter has a higher-ranking position than him.

23. "The knowledge of an aircraft engineer is acquired through years of education." Which statement serves to support this claim?
    a. Aircraft engineers are compensated with generous salaries.
    b. Such advanced degrees enable an individual to position himself or herself for executive, faculty, or research opportunities.
    c. Ideally, an individual will begin their preparation for the profession in high school by taking chemistry, physics, trigonometry, and calculus.
    d. Aircraft engineers who know how to utilize modeling and simulation programs, fluid dynamic software, and robotic engineering tools will be the most employable.

The next question is based on the following passage:

> Aircraft engineers are compensated with generous salaries. In fact, in May 2014, the lowest 10 percent of all American aircraft engineers earned an average of $60,110 while the highest paid 10 percent of all American aircraft engineers earned $155,240. In May 2015, the United States Bureau of Labor Statistics (BLS) reported that the median annual salary of aircraft engineers was $107,830. Conversely, employment opportunities for aircraft engineers are projected to decrease by two percent by 2024. This decrease may be the result of a decline in the manufacturing industry.

24. Which of the following would be the best replacement for the underlined portion of the sentence reproduced below?

> <u>Conversely,</u> employment opportunities for aircraft engineers are projected to decrease by two percent by 2024.

    a. NO CHANGE
    b. Similarly,
    c. In other words,
    d. Accordingly,

25. Which of the following would be the best replacement for the underlined sentence below?

As the leader of the BPP, Hampton organized rallies, taught political education classes, and established a free medical clinic.

a. NO CHANGE
b. As the leader of the BPP, Hampton: organized rallies, taught political education classes, and established a free medical clinic.
c. As the leader of the BPP, Hampton; organized rallies, taught political education classes, and established a free medical clinic.
d. As the leader of the BPP, Hampton—organized rallies, taught political education classes, and established a medical free clinic.

26. Which of the following would be the best replacement for the underlined portion of the sentence below?

There is substantial evidence that global oceans levels have already begun to rise due to human activities.

a. NO CHANGE
b. ocean levels
c. ocean's levels
d. levels of the oceans

27. Which of the following would be the best replacement for the underlined portion of the sentence below?

New technologies can be used has project the severity of an anticipated flood, which can help mitigate such disasters.

a. NO CHANGE
b. to project
c. project
d. projecting

Reading and Writing: Module 2

The next question is based on the following texts:

Text 1: The key concept of utilitarian ethics is that each person should act to maximize happiness. A few utilitarians focus on maximizing other values, such as pleasure (hedonistic utilitarianism). If each person makes their everyday choices in accordance with this principle, then happiness will be increased throughout society. The beauty of utilitarianism is its simplicity—it seeks to cut through as many problems as possible by pursuing an obvious and unobjectionable good.

Text 2: Few people realize how easy it is to change the world. We use the phrase "change the world" like it's this beautiful, impossible dream. We smile condescendingly at kids who want to "change the world," just like we do at the kid who wants to become a professional football player or a top-chart rock star. We act as if "changing the world" is unrealistic. But that isn't true—each one of us can change the world with every smile at a stranger, every shared meal, every held door.

1. Is Text 2 making the same argument as Text 1? Why or why not?

a. Yes, because both texts express a desire to make the world a better place.
b. No, because Text 1 presents a rational philosophy, not an emotional impulse.

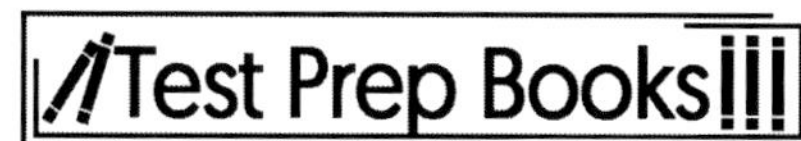

c. Yes, because both texts claim that mundane choices have ethical value.
d. No, because both texts define a phrase rather than make an argument.

2. Which of the following would be the best choice for the underlined portion of the following sentence?

In natural evolution, animals must adapt to their environments increase their chance of survival.

a. NO CHANGE
b. animals must adapt to their environments to increase their chance of survival.
c. animals must adapt to their environments, increase their chance of survival.
d. animals must adapt to their environments, increasing their chance of survival.

3. Which of the following would be the best choice for the underlined portion of the following sentence?

For example, Bloodhounds have broad snouts and droopy ears that fall to the ground when they smell.

a. NO CHANGE
b. For example, Bloodhounds,
c. For example Bloodhounds
d. For example, bloodhounds

4. Which of the following would be the best choice for the underlined portion of the following sentence?

Sometimes I get tired during classes; usually I turn to doodling in order to keep awake.

a. NO CHANGE
b. usually I turn to doodling in order to keep awakened.
c. usually I turn to doodling, in order, to keep awake.
d. usually I turns to doodling in order to keep awake.

5. Which of the following would be the best choice for the underlined portion of the following sentence?

Discussions that make people think about the content and how it applies to there lives world and future are key.

a. NO CHANGE
b. how it applies to their lives, world, and future are key.
c. how it applied to there lives world and future are key.
d. how it applies to their lives, world, and future, are key.

6. Which of the following would be the best choice for the underlined portion of the following sentence?

Since the first discovery of dinosaur bones, scientists has made strides in technological development and methodologies used to investigate these extinct animals.

a. NO CHANGE
b. scientists has made strides in technological development, and methodologies, used to investigate
c. scientists have made strides in technological development and methodologies used to investigate
d. scientists, have made strides in technological development and methodologies used, to investigate

7. Which of the following would be the best choice for the underlined portion of the sentence below?

> Finer details are usually expanded on in written articles, often people who read newspapers or go online for web articles want more than a quick blurb.

a. NO CHANGE
b. in written articles. Often, people who
c. in written articles, often, people who
d. in written articles often people who

The next question is based on the following passage:

> Pour alcohol into a test tube (square-bottomed test tubes are best for this experiment), standing the tube up beside a ruler. When the alcohol is just one inch high in the tube, stop pouring. Put exactly the same amount of water in another test tube of the same size. When you pour them together, how many inches high do you think the mixture will be? Pour the water into the alcohol, shake the mixture a little, and measure to see how high it comes in the test tube. Did you notice the warmth when you shook the tube?
>
> If you use denatured alcohol, you are likely to have an emulsion as a result of the mixing. The alcohol part of the denatured alcohol dissolves in the water well enough, but the denaturing substance in the alcohol will not dissolve in water; so it forms tiny droplets that make the mixture of alcohol and water cloudy.
>
> The purpose of this experiment is to show that the molecules of water get into the spaces between the molecules of alcohol. It is as if you were to add a pail of pebbles to a pail of apples. The pebbles would fill in between the apples, and the mixture would not nearly fill two pails.

Excerpt from "Common Science" by Carleton W. Washburne

8. What can be inferred about denatured alcohol from the passage above?
a. It can be dangerous to work with in a laboratory.
b. It has the same basic properties as regular alcohol.
c. It needs to be heated in order to completely dissolve.
d. There are better alternatives to form true solutions.

The next question is based on the following passage:

> A lane was forthwith opened through the crowd of spectators. Preceded by the beadle, and attended by an irregular procession of stern-browed men and unkindly visaged women, Hester Prynne set forth towards the place appointed for her punishment. A crowd of eager and curious school-boys, understanding little of the matter in hand, except that it gave them a half-holiday, ran before her progress, turning their heads continually to stare into her face, and at the winking baby in her arms, and at the ignominious letter on her breast. It was no great distance, in those days, from the prison-door to the market-place. Measured by the prisoner's experience, however, it might be reckoned a journey of some length; for, haughty as her demeanor was, she perchance underwent an agony from every footstep of those that thronged to see her, as if her heart had been flung into the street for them all to spurn and trample upon. In our nature, however, there is a provision, alike marvelous and merciful, that the sufferer should never know the intensity of what he endures by its present torture, but chiefly by the pang that rankles after it. With almost a serene deportment, therefore, Hester Prynne passed through this portion of her ordeal, and came to a

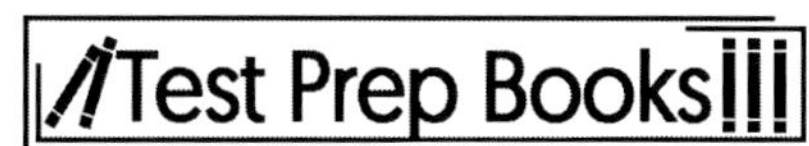

sort of scaffold, at the western extremity of the market-place. It stood nearly beneath the eaves of Boston's earliest church, and appeared to be a fixture there.

Excerpt from *The Scarlet Letter*, Nathaniel Hawthorne, 1878

9. Based on the passage, what might Hester Prynne have felt on her walk from the prison to the marketplace?
   a. Anger
   b. Fear
   c. Agony
   d. Proud

The next question is based on the following passage:

Sometimes the processes of democracy are slow, and I have known some of our leaders to say that a benevolent dictatorship would accomplish the ends desired in a much shorter time than it takes to go through the democratic processes of discussion and the slow formation of public opinion. But there is no way of insuring that a dictatorship will remain benevolent or that power once in the hands of a few will be returned to the people without struggle or revolution. This we have learned by experience and we accept the slow processes of democracy because we know that shortcuts compromise principles on which no compromise is possible.

Excerpt from Eleanor Roosevelt's "The Struggle for Human Rights," September 28, 1948

10. According to Roosevelt, why do some people argue in favor of dictatorship?
   a. Dictatorships need not be tyrannical.
   b. Dictators come to power for a reason.
   c. Some dictators have been quite successful and popular.
   d. They believe that a dictator could achieve goals more quickly.

The next question is based on the following passage:

For the cries of pain and the hymns and protests of oppressed people have summoned into convocation all the majesty of this great government—the government of the greatest nation on earth. Our mission is at once the oldest and the most basic of this country: to right wrong, to do justice, to serve man.

Excerpt from Lyndon Johnson's "Address to Joint Session of Congress," March 15, 1965

11. In this passage, what does the word *convocation* mean?
   a. A vocal duet
   b. A second career
   c. A gathering or assembly
   d. Closure

12. Which of the following would be the best choice for the underlined portion of the following sentence?

Ancient civilizations have reported <u>seeing Bigfoot as well including Native Americans.</u>

   a. NO CHANGE
   b. seeing Bigfoot, Native Americans as well.
   c. seeing Bigfoot also the Native Americans.
   d. seeing Bigfoot, including Native Americans.

The next question is based on the following passage:

According to myth, Prometheus was the titan who gave fire to mankind. Because fire advanced civilization, Prometheus symbolically gave humanity knowledge and power. Yet, for giving fire to man, Prometheus was punished by the gods bound to a rock and tormented for his act.

13. Which of the following would be the best choice for the underlined portion of the following sentence?

Yet, for giving fire to man, Prometheus was <u>punished by the gods bound to a rock and tormented for his act.</u>

a. NO CHANGE
b. punished by the gods, bound to a rock and tormented for his act.
c. bound to a rock and tormented by the gods as punishment.
d. punished for his act by being bound to a rock and tormented as punishment from the gods.

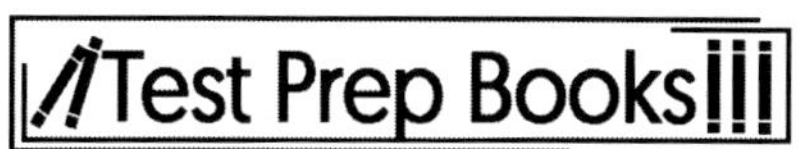

The next question is based on the following graphs:

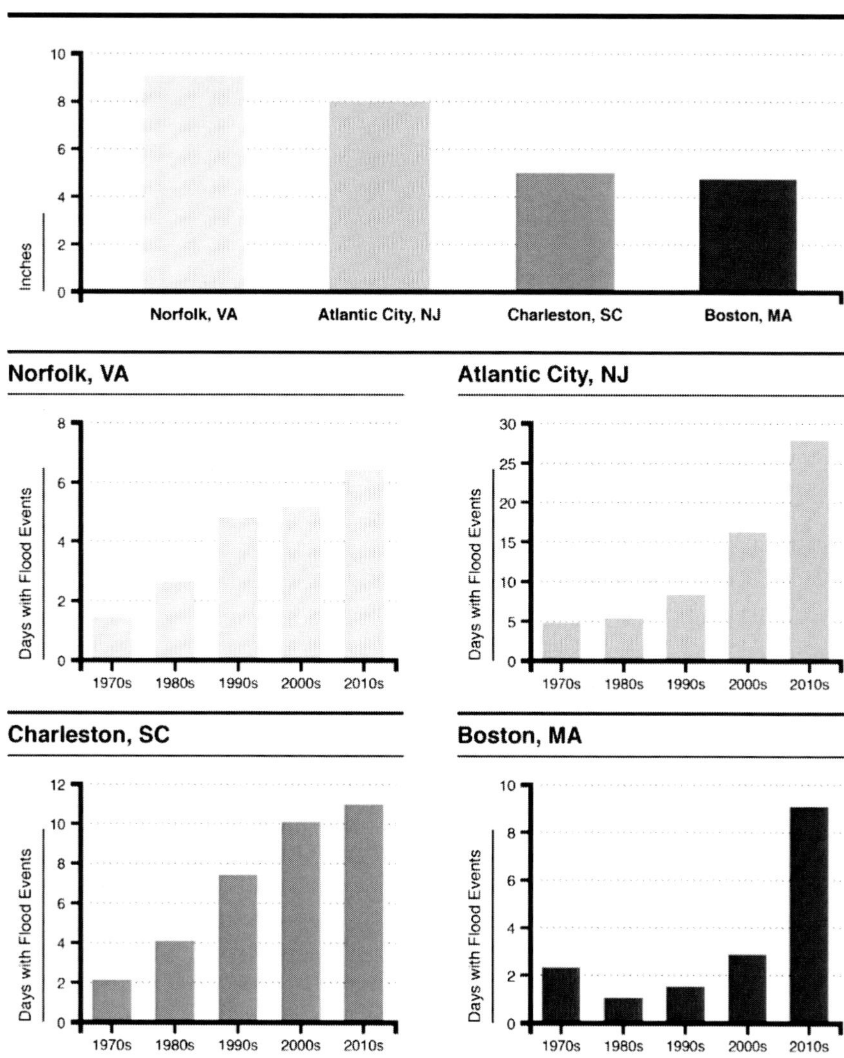

Global warming is the result of air pollution that prevents the sun's radiation from being emitted back into space. Instead, the radiation is trapped in the Earth's atmosphere and results in global warming. The warming of the Earth has resulted in climate changes. As a result, floods have been occurring with increasing regularity. Some claim that the increased temperatures on Earth may cause the icebergs to melt. They fear that the melting of icebergs will cause the ocean levels to rise and flood coastal regions.

14. What information from the graphs could be used to support the claims found in the paragraph above?
    a. Between 1970–1980, Boston experienced an increase in the number of days with flood events.
    b. Between 1970–1980, Atlantic City, New Jersey did not experience an increase in the number of days with flood events.
    c. Since 1970, the number of days with floods has decreased in major coastal cities across America.
    d. Since 1970, sea levels have risen along the East Coast.

The next question is based on the timeline of the life of Alexander Graham Bell:

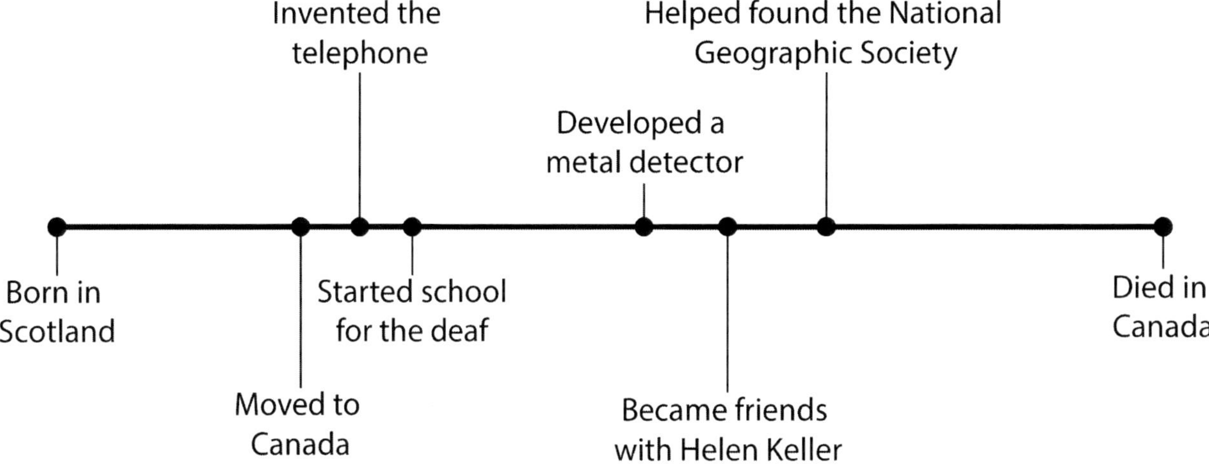

15. Which one of the following statements is accurate based on the timeline?
    a. Bell did nothing significant after he helped found the National Geographic Society.
    b. Bell started a school for the deaf in Canada.
    c. Bell lived in at least two countries.
    d. Developing a metal detector allowed Bell to meet Helen Keller.

The next question is based on the following passage:

> There are two major kinds of cameras on the market right now for amateur photographers. Camera enthusiasts can either purchase a digital single-lens reflex camera (DSLR) camera or a compact system camera (CSC). The main difference between a DSLR and a CSC is that the DSLR has a full-sized sensor, which means it fits in a much larger body. The CSC uses a mirrorless system, which makes for a lighter, smaller camera. While both take quality pictures, the DSLR generally has better picture quality due to the larger sensor. CSCs still take very good quality pictures and are more convenient to carry than a DSLR. This makes the CSC an ideal choice for the amateur photographer looking to step up from a point-and-shoot camera.

16. What is the main difference between the DSLR and CSC?
    a. The picture quality is better in the DSLR.
    b. The CSC is less expensive than the DSLR.
    c. The DSLR is a better choice for amateur photographers.
    d. The DSLR's larger sensor makes it a bigger camera than the CSC.

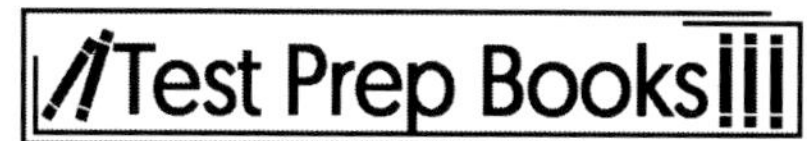

The next question is based on the following passage:

> From that time forward, Mr. Utterson began to haunt the door in the by-street of shops. In the morning before office hours, at noon when business was plenty and time scarce, at night under the face of the full city moon, by all lights and at all hours of solitude or concourse, the lawyer was to be found on his chosen post.
>
> Excerpt from *The Strange Case of Dr. Jekyll and Mr. Hyde* by Robert Louis Stevenson

17. What is the definition of the word *haunt* in the passage above?
    a. To levitate
    b. To constantly visit
    c. To terrorize
    d. To daunt

18. If a writer changes the phrase *mazes of roads lit by streetlights* to the phrase *labyrinths of the lamp-lighted city*, what literary device are they employing?
    a. Hyperbole
    b. Simile
    c. Juxtaposition
    d. Alliteration

The next question is based on the following passage:

> A good résumé is essential in the professional world and can be the deciding factor in whether or not the hiring manager decides to go through with an interview. A well-crafted résumé should show off skills, experiences, and progression. Employers will look at the résumé and determine if they are interested in hearing more about the candidate based on what they see and offer an interview.

19. Which portion of the text should be revised or deleted?
    a. NO CHANGE
    b. is essential in the professional world and
    c. skills, experiences, and progression
    d. and offer an interview

The next question is based on the following passage:

> Privacy is a major concern that has greatly evolved in recent years. Major cyberattacks and data breaches have affected governments, banks, businesses, and individuals. For example, in 2017, a data breach of a popular credit reporting agency led to more than 147 million individuals having their data leaked. This included sensitive information such as Social Security numbers. However, hackers can do damage to more than just privacy.

20. Which sentence would best strengthen the author's argument after the last sentence?
    a. They can also invade home cameras without anyone taking notice.
    b. In 2021, they managed to cut off fuel supply to the East Coast of the United States via the Colonial Pipeline.
    c. Cybersecurity is a vital part of legislation for this reason.
    d. They may choose to release sensitive information about the government, which could hurt foreign affairs.

The next question is based on the following passage:

(1) It was a clear, sunny day with a light breeze. (2) It was perfect weather for a special event. (3) Family and friends were called to gather at the beach to witness the vow renewal of Sherry and Jim. (4) The ceremony was short and sweet with the main event being the celebration afterward. (5) There was good music, food, and drinks for the guests to enjoy. (6) It was most definitely a night to remember for all in attendance.

21. Where should the following sentence be placed in the text?

Before the ceremony began, a photographer snapped photos of everyone arriving in their beautiful dresses and suits.

a. After Sentence 1
b. After Sentence 2
c. After Sentence 3
d. After Sentence 4

The next question is based on the following passage:

These community assessments conducted during the Zika outbreak, hurricane responses, and hurricane recovery in US Virgin Islands (USVI) found that households were more concerned about contracting mosquito-borne diseases shortly after the Zika outbreak than during the hurricane response and hurricane recovery, even though reported mosquito biting activity increased, and environmental conditions were more favorable for mosquito breeding and exposure to bites following the hurricanes. In addition, although mosquito-borne diseases are endemic in USVI, and the population might be aware of the risk, households had concerns after the hurricanes that did not exist during the Zika outbreak, such as lack of shelter, clean water, and electricity. These differing levels of concern did not, however, change the community's support for mosquito spraying, although support for specific spray methods varied.

Excerpt from "Community Assessments for Mosquito Prevention and Control Experiences, Attitudes, and Practices—US Virgin Islands, 2017 and 2018," in *Morbidity and Mortality Weekly Report*

22. The research in this paragraph attempts to draw a correlation between which two things?
a. Zika and hurricanes
b. Resident concerns and Zika spread
c. Hurricanes and mosquito spraying
d. Basic necessities and mosquito-borne diseases

The next question is based on the following passages:

Text 1: The Salem witch trials occurred in 1692 in Salem, Massachusetts. Around 20 people, most of them women, were accused of witchcraft. They were then put on trial, convicted, and in many cases, executed for their supposed crimes. These trials are often used as an example of mass hysteria and paranoia. Anything that seemed relatively out of the norm could be considered a sign of witchcraft.

Text 2: Bridget Bishop was a young woman who was executed in Salem, Massachusetts in 1692 after being accused of witchcraft. She was considered suspicious for running an inn. Also, peculiarly, her first two

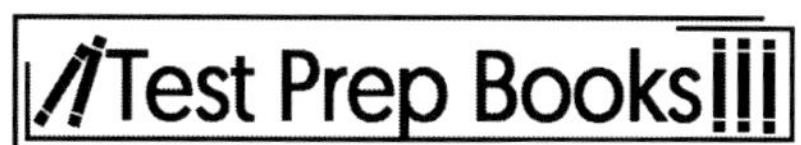

husbands faced early deaths. She dressed in colorful, provocative clothing, which was frowned upon at that time.

23. Based on these two texts, why was Bridget Bishop executed?
    a. Having multiple husbands was considered illegal.
    b. She was believed to be a witch due to paranoia.
    c. Women were not allowed to run inns.
    d. Her clothing was too provocative for the religious community.

The next question is based on the following passages:

Text 1: The archaeologists in the field recently uncovered a remarkable find in Pakistan. The discovery could be one of the earliest Buddhist temples to ever exist. It may even date back to second century BC. It is a 10-foot circular structure and contains a Buddhist stupa.

Text 2: The Venus of Willendorf is a small figurine that dates back to 25,000 to 30,000 years ago. This makes it one of the earliest depictions of art from the Paleolithic era. It is thought to depict a fertility deity, hence its name. It was discovered in 1908 by archaeologists in Willendorf, Lower Austria.

24. Based on the texts, what can be reasonably said about the discoveries?
    a. Both discoveries revealed civilizations that people did not know existed.
    b. The temple is a more significant find because it is older than the figurine.
    c. The temple is a significant religious discovery, while the figurine is important to art history.
    d. The two excavations were done by the same group of archaeologists.

The next question is based on the following passage:

An accomplished wizard once lived on the top floor of a tenement house and passed his time in thoughtful study and studious thought. What he didn't know about wizardry was hardly worth knowing, for he possessed all the books and recipes of all the wizards who had lived before him; and, moreover, he had invented several wizardments himself. This admirable person would have been completely happy but for the numerous interruptions to his studies caused by folk who came to consult him about their troubles (in which he was not interested), and by the loud knocks of the iceman, the milkman, the baker's boy, the laundryman and the peanut woman.

Excerpt based on "The Glass Dog" in *American Fairy Tales* by L. Frank Baum

25. What inference can be made about the wizard?
    a. He greatly enjoys the company of the people in his community.
    b. The people in the community see him as competent.
    c. He has many friends whom he wants to help.
    d. The community has shunned the wizard due to his magical abilities.

The next question is based on the following passage:

I wandered lonely as a cloud
That floats on high o'er vales and hills,
When all at once I saw a crowd,
A host, of golden daffodils;
Beside the lake, beneath the trees,
Fluttering and dancing in the breeze.

Continuous as the stars that shine
And twinkle on the milky way,
They stretched in never-ending line
Along the margin of a bay:
Ten thousand saw I at a glance,
Tossing their heads in sprightly dance.

The waves beside them danced; but they
Out-did the sparkling waves in glee:
A poet could not but be gay,
In such a jocund company:
I gazed—and gazed—but little thought
What wealth the show to me had brought:

For oft, when on my couch I lie
In vacant or in pensive mood,
They flash upon that inward eye
Which is the bliss of solitude;
And then my heart with pleasure fills,
And dances with the daffodils.

"I Wandered Lonely as a Cloud" by William Wordsworth

26. How does the structure of the poem contribute to its purpose?
    a. The stanzas parallel the speaker's feelings with the environmental destruction around them.
    b. The lines are short to emphasize the speaker's changing state of mind.
    c. The rhyme scheme creates a harmonious quality that reflects the beauty of nature.
    d. The structure does not contribute to the purpose of the text.

27. Which of the following would be the best choice for the underlined portion of the following sentence?

    In the modern age of technology, a teacher's focus is no longer the "what" of the content, <u>but more importantly, the 'why.'</u>

    a. NO CHANGE
    b. but more importantly, the "why."
    c. but, more importantly, the 'why'.
    d. but more importantly, the "why".

Math: Module 1

1. Which of the following inequalities is equivalent to $3 - \frac{1}{2}x \geq 2$?
    a. $x \geq 2$
    b. $x \leq 2$
    c. $x \geq 1$
    d. $x \leq 1$

2. If $g(x) = x^3 - 3x^2 - 2x + 6$ and $f(x) = 2$, then what is $g(f(x))$?
   a. -26
   b. 6
   c. $2x^3 - 6x^2 - 4x + 12$
   d. -2

3. A hospital has a bed-to-room ratio of two to one. If there are 145 rooms, how many beds are there?

4. What are the coordinates of the focus of the parabola $y = -9x^2$?
   a. $(-3, 0)$
   b. $\left(-\frac{1}{36}, 0\right)$
   c. $(0, -3)$
   d. $\left(0, -\frac{1}{36}\right)$

5. In cubic inches, what is the volume of a cube with the side length equal to 3 inches?

6. What is the volume of a rectangular prism with a height of 3 centimeters, a width of 5 centimeters, and a depth of 11 centimeters?
   a. 19 cm^3
   b. 165 cm^3
   c. 225 cm^3
   d. 150 cm^3

7. What is the volume of a cylinder, in terms of π, with a radius of 5 inches and a height of 10 inches?
   a. $250\pi \text{ in}^3$
   b. $50\pi \text{ in}^3$
   c. $100\pi \text{ in}^3$
   d. $200\pi \text{ in}^3$

8. What is the solution to the following system of equations?

$$x^2 - 2x + y = 8$$

$$x - y = -2$$

   a. $(-2, 3)$
   b. There is no solution.
   c. $(-2, 0), (1, 3)$
   d. $(-2, 0), (3, 5)$

9. What is the equation for the line passing through the origin and the point $(2, 1)$?
   a. $y = 2x$
   b. $y = \frac{1}{2}x$
   c. $y = x - 2$
   d. $2y = x + 1$

10. The scatterplot below shows the distance traveled in hundreds of miles for a small Cessna airplane over the course of several trips. Approximate how many miles the plane would travel over a seven-hour time frame by creating a line of best fit.

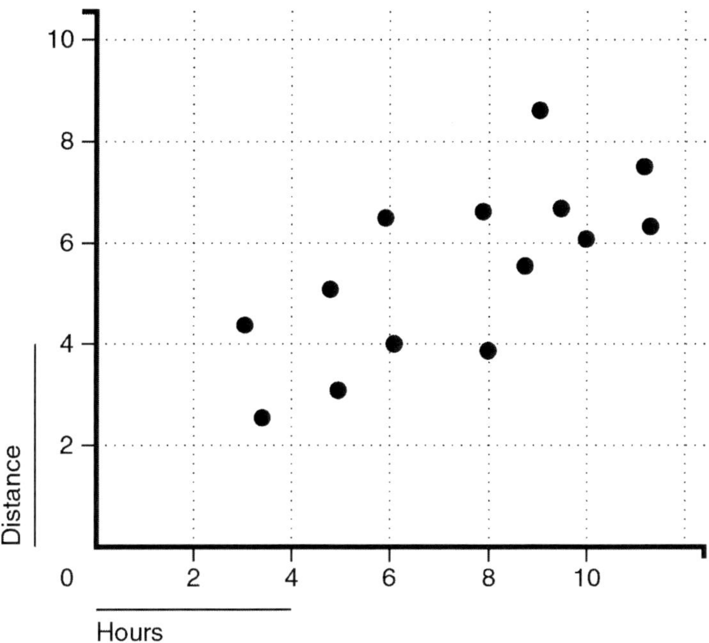

a. 6 miles
b. 550 miles
c. 5.5 miles
d. 600 miles

11. What type of function is modeled by the values in the following table?

x	$f(x)$
1	2
2	4
3	8
4	16
5	32

a. Linear
b. Exponential
c. Quadratic
d. Cubic

12. A shuffled deck of 52 cards contains four kings. One card is drawn and is not put back in the deck. Then, a second card is drawn. What's the probability that both cards are kings?

a. $\frac{1}{169}$

b. $\frac{1}{221}$

c. $\frac{1}{13}$

d. $\frac{4}{13}$

13. In the image below, what is demonstrated by the two triangles?

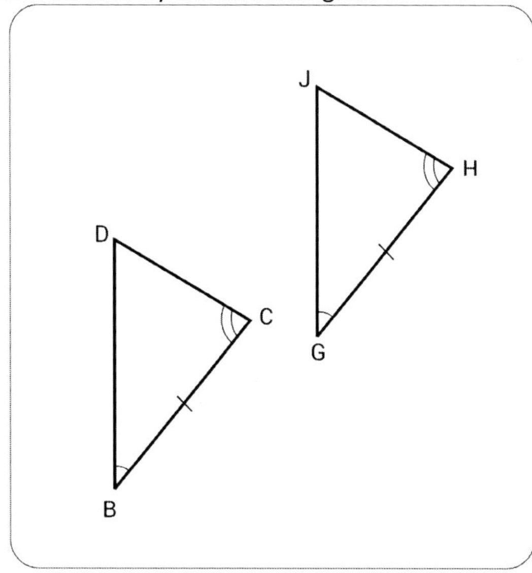

a. According to Side-Side-Side, the triangles are congruent.
b. According to Angle-Angle-Angle, the triangles are congruent.
c. According to Angle-Side-Angle, the triangles are congruent.
d. There is not enough information to prove the two triangles are congruent.

14. On Monday, Robert mopped the floor in four hours. On Tuesday, he did it in three hours. If on Monday, his average rate of mopping was p sq. ft. per hour, what was his average rate on Tuesday?

a. $\frac{4}{3}p$ sq. ft. per hour

b. $\frac{3}{4}p$ sq. ft. per hour

c. $\frac{5}{4}p$ sq. ft. per hour

d. $p + 1$ sq. ft. per hour

15. If $\sqrt{5 + x} = 5$, what is x?

16. Which of the following polynomials is equal to $(2x - 4y)^2$?
   a. $4x^2 - 16xy + 16y^2$
   b. $4x^2 - 8xy + 16y^2$
   c. $4x^2 - 16xy - 16y^2$
   d. $2x^2 - 8xy + 8y^2$

17. What are the zeros of $f(x) = x^2 + 4$?
   a. $x = -4$
   b. $x = \pm 2i$
   c. $x = \pm 2$
   d. $x = \pm 4i$

18. What is the simplified form of the expression $(7n + 3n^3 + 3) + (8n + 5n^3 + 2n^4)$?
   a. $9n^4 + 15n - 2$
   b. $2n^4 + 5n^3 + 15n - 2$
   c. $9n^4 + 8n^3 + 15n$
   d. $2n^4 + 8n^3 + 15n + 3$

19. What is the simplified result of $\frac{15}{23} \times \frac{54}{127}$?
   a. $\frac{810}{2{,}921}$
   b. $\frac{81}{292}$
   c. $\frac{69}{150}$
   d. $\frac{810}{2{,}929}$

20. What is the product of the following expressions?

$$(4x - 8)(5x^2 + x + 6)$$

   a. $20x^3 - 36x^2 + 16x - 48$
   b. $6x^3 - 41x^2 + 12x + 15$
   c. $20\text{x}^3 + 11x^2 - 37x - 12$
   d. $2x^3 - 11x^2 - 32x + 20$

21. What is the solution for the following equation?

$$\frac{x^2 + x - 30}{x - 5} = 11$$

   a. $x = -6$
   b. There is no solution.
   c. $x = 16$
   d. $x = 5$

22. If x is not zero, then $\frac{3}{x} + \frac{5u}{2x} - \frac{u}{4} =$
   a. $\frac{12+10u-ux}{4x}$
   b. $\frac{3+5u-ux}{x}$
   c. $\frac{12x+10u+ux}{4x}$
   d. $\frac{12+10u-u}{4x}$

Math: Module 2

1. What are the zeros of the function: $f(x) = x^3 + 4x^2 + 4x$?
   a. -2
   b. 0, -2
   c. 2
   d. 0, 2

2. Is the following function even, odd, neither, or both?

$$y = \frac{1}{2}x^4 + 2x^2 - 6$$

   a. Even
   b. Odd
   c. Neither
   d. Both

3. Store-brand coffee beans cost $1.23 per pound. A local coffee bean roaster charges $1.98 per $1\frac{1}{2}$ pounds. How much more would 5 pounds from the local roaster cost than 5 pounds of the store-brand coffee?
   a. $0.55
   b. $1.55
   c. $1.45
   d. $0.45

4. Paint Inc. charges $2,000 for painting the first 1,800 feet of trim on a house and an additional $1.00 per foot for each foot beyond that. In dollars, how much would it cost to paint a house with 3,125 feet of trim?

5. Given the following triangle, what's the length of the missing side? Round the answer to the nearest tenth.

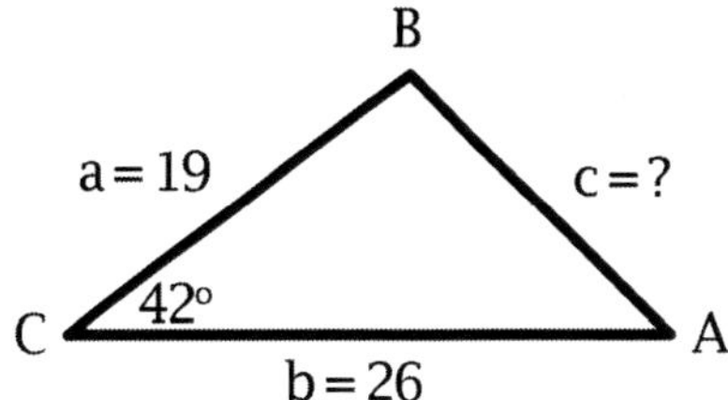

a. 17.0
b. 17.4
c. 18.0
d. 18.4

6. For the following similar triangles, what are the values of x and y (rounded to one decimal place)?

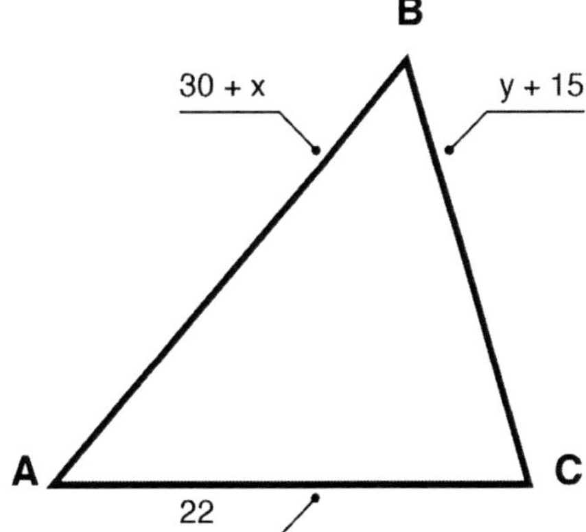

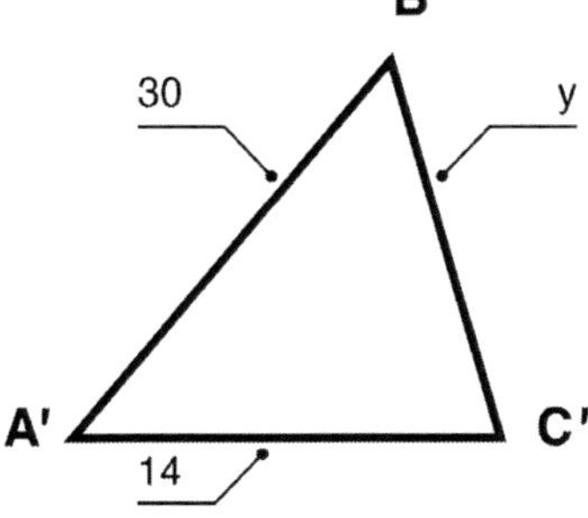

a. $x = 16.5, y = 25.1$
b. $x = 19.5, y = 24.1$
c. $x = 17.1, y = 26.3$
d. $x = 26.3, y = 17.1$

7. What are the center and radius of the circle with the equation $4x^2 + 4y^2 - 16x - 24y + 51 = 0$?
a. Center $(3, 2)$ and radius $1/2$
b. Center $(2, 3)$ and radius $1/2$
c. Center $(3, 2)$ and radius $1/4$
d. Center $(2, 3)$ and radius $1/4$

8. What is $(2 \times 20) \div (7 + 1) + (6 \times 0.01) + (4 \times 0.001)$?
a. 5.064
b. 5.64
c. 5.0064
d. 48.064

9. A piggy bank contains 12 dollars' worth of nickels. A nickel weighs 5 grams, and the empty piggy bank weighs 1,050 grams. In grams, what is the total weight of the full piggy bank?

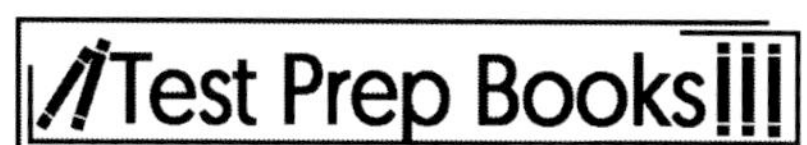

10. Last year, the New York City area received approximately $27\frac{3}{4}$ inches of snow. The Denver area received approximately three times as much snow as New York City. How much snow fell in Denver?

a. 60 inches
b. $27\frac{1}{4}$ inches
c. $9\frac{1}{4}$ inches
d. $83\frac{1}{4}$ inches

11. If $-3(x + 4) \geq x + 8$, what is the value of x?

a. $x = 4$
b. $x \geq 2$
c. $x \geq -5$
d. $x \leq -5$

12. Karen gets paid a weekly salary and a commission for every sale that she makes. The table below shows the number of sales and her pay for different weeks.

Sales	2	7	4	8
Pay	\$380	\$580	\$460	\$620

Which of the following equations represents Karen's weekly pay?

a. $y = 90x + 200$
b. $y = 90x - 200$
c. $y = 40x + 300$
d. $y = 40x - 300$

13. The square and circle have the same center. The circle has a radius of r. What is the area of the shaded region?

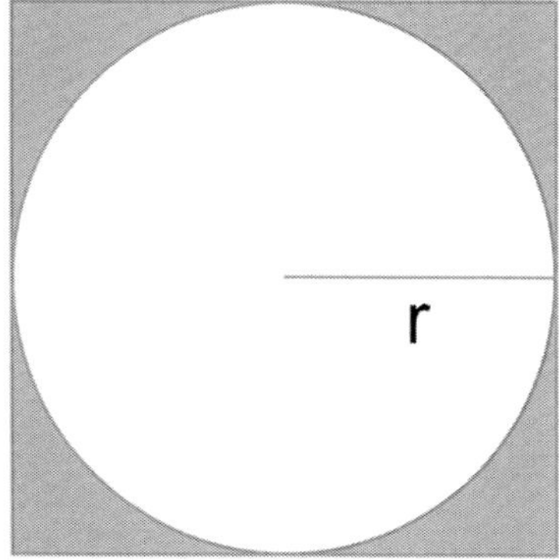

a. $r^2 - \pi r^2$
b. $4r^2 - 2\pi r$
c. $(4 - \pi)r^2$
d. $(\pi - 1)r^2$

14. The graph shows the position of a car over a 10-second time interval. Which of the following is the correct interpretation of the graph for the interval 1 to 3 seconds?

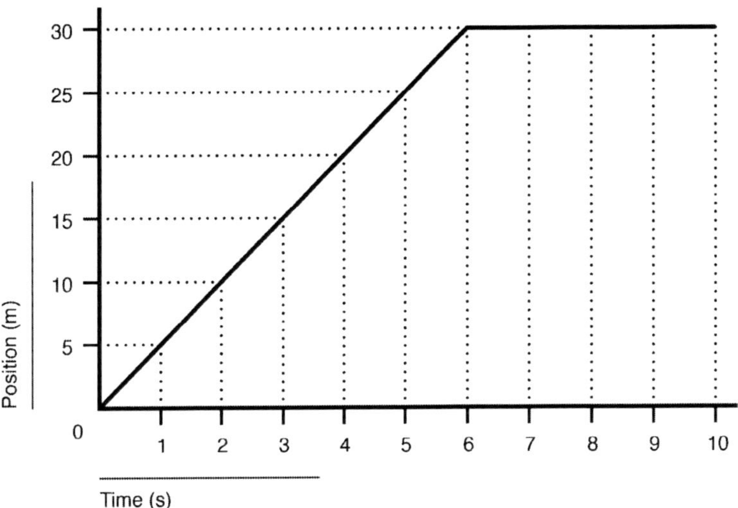

a. The car remains in the same position.
b. The car is traveling at a speed of 5 m/s.
c. The car is traveling up a hill.
d. The car is traveling at 5 mph.

15. Which of the ordered pairs below is a solution to the following system of inequalities?

$$y > 2x - 3$$

$$y < -4x + 8$$

a. $(4,5)$
b. $(-3,-2)$
c. $(3,-1)$
d. $(5,2)$

16. Which equation best represents the scatter plot below?

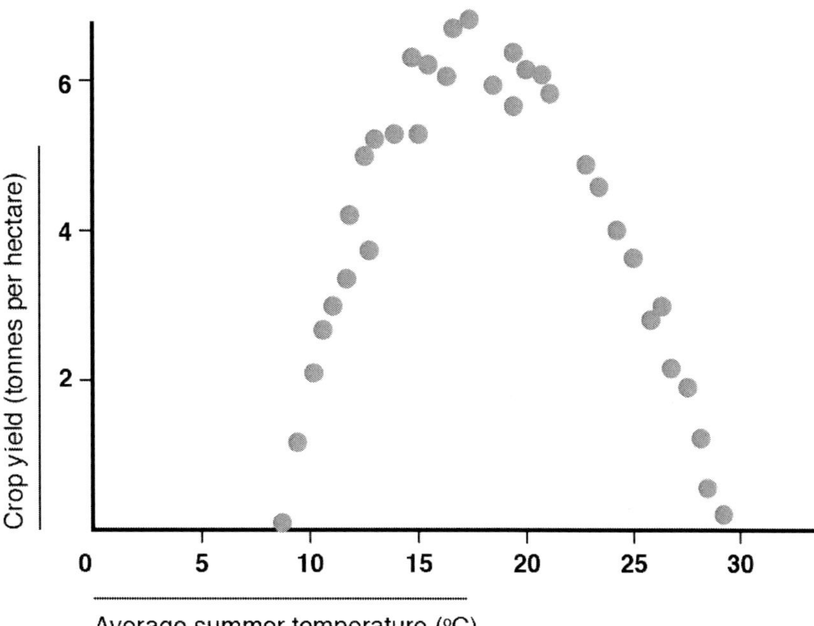

a. $y = 3x - 4$
b. $y = 2x^2 + 7x - 9$
c. $y = (3)(4^x)$
d. $y = -\frac{1}{14}x^2 + 2x - 8$

17. Bill can make two wicker baskets every day. He already has some wicker baskets made. In five days, he will have a total of 17 wicker baskets. How many wicker baskets did he have before he started working on more?

18. What is the solution to the radical equation $\sqrt[3]{2x + 11} + 9 = 12$?

a. –8
b. 8
c. 0
d. 12

19. A hospital has a nurse-to-patient ratio of $1:25$. If the hospital has the capacity for 325 patients, how many nurses are there?

a. 13 nurses
b. 25 nurses
c. 325 nurses
d. 12 nurses

20. What is $4 \times 7 + (25 - 21)^2 \div 2$?

21. If $\frac{2x}{5} - 1 = 59$, what is the value of x?
   a. 60
   b. 145
   c. 150
   d. 115

22. A National Hockey League store in the state of Michigan advertises 50% off all items. Sales tax in Michigan is 6%. How much would a hat originally priced at $32.99 and a jersey originally priced at $64.99 cost during this sale? Round to the nearest penny.
   a. $97.98
   b. $103.86
   c. $51.93
   d. $48.99

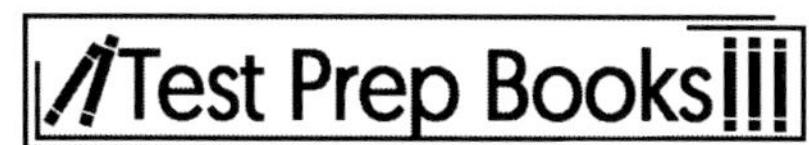

Answers Explanation

Reading and Writing: Module 1

1. D: The sentence uses personification, whereby darkness is given a human quality—being able to swallow. There is no comparison being made, making *metaphor*, Choice *A,* incorrect. A synecdoche, which is a device that uses a part to represent a whole or vice versa, is not present, making Choice *B* incorrect. The sentence has no interjected scenes from a previous point in the narrative, making *flashback*, Choice *C,* incorrect.

2. C: Jimmy Carter talks about how Americans are losing confidence in their government, their ability to self-govern, and democracy. He basically says America has lost its way and must find it again. That will be hard and will require facing the truth. In the last paragraph, he says that we need to change course and restore confidence and faith. Choice *A* is incorrect because Carter believes that faith can be restored, meaning there is hope for the future. Choice *B* only addresses part of the speech, so it is not the best answer. While Carter does reference other people in the Western world, that is irrelevant to the underlying message, making Choice *D* incorrect.

3. C: In the first way of life, countries are ruled by a majority, with representative government, free elections, and freedom of speech. In the second way of life, the will of a small number of people is forcibly imposed upon the majority. These countries are characterized by terror and oppression. Choice *A* is wrong because both parts of the sentence describe the first way of life. Choice *B* is wrong because both qualities describe the second way of life. Choice *D* is incorrect because it is the opposite of what Truman describes; the first part describes the second way of life and vice versa.

4. B: The word *subterfuges* could be replaced with *tricky deceptions* and the sentence would retain the same meaning. This can be gathered from nearby words like *violation*, *coercion*, and *infiltration*. *Helpful pieces of intel* would be information of military or political value, not deceit, which makes Choice *A* wrong. Political infiltration may be a time-consuming activity, but it does not address the deception of subterfuge. This makes Choice *C* incorrect. The prefix "sub-" in the word *subterfuge* does mean "under," but it would only mean underground in a word like *subterranean*. This makes Choice *D* wrong.

5. D: Choice *D* conveys a grammatically correct question about technology and development. Choice *A* does not make sense the way it is worded. Choice *B* doesn't make sense in context because the sentence does not introduce the rest of a question. Choice *C* adds unnecessary commas.

6. C: The passage by Jean-Henri Fabre was written for a children's storybook, which is why he uses whimsical language. Personifying both the bee and the flower and using phrases like "merry little people" evokes the mood of a fairytale or fable. Pedantic word choice suggests a pompous scholarly paper; this passage is anything but pompous and scholarly, making Choice *A* incorrect. This passage is light-hearted, while something emotional usually plays on deep or dark emotions. This is why Choice *B* is incorrect. Choice *D* is incorrect because, despite whimsical storytelling, the message and information are clear, not ambiguous.

7. D: The best substitution for the word *posterior* is *rear*. This answer can be drawn from realizing posterior legs means the opposite of "forward appendages." Also, the prefix *post*- means behind or after. While the word *strongest* fits in the sentence nicely, nothing implies that that particular set of legs is the strongest. This makes Choice *A* incorrect. *Anterior*, meaning front, is actually the antonym for the word *posterior*, so Choice *B* is wrong. *Ambulatory* is a word that could describe any pair of functioning legs and does not differentiate the hind legs from the front or middle, which makes Choice *C* incorrect.

8. B: After the experimenter is asked to add more salt than can be dissolved and then to use a Bunsen burner to heat the test tube, a logical result would be that the heat acts as an agent to dissolve the salt more readily. Choice *A* is the opposite of the expected result. The rhetorical question that follows the instructions implies that the salt will not impede the heating element, making Choice *C* incorrect. While the author does mention washing dishes, using the saltwater solution as soap is an inaccurate connection, leaving Choice *D* incorrect.

9. A: Choice *A* is correct because in both Text 1 and Text 2 the speakers argue that a writer's word choice is important. Choice *B* is incorrect because the texts disagree with how to describe the "best word." Choice *C* is incorrect because Text 1 does not include an opinion about literature courses. Choice *D* is incorrect because Text 2 *does* believe simple words can inspire strong emotions.

10. B: Choice *B* is correct because both texts recognize that creative expression is important when making a painting. Choice *A* is incorrect because Text 1 does not place importance on a painting's message. Choice *C* is incorrect because Text 2 does not value a painting's fidelity to real life. Choice *D* is incorrect because neither text discusses the subject matter of a painting.

11. C: Choice *C* correctly uses *from* to describe the fact that dogs are related to wolves. The word *through* is incorrectly used here, so Choice *A* is incorrect. Choice *B* does not make sense. Choice *D* unnecessarily changes the verb tense in addition to incorrectly using *through*.

12. A: Choice *A* is correct since there are no errors in the sentence. Choices *B* and *C* both have extraneous commas, disrupting the flow of the sentence. Choice *D* unnecessarily rearranges the sentence.

13. B: Choice *B* correctly adds a comma after the word *person*. Choice *C* inserts a semicolon where a comma is needed. Choice *D* adds a period to the middle of the sentence.

14. B: Choice *B* changes *its*, which is possessive, to *it's*, which is a contraction of "it is." It also separates the two independent clauses with a comma and streamlines the sentence by eliminating *and*. Choices *C* and *D* are run-on sentences.

15. D: By reorganizing the sentence, the context becomes clearer with Choice *D*. Choice *A* has an awkward sentence structure and is less direct than Choice *D*. Choice *B* offers a revision that doesn't correspond well with the original sentence's intent. Choice *C* cuts out too much of the original content, losing the full meaning.

16. D: Choice *D* correctly adds a comma after *media*. Choice *A* is missing this comma, while Choice *B* inserts an unnecessary comma. Choice *C* repeats information from the previous sentence.

17. C: Roosevelt notes that secrecy ensures an individual's right to vote as they choose. Choice *A* and Choice *D* may be true; public votes were known for their carnivalesque atmosphere, and private votes protect voters from violent confrontations with their political foes. However, these ideas are not stated in the passage. Choice *B* is incorrect as the opposite may be true. Privacy might increase the likelihood that, because the vote is secret, an individual can attest to voting one way but actually vote another without any accountability. This would make bribery a risk.

18. B: Johnson notes that Selma is an opportunity to right wrongs and seek justice as it relates to the denial of equal rights. Although a bridge played a prominent role in the Selma protest march, it was not the cause, so Choice *A* is incorrect. A man was killed, but that happened during the protest, so it could not be the cause. Therefore, Choice *C* is not correct. Finally, though Johnson discusses wealth in this passage, he does not say it is the cause of the events in Selma, so Choice *D* is incorrect.

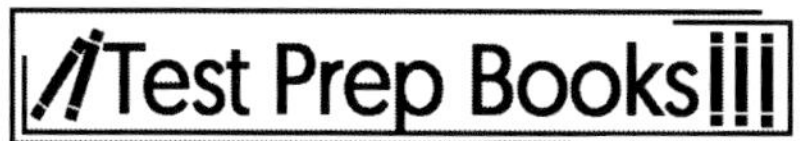

19. C: Choice *C* correctly adds a comma after *style*, successfully joining the dependent and the independent clauses as a single sentence. Choice *A* is incorrect because the dependent and independent clauses remain unsuccessfully combined without the comma. Choices *B* and *D* do nothing to fix this.

20. D: The graph shows the number of people (in millions) boarding United States flights between 1996 and 2005. In the first few months following the September 11 attacks, the number of passengers boarding US flights dropped to around 50 million, compared to around 70 million before the attacks. Therefore, the correct answer is Choice *D*. The graph does not show where the flights were redirected, the number of passengers that other countries received as a result of the redirected air travel, or the resulting flight schedule implications, making the other choices incorrect.

21. D: Choice *D* is the correct answer because the subject of the analogy is resting at the side of a fountain on a weary summer day. Thus, it is reasonable to conclude that they are experiencing relaxation. Choice *A* is incorrect because strain is the opposite of the restful experience at the fountain. Choice *B* is incorrect because the person is not being newly warmed; they are merely enjoying a state of tranquility after a likely warm summer day. Choice *C* is incorrect because the text describes only restfulness at the fountain, not excitement.

22. B: Choice *B* is the correct answer, as the narrator is describing the poor appearance of Sir Walter compared to the last time he saw him, including weight loss and a loss of color from his face. Choice *A* cannot be inferred because there is nothing to suggest that this is the narrator's first time in Sir Walter's office. Choice *C* is incorrect because there is no indication that Sir Walter has just accepted a new position. Choice *D* is incorrect because the narrator expresses no opinion about Sir Walter's position.

23. C: Any time a writer wants to validate a claim, he or she ought to provide factual information that proves or supports that claim: "beginning their preparation for the profession in high school" supports the claim that aircraft engineers undergo years of education. For this reason, Choice *C* is the correct response. However, completing such courses in high school does not guarantee that aircraft engineers will earn generous salaries, Choice *A*, become employed in executive positions, Choice *B*, or stay employed, Choice *D*.

24. A: The word *conversely* best demonstrates the opposing sentiments in this passage. Choice *B* is incorrect because it denotes agreement with the previous statement. Choice *C* is incorrect because the sentiment is not restated but opposed. Choice *D* is incorrect because the previous statement is not a cause for the sentence in question.

25. A: The sentence is correct as-is; therefore, Choice *A* is correct. The list of events accomplished by Hampton is short enough that each item in the list can be separated by a comma. Choice *B* is incorrect. Although a colon can be used to introduce a list of items, it is not a conventional choice for separating items within a series. Semicolons are used to separate at least three items in a series that have an internal comma. Semicolons can also be used to separate clauses in a sentence that contain internal commas intended for clarification purposes. Neither of the two latter uses of semicolons is required in the example sentence. Therefore, Choice *C* is incorrect. Choice *D* is incorrect because a dash is not a conventional choice for punctuating items in a series.

26. B: In this sentence, the word "*ocean*" does not require an 's' after it to make it plural because "ocean levels" is plural. Therefore, Choice *A* is incorrect. Because the passage is referring to multiple—if not all—ocean levels, *ocean* does not require an apostrophe (*'s*) because that would indicate that only one ocean is the focus, which is not the case. Therefore, Choice *C* is incorrect. Choice *D* does not fit well into the sentence. This leaves Choice *B,* which correctly completes the sentence and maintains the intended meaning.

27. B: To project means to anticipate or forecast. This goes very well with the sentence because it describes how new technology is trying to estimate flood activity in order to prevent damage and save lives. *Project* in this case needs to be assisted by *to* in order to function in the sentence. Therefore, Choice *C* is incorrect. Choices *A* and *D* have incorrect tenses.

Reading and Writing: Module 2

1. C: Choice *C* is correct because Text 1 applies utilitarianism to "everyday choices" and Text 2 lists simple ways a person can change the world. Choice *A* is incorrect because a shared motive does not logically mean that both texts have the same argument. Choice *B* is incorrect because Text 2 uses more emotional language as rhetoric supporting the shared argument. Choice *D* is incorrect because both texts create definitions as part of an argument calling for action.

2. B: Choice *B* is correct because the sentence is talking about a continuing process. Therefore, the best modification is to add the word *to* in front of *increase*. Choice *A* is incorrect because this modifier is missing. Choice *C* is incorrect because, with the additional comma, the present tense of *increase* is inappropriate. Choice *D* makes more sense, but the tense is still not the best to use.

3. D: Choice *D* is correct, since only proper names should be capitalized. Because *bloodhound* is not a proper name, Choice *A* is incorrect. Only the proper nouns within breed names need to be capitalized, such as *German shepherd*. In terms of punctuation, only one comma after *example* is needed, so Choices *B* and *C* are incorrect.

4. A: Choice *B* incorrectly changes *awake* to *awakened*. Choice *C* adds unnecessary commas. Choice *D* incorrectly changes *turn* to *turns*.

5. B: Choice *B* fixes the homophone issue. Because the author is talking about people, *their* must be used instead of *there*. This revision also appropriately uses the Oxford comma, separating and distinguishing *lives, world,* and *future*. Choice *A* uses the wrong homophone and is missing commas. Choice *C* incorrectly changes *applies* to *applied*, fails to change *there* to *their*, and fails to add the necessary punctuation. Choice *D* incorrectly adds a comma between the subject (*Discussions that make people think about the content and how it applies to their lives, world, and future*) and the predicate (*are key*).

6. C: Choice *C* is correct because it fixes the core issue with this sentence: the singular *has* does not agree with the plural *scientists*. Choices *B* and *D* add unnecessary commas.

7. B: Choice *B* correctly separates the section into two sentences and adds a comma after *Often*. Choice *A* is incorrect because it is a run-on sentence. Choice *C* adds an extraneous comma, while Choice *D* makes the run-on issue worse and does not coincide with the overall structure of the sentence.

8. D: Even if you do not know that *denatured* means the alcohol has been altered in some fashion, there are context clues that imply the solution will not be pure due to the denatured substances. There is no evidence to indicate denatured alcohol is dangerous or unfit for a laboratory, making Choice *A* wrong. Choice *B* is incorrect because the author wrote an entire paragraph differentiating denatured alcohol from regular alcohol. Lastly, there is no amount of heating that will cause the denatured components to dissolve, which is what makes Choice *C* incorrect.

9. C: It is easy to imagine that Hester may have felt either anger, Choice *A*, or fear, Choice *B*, but those are not expressed in the text. Instead, while the passage mentions that her appearance was haughty, Choice *D*, it goes on to say that she likely felt agony, Choice *C*.

10. D: Roosevelt notes that without the processes and discussions that democracy requires, a dictatorship can achieve the same results much more quickly. While it is true that dictatorships may be benevolent, this is not the argument Roosevelt offers, so Choice *A* is incorrect. It is true that multiple factors enable dictators to rise to power, but this is not the reason Roosevelt offers, so Choice *B* is incorrect. Finally, Choice *C* suggests that dictators have

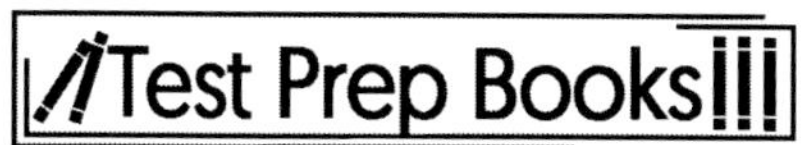

been successful and popular, and though that might be true in some instances, it is also not what the passage discusses.

11. C: *Convocation* means a gathering or a formal assembly. In this case, the people are summoning the leaders of government to an assembly. Based on context and conventional definitions of the words, Choices *A, B*, and *D* are incorrect.

12. D: Choice *D* is correct because it moves the modifying clause "including Native Americans" so that it comes after what it describes: "Ancient civilizations." This adds clarity to the sentence and makes it more direct. Choice *A* uses redundant phrases *as well* and *including*. It also lacks punctuation. Choice *B* is poorly constructed, taking out the clearer *including*. Choice *C* also makes little sense.

13. C: Choice *C* reverses the order of the section, making the sentence more direct. Choice *A* lacks a comma after *gods*, and although Choice *B* adds this, the structure is too different from the first half of the sentence to flow correctly. Choice *D* is overly complicated and repetitious in its structure, even though it doesn't need any punctuation.

14. D: All of the cities included in the graphs are along the East Coast of the United States. All of the bars on the graphs show an increase in sea level or the number of days with flood events since 1970. Therefore, the author chose to include the graphs to support the claim that sea levels have risen along the East Coast since 1970, Choice *D*. Choice *A* is incorrect because the bar above 1970 on Boston's graph is longer than the graph's bar above 1980. Between 1970-1980, Boston experienced a decrease in the number of days with flood events. It's important to note that while there was a decrease from one decade to another, it does not negate the overall trend of increase in flooding events. Choice *B* is incorrect because the bar above 1970 on Atlantic City's graph is shorter than the graph's bar above 1980. Therefore, between 1970-1980, Atlantic City experienced an increase in the number of days with flood events. Choice *C* is incorrect because the bars increase in height on all of the cities' graphs, showing an increase in the number of days with floods along the entire East Coast.

15. C: This question is testing whether you can discern accurate conclusions from a timeline. Although the incorrect answer choices can seem correct, they cannot be confirmed from the information presented on the timeline. Choice *A* is incorrect; while it may be reasonable to assume that the timeline documents all major life events, we do not know for certain that Bell did not engage in any notable activities after founding the National Geographic Society. Choice *B* is incorrect because the timeline does not confirm that the school was in Canada; Bell actually started it in the United States. Choice *D* is incorrect because nothing on the timeline shows causation between the two events. Choice *C* is the only verifiable statement based on the timeline, so it must be the correct answer.

16. D: The passage directly states that the larger sensor is the main difference between the two cameras. Choices *A* and *B* may be true, but these answers do not identify the major difference between the two cameras. Choice *C* states the opposite of what the paragraph suggests is the best option for amateur photographers, so it is incorrect.

17. B: The mention of *morning*, *noon*, and *night* make it clear that the word *haunt* refers to frequent appearances at this location. Choice *A* doesn't work because the text makes no mention of levitating. Choices *C* and *D* are not correct because the text does not mention of Mr. Utterson's actions negatively affecting anyone else.

18. D: Choice *D* is the correct answer because of the repetition of words that start with the letter "L." Hyperbole is an exaggeration, so Choice *A* doesn't work. No comparison is being made, so no simile or metaphor is being used, thus eliminating Choices *B* and *C*.

19. D: Choice *D* is the correct answer because that is the portion of text that should be deleted. It is redundant because the first sentence already mentions that a résumé can lead to an interview. Choice *A* is incorrect because "and offer an interview" should be deleted to fix redundancy. Choice *B* is incorrect because that portion of the text stresses where a résumé is essential, which is in the professional world. Choice *C* is incorrect because those are the main parts of a good résumé. That portion of the text explains the composition of the résumé.

20. B: Choice *B* is the correct answer because it is a real-life example of how hackers can affect more than just privacy; they can also affect infrastructure. This strengthens the author's argument. Choice *A* is incorrect because it is another invasion of privacy and the text is talking about other types of damage. Choice *C* is incorrect because it does not strengthen the argument; it is introducing another related subject, which is cybersecurity law. Choice *D* is incorrect because it brings up another privacy concern when the end of the text brings up other concerns.

21. C: Choice *C* is the correct answer because the sentence in question should come before the ceremony begins, which is mentioned in Sentence 4. It is appropriate to come after Sentence 3 because the photographs could only be taken after the friends and family began to gather. Choices *A*, *B*, and *D* are incorrect because they do not fit the logical sequence.

22. D: According to the research, one can infer that concerns about basic necessities like shelter post-hurricane may impact rates of mosquito-borne illnesses. There is no connection mentioned between Zika and hurricanes, though the research does compare the two in terms of mosquito problems, so Choice *A* is incorrect. Similarly, Choice *B* is incorrect since, while the passage discusses resident concerns of risk and Zika, it does so in connection with mosquito-borne illnesses, not in regard to the spread of Zika specifically. Choice *C* is also incorrect because, again, though discussed together, there's no real correlation between hurricanes and mosquito spraying discussed in the passage.

23. B: Choice *B* is the correct answer because young women in Salem were executed due to mass hysteria, as the first text states. Bridget Bishop had peculiarities about her that made her suspicious due to the paranoia, which is why she was executed. Choice *A* is incorrect because having multiple husbands is not mentioned as being illegal. Choice *C* is incorrect because there is no indication that women were not allowed to run inns, only that it was strange. Choice *D* is incorrect because her clothing was not the main reason she was executed, and the text does not specify whether the community was religious.

24. C: Choice *C* is the correct answer because both archaeological discoveries were important to different areas of study. The Buddhist temple is significant for the religion it pertains to, while the figurine is a marker of the earliest era of art history. Choice *A* is incorrect because the discoveries were not stated to reveal new civilizations. Choice *B* is incorrect because the figurine is older than the temple. Choice *D* is incorrect because these two discoveries were unveiled over 100 years apart.

25. B: Choice *B* is the correct answer because, according to the text, the wizard regularly receives people at his door asking for advice. This suggests that the community deems him competent enough to help with their issues. Choices *A* and *C* are incorrect because the people who seek the wizard's help are not described as his friends, and the text suggests that he dislikes the company of the people who visit him, preferring to be left alone with his studies. Choice *D* is incorrect because the community continually engages with the wizard, so he is not shunned.

26. C: Choice *C* is the correct answer because the rhyme scheme is ABABCC, which creates a seamless flow with its rhythmic quality. This flow aligns with the beauty of nature that surrounds the speaker. Choice *A* is incorrect because there is no mention of environmental destruction in this poem. Choice *B* is incorrect because the lines are short because that is characteristic of this type of poetry, not because of the speaker's thoughts. Choice *D* is incorrect because the structure does contribute to the purpose of the text, which is to celebrate nature's beauty.

27. B: Choice *B* uses all punctuation correctly in this sentence. In American English, single quotes should only be used if they are quotes within a quote, making Choices *A* and *C* incorrect. Additionally, punctuation here should go inside the quotes, making Choice *D* incorrect.

Math: Module 1

1. B: To simplify this inequality, subtract 3 from both sides:

$$3 - 3 - \frac{1}{2}x \geq 2 - 3$$

$$-\frac{1}{2}x \geq -1$$

Then, multiply both sides by –2 (remembering this flips the direction of the inequality):

$$(-\frac{1}{2}x)(-2) \geq (-1)(-2)$$

$$x \leq 2.$$

2. D: This problem involves a composition function, where one function is plugged into the other function. In this case, the $f(x)$ function is plugged into the $g(x)$ function for each x value. Since $f(x) = 2$, the composition equation becomes:

$$g(f(x)) = g(2) = (2)^3 - 3(2)^2 - 2(2) + 6$$

Simplifying the equation gives the answer:

$$g(f(x)) = 8 - 3(4) - 2(2) + 6$$

$$g(f(x)) = 8 - 12 - 4 + 6$$

$$g(f(x)) = -2$$

3. 290: Using the given information of two beds to one room and 145 rooms, set up an equation to solve for the number of beds (B):

$$\frac{B}{145} = \frac{2}{1}$$

Multiply both sides by 145 to get B by itself on one side.

$$\frac{B}{1} = \frac{290}{1} = 290 \text{ beds}$$

4. D: A parabola of the form $y = \frac{1}{4f}x^2$ has a focus $(0, f)$.

Because $y = -9x^2$, set $-9 = \frac{1}{4f}$.

Solving this equation for f results in $f = -\frac{1}{36}$. Therefore, the coordinates of the focus are $\left(0, -\frac{1}{36}\right)$.

5. 27: The volume of a cube is the length of the side cubed, and 3 inches cubed is 27 in^3.

6. B: The volume of a rectangular prism is $length \times width \times height$, and $3 \text{ cm} \times 5 \text{ cm} \times 11 \text{ cm}$ is 165 cm^3.

7. A: The volume of a cylinder is $\pi r^2 h$, and $\pi \times 5^2 \times 10$ is $250\pi \text{ in}^3$.

8. D: This system of equations involves one quadratic function and one linear function, as seen from the degree of each equation. One way to solve this is through substitution.

Solving for y in the second equation yields:

$$y = x + 2$$

Plugging this equation in for the y of the quadratic equation yields:

$$x^2 - 2x + x + 2 = 8$$

Simplifying the equation, it becomes:

$$x^2 - x + 2 = 8$$

Setting this equal to zero and factoring, it becomes:

$$x^2 - x - 6 = 0 = (x - 3)(x + 2)$$

Solving these two factors for x gives the zeros:

$$x = 3, -2$$

To find the y-values for the points, each number can be plugged into either original equation. Solving each one for y yields the points $(3, 5)$ and $(-2, 0)$.

9. B: The origin is (0,0). The slope is given by $\frac{y_2 - y_1}{x_2 - x_1} = \frac{1-0}{2-0} = \frac{1}{2}$.

The y-intercept will be 0 since it passes through the origin. Using slope-intercept form, the equation for this line is $y = \frac{1}{2}x$.

10. B: The line of best fit reaches approximately $d = 5.5$ on the graph. Since the unit of d is 100 miles, multiply 5.5 times 100 to obtain 550 miles.

11. B: The table shows values that are increasing exponentially. The differences between the inputs are the same, while the differences in the outputs are changing by a factor of 2. The values in the table can be modeled by the equation $f(x) = 2^x$.

12. B: For the first card drawn, the probability of a king being pulled is $\frac{4}{52}$. Since this card isn't replaced, if a king is drawn first, the probability of a king being drawn second is $\frac{3}{51}$. The probability of a king being drawn in both the first and second draw is the product of the two probabilities:

$$\frac{4}{52} \times \frac{3}{51} = \frac{12}{2{,}652}$$

To reduce this fraction, divide the top and bottom by 12 to get $\frac{1}{221}$.

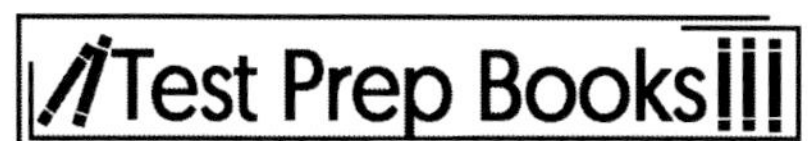

13. C: The picture demonstrates Angle-Side-Angle congruence. Choices *A* and *B* are incorrect because the picture does not show Side-Side-Side congruence and angles alone cannot prove congruence. Choice *D* is not the correct answer because there is already enough information to prove congruence.

14. A: If s is the size of the floor in square feet and r is the rate on Tuesday, then, based on the information given, $p = \frac{s}{4}$ and $r = \frac{s}{3}$. Solve the Monday rate for s, $s = 4p$, and then substitute that in the expression for Tuesday.

15. 20: To solve this equation, square both sides to eliminate the radical, resulting in $x + 5 = 25$. Subtracting 5 from both sides to solve for x gives $x = 20$.

16. A: To expand a squared binomial, it's necessary to use the FOIL (First, Outer, Inner, Last) method:

$$(2x - 4y)^2$$

$$2x \times 2x + 2x(-4y) + (-4y)(2x) + (-4y)(-4y)$$

$$4x^2 - 8xy - 8xy + 16y^2$$

$$4x^2 - 16xy + 16y^2$$

17. B: The zeros of this function can be found by setting $f(x)$ equal to 0 and solving for x.

$$0 = x^2 + 4$$

$$-4 = x^2$$

$$\sqrt{-4} = x$$

Taking the square root of a negative number results in an imaginary number, so the solution is $x = \pm 2i$.

18. D: The expression is simplified by collecting like terms. Terms with the same variable and exponent are like terms, and their coefficients can be added.

19. A: Multiply across the top and across the bottom.

$$\frac{15 \times 54}{23 \times 127} = \frac{810}{2{,}921}$$

This matches Choice *A*, but we must decide whether it can be reduced. Because the numbers are so large, it may be difficult to tell, so the easiest method may be to look at each of the other answer choices. With Choice *B*, we can tell that the denominator, 292, is not a factor of 2,921 because $292 \times 10 = 2{,}920$, not 2,921, so that doesn't work. With Choice *C*, again, we can see that the denominator, 150, is not a factor of 2,921, because 150 is a multiple of 10 and 2,921 isn't. Finally, in Choice *D*, the numerator is the same as in our original fraction, but the denominator isn't, so this can't have the same value. The other choices are eliminated, so the answer must be Choice *A*.

20. A: Finding the product means distributing one polynomial to the other so that each term in the first is multiplied by each term in the second. Then, like terms can be collected. Multiplying the factors yields the expression:

$$20x^3 + 4x^2 + 24x - 40x^2 - 8x - 48$$

Collecting like terms means adding the x^2 terms and adding the x terms. The final answer after simplifying the expression is:

$$20x^3 - 36x^2 + 16x - 48$$

21. B: The equation can be solved by factoring the numerator into $(x+6)(x-5)$. Since $(x-5)$ exists on top and bottom, that factor cancels. This leaves the equation $x + 6 = 11$. Solving the equation gives the answer $x = 5$. When this value is plugged into the equation, it yields a zero in the denominator of the fraction. Since this is undefined, there is no solution.

22. A: The common denominator here will be $4x$. Rewrite these fractions as:

$$\frac{3}{x} + \frac{5u}{2x} - \frac{u}{4}$$

$$\frac{12}{4x} + \frac{10u}{4x} - \frac{ux}{4x}$$

$$\frac{12 + 10u - ux}{4x}$$

Math: Module 2

1. B: There are two zeros for the given function. They are $x = 0, -2$. The zeros can be found a number of ways, but this particular equation can be factored into:

$$f(x) = x(x^2 + 4x + 4) = x(x+2)(x+2)$$

By setting each factor equal to zero and solving for x, there are two solutions: $x = 0$ and $x = -2$. On a graph, these zeros can be seen where the line crosses the x-axis.

2. A: The equation is *even* because $f(-x) = f(x)$. Plugging in a negative value will result in the same answer as when plugging in the positive of that same value. The function:

$$f(-2) = \frac{1}{2}(-2)^4 + 2(-2)^2 - 6$$

$$8 + 8 - 6 = 10$$

This function yields the same value as:

$$f(2) = \frac{1}{2}(2)^4 + 2(2)^2 - 6$$

$$8 + 8 - 6 = 10$$

3. D: First, list the givens:

$$\text{Store-brand coffee} = \$1.23/\text{lb}$$

$$\text{Local roaster's coffee} = \frac{\$1.98}{1.5 \text{ lb}}$$

Calculate the cost for five pounds of store-brand coffee:

$$\frac{\$1.23}{1\text{ lb}} \times 5\text{ lb} = \$6.15$$

Calculate the cost for five pounds of the local roaster's coffee:

$$\frac{\$1.98}{1.5\text{ lb}} \times 5\text{ lb} = \$6.60$$

Subtract to find the difference in price for five pounds of coffee:

$$\$6.60 - \$6.15 = \$0.45$$

4. 3,325: First, list the givens:

$$1{,}800\text{ ft} = \$2{,}000$$

$$\text{Cost after } 1{,}800\text{ ft} = \$1.00/\text{ft}$$

Find how many feet are left after the first 1,800 ft:

$$3{,}125\text{ ft} - 1{,}800\text{ ft} = 1{,}325\text{ ft}$$

Calculate the cost for the feet over 1,800 ft:

$$1{,}325\ ft \times \frac{\$1.00}{1\ ft} = \$1{,}325$$

Add this to the cost for the initial 1,800 feet to find the total cost:

$$\$2{,}000 + \$1{,}325 = \$3{,}325$$

5. B: Because this isn't a right triangle, the SOHCAHTOA mnemonic can't be used. However, the law of cosines can be used:

$$c^2 = a^2 + b^2 - 2ab\cos C$$

$$c^2 = 19^2 + 26^2 - 2 \times 19 \times 26 \times \cos 42° = 302.773$$

Taking the square root and rounding to the nearest tenth results in $c = 17.4$.

6. C: Because the triangles are similar, the lengths of the corresponding sides are proportional. Therefore:

$$\frac{30 + x}{30} = \frac{22}{14} = \frac{y + 15}{y}$$

Using cross multiplication on the first two terms results in the equation:

$$14(30 + x) = 22 \times 30$$

When solved, this gives:

$$x \approx 17.1$$

Using cross multiplication on the last two terms results in the equation:

$$14(y + 15) = 22y$$

When solved, this gives:

$$y \approx 26.3$$

7. B: The technique of completing the square must be used to change the equation below into the standard equation of a circle:

$$4x^2 + 4y^2 - 16x - 24y + 51 = 0$$

First, the constant must be moved to the right-hand side of the equals sign, and each term must be divided by the coefficient of the x^2-term (which is 4). The x- and y-terms must be grouped together to obtain:

$$x^2 - 4x + y^2 - 6y = -\frac{51}{4}$$

Then, the process of completing the square must be completed for each variable. This gives:

$$(x^2 - 4x + 4) + (y^2 - 6y + 9) = -\frac{51}{4} + 4 + 9$$

The equation can be written as:

$$(x - 2)^2 + (y - 3)^2 = \frac{1}{4}$$

Therefore, the center of the circle is $(2, 3)$, and the radius is:

$$\sqrt{\frac{1}{4}} = \frac{1}{2}$$

8. A: Operations within the parentheses must be completed first. Division is completed next, and finally, addition. When adding decimals, digits within each place value are added together. Therefore, the expression is evaluated as:

$$(2 \times 20) \div (7 + 1) + (6 \times 0.01) + (4 \times 0.001)$$

$$40 \div 8 + 0.06 + 0.004 = 5 + 0.06 + 0.004 = 5.064$$

9. 2250: A dollar contains 20 nickels. Therefore, if there are 12 dollars' worth of nickels, there are $12 \times 20 = 240$ nickels. Each nickel weighs 5 grams. Therefore, the weight of the nickels is $240 \times 5 = 1{,}200$ grams. To find the total weight of the filled piggy bank, add the weight of the nickels and the weight of the empty bank:

$$1{,}200 + 1{,}050 = 2{,}250 \text{ grams.}$$

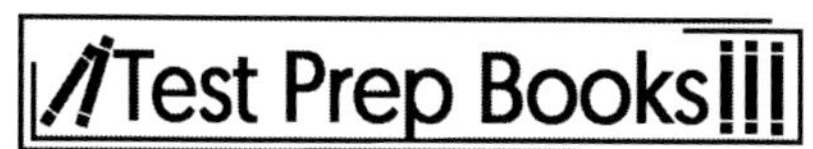

10. D: To find Denver's total snowfall, multiply $27\frac{3}{4}$ by 3. To do this, convert the mixed number into an improper fraction.

$$27\frac{3}{4} = \frac{27 \times 4 + 3}{4} = \frac{111}{4}$$

Therefore, Denver had approximately $\frac{3\times111}{4} = \frac{333}{4}$ inches of snow. The improper fraction can be converted back into a mixed number through division.

$$\frac{333}{4} = 83\frac{1}{4} \text{ inches}$$

11. D: Solve a linear inequality in a similar way to solving a linear equation. First, start by distributing the -3 on the left side of the inequality.

$$-3x - 12 \geq x + 8$$

Then, add 12 to both sides.

$$-3x \geq x + 20$$

Next, subtract x from both sides.

$$-4x \geq 20$$

Finally, divide both sides of the inequality by –4. Don't forget to flip the inequality sign because you are dividing by a negative number.

$$x \leq -5$$

12. C: In this scenario, the variables are the number of sales and Karen's weekly pay. The weekly pay depends on the number of sales. Therefore, weekly pay is the dependent variable (y), and the number of sales is the independent variable (x). Each pair of values from the table can be written as an ordered pair (x, y): $(2, 380)$, $(7, 580)$, $(4, 460)$, $(8, 620)$. The ordered pairs can be substituted into the equations to see which create true statements (where both sides are equal) for each pair. Even if one ordered pair produces equal values for a given equation, the other three ordered pairs must be checked. The only equation which is true for all four ordered pairs is $y = 40x + 300$:

$$380 = 40(2) + 300 \rightarrow 380 = 380$$

$$580 = 40(7) + 300 \rightarrow 580 = 580$$

$$460 = 40(4) + 300 \rightarrow 460 = 460$$

$$620 = 40(8) + 300 \rightarrow 620 = 620$$

13. C: The area of the shaded region is the area of the square minus the area of the circle. The area of the circle is πr^2. The side of the square will be $2r$, so the area of the square will be $4r^2$. Therefore, the difference is:

$$4r^2 - \pi r^2 = (4 - \pi)r^2$$

14. B: The car is traveling at a speed of 5 meters per second. On the interval from 1 to 3 seconds, the position changes by 10 meters. This is 10 meters in 2 seconds, or 5 meters in each second.

15. B: For an ordered pair to be a solution to a system of inequalities, it must make a true statement for both inequalities when substituting its values for x and y. Substituting $(-3, -2)$ into the inequalities produces $(-2) > 2(-3) - 3$, which is $-2 > -9$, and $(-2) < -4(-3) + 8$, or $-2 < 20$. Both are true statements.

16. D: The shape of the scatter plot is a parabola (U-shaped). This eliminates Choices *A* (a linear equation that produces a straight line) and *C* (an exponential equation that produces a smooth curve upward or downward). The value of a for a quadratic function in standard form ($y = ax^2 + bx + c$) indicates whether the parabola opens up (U-shaped) or opens down (upside-down U). A negative value for a produces a parabola that opens down; therefore, Choice *B* can also be eliminated.

17. 7: Bill's progress in making wicker baskets can be visualized as a linear equation using slope-intercept form. Let $y =$ how many wicker baskets Bill has, and let $x =$ how many days have passed. He can make two wicker baskets per day, so the slope of the line is 2. The information we want to know is the y-intercept value, which we can find by inserting $x = 5$ and $y = 17$ and then solving for the unknown y-intercept. The equation starts as $17 = 2(5) + b$. Multiply 2 by 5 to get 10, then subtract 10 from both sides, resulting in $7 = b$. The y-intercept is 7, meaning that Bill had seven baskets before he started working on more.

18. B: First, subtract 9 from both sides to isolate the radical.

$$\sqrt[3]{2x + 11} + 9 = 12$$

$$\sqrt[3]{2x + 11} = 3$$

Then, cube each side of the equation to obtain:

$$2x + 11 = 27$$

Subtract 11 from both sides, and then divide by 2.

$$2x = 16$$

The result is $x = 8$.

Plug 8 back into the original equation to check the answer:

$$\sqrt[3]{16 + 11} + 9 = 12$$

$$\sqrt[3]{27} + 9 = 12$$

$$3 + 9 = 12$$

19. A: Using the given information of one nurse to 25 patients and 325 total patients, set up an equation to solve for the number of nurses (N):

$$\frac{N}{325} = \frac{1}{25}$$

Multiply both sides by 325 to get N by itself on one side:

$$\frac{N}{1} = \frac{325}{25} = 13 \text{ nurses}$$

20. 36: To solve this correctly, keep in mind the order of operations with the mnemonic PEMDAS (Please Excuse My Dear Aunt Sally). This stands for Parentheses, Exponents, Multiplication, Division, Addition, Subtraction. Taking it step by step, solve inside the parentheses first:

$$4 \times 7 + (4)^2 \div 2$$

Then, apply the exponent:

$$4 \times 7 + 16 \div 2$$

Multiplication and division are both performed next.

$$28 + 8$$

Addition and subtraction are done last.

$$28 + 8 = 36$$

The solution is 36.

21. C: Set up the initial equation:

$$\frac{2x}{5} - 1 = 59$$

Add 1 to both sides:

$$\frac{2x}{5} - 1 + 1 = 59 + 1$$

Multiply both sides by $\frac{5}{2}$:

$$\frac{2x}{5} \times \frac{5}{2} = 60 \times \frac{5}{2} = 150$$

$$x = 150$$

22. C: First, list the givens:

$$Tax = 6.0\% = 0.06$$

$$Sale = 50\% = 0.5$$

$$Hat = \$32.99$$

$$Jersey = \$64.99$$

Calculate the sale prices for hats and jerseys:

$$Hat\ sale = 0.5\ (\$32.99) = \$16.495$$

$$Jersey\ sale = 0.5\ (\$64.99) = \$32.495$$

Total the sale prices:

$$Hat\ sale + jersey\ sale = \$16.495 + \$32.495 = \$48.99$$

Finally, calculate the sales tax, and add it to the total sale prices:

$$Total\ after\ tax = \$48.99 + (\$48.99 \times 0.06) = \$51.93$$

Practice Test #2

Reading and Writing: Module 1

The next question is based on the following passages:

Text 1: Benny turned to go back with a light step. It was late in the afternoon, and already growing shadowy in the deep pine grove through which he had to pass. He was not afraid, however, for he had sense enough to know that there were neither bears nor wildcats thereabouts, and he did not even consider whether he would encounter a snake. He caught sight of a gray squirrel scampering up a tree, and saw a clumsy land turtle traveling slowly along.

Text 2: He kept on steadily till he was about in the middle of the woods, when presently there came from the thicket close by a sound between a growl and a moan, and the boy stood still to listen. The sound was repeated, and this time it sounded nearer. Benny was no coward, but it must be confessed that his heart misgave him, and for a moment he stood uncertain whether to run or whether to investigate the matter. "I'll see what it is, I won't be silly," he told himself. "Maybe somebody is hurt in there." And he dauntlessly followed the sound as a cry of distress reached his ears. Then he seized a stick and rushed forward.

1. What does the juxtaposition between these two passages reveal about Benny's character?
   a. Benny is an easily startled person.
   b. Benny is headstrong and tries to ignore his feelings of fear for the greater good.
   c. Benny's hubris gets him into trouble.
   d. Benny is an adventurous soul who isn't afraid of danger.

The next question is based on the following passages:

Text 1: The great capitals of the later Greece, Alexandria, Antioch, Pergamum, rivaled Athens itself in their devotion to the stage. Another development of drama, independent of Athens, in Sicily and Magna Graecia, may be distinguished as farcical rather than comic. After receiving sophisticated, literary treatment at the hands of Epicharmus and Sophron in the fifth century, it continued its existence under the name of *mime* (μῖμος), upon a more popular level.

Text 2: The vast popular audiences of the period under consideration cared but little for the literary drama. In the Roman theater of Pompey, thronged with slaves and foreigners of every tongue, the finer histrionic effects must necessarily have been lost. Something more spectacular and sensuous, something appealing to a cruder sense of humor, almost inevitably took their place. There is evidence indeed that, while the theaters stood, tragedy and comedy never wholly disappeared from their boards. But it was probably only the ancient masterpieces that got a hearing.

2. What was the main difference between works of the stage in ancient Greece and ancient Rome?
   a. The Greek stage was rife with comedy, whereas the Roman stage was far more serious and deliberate about their choice of plays.
   b. The Greek tradition featured a need to innovate past their origins, whereas the Romans respected the classics that the Greeks rejected.
   c. The Greek stage had a refined sense of humor and was presented in a literary style, whereas Roman plays were meant to entertain plebeian audiences with limited access to literature.
   d. The Greek plays were silent and featured mimes, whereas the Roman stage was often loud and bombastic.

The next question is based on the following passage:

> "My prince," said Aramis, turning in the carriage towards his companion, "weak creature as I am, so unpretending in genius, so low in the scale of intelligent beings, it has never yet happened to me to converse with a man without penetrating his thoughts through that living mask which has been thrown over our mind, in order to retain its expression. But to-night, in this darkness, in the reserve which you maintain, I can read nothing on your features, and something tells me that I shall have great difficulty in <u>wresting</u> from you a sincere declaration."

3. Given the context, what is the most likely meaning of the underlined word in the passage?
   a. Comprehending
   b. Eliciting
   c. Requesting
   d. Barring

The next question is based on the following passage:

> The duke was lodged magnificently in Paris. He had one of those superb establishments pertaining to great fortunes, the like of which certain old men remembered to have seen in all their glory in the times of wasteful liberality of Henry III's reign. Then, really, several great nobles were richer than the king. They knew it, used it, and never deprived themselves of the pleasure of humiliating his royal majesty when they had an opportunity. From Louis XI—that terrible mower-down of the great—to Richelieu, how many families had raised their heads! How many, from Richelieu to Louis XIV, had bowed their heads, never to raise them again! <u>But M. de Beaufort was born a prince, and of a blood which is not shed upon scaffolds, unless by the decree of peoples,—a prince who had kept up a grand style of living.</u>

4. Which choice best describes the function of the underlined sentence in the passage as a whole?
   a. It illustrates a striking contrast between M. de Beaufort and nobles of earlier generations.
   b. It creates unity between M. de Beaufort and his royal predecessors in Paris.
   c. It establishes a familial connection between M. de Beaufort and King Louis XI.
   d. It explains M. de Beaufort's motivation for living in Paris.

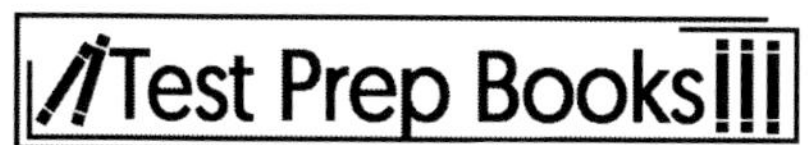

The next question is based on the following passage of untitled poetry by Fernando Pessoa:

> Whether we write or speak or do but look
> We are ever unapparent. What we are
> Cannot be transfused into word or book.
> Our soul from us is infinitely far.
> However much we give our thoughts the will
> To be our soul and gesture it abroad,
> Our hearts are incommunicable still.
> In what we show ourselves we are ignored.
> The abyss from soul to soul cannot be bridged
> By any skill of thought or trick of seeming.
> Unto our very selves we are abridged
> When we would utter to our thought our being.
> We are our dreams of ourselves, souls by gleams,
> And each to each other dreams of others' dreams.

5. What is the main idea of the text?
   a. Artistic expression is the only way to express oneself authentically.
   b. Writing is the best medium to express one's innermost thoughts, motivations, and feelings.
   c. People's true souls or identities cannot be fully communicated through artistic expression.
   d. Creating art or poetry is a distraction from other things in life that matter more.

The next question is based on the following passage:

> The research team evaluated various options but found that the proposed solution was not __________. Factors such as the high cost and limited potential for success informed their conclusion.

6. Which choice completes the text with the most logical and precise word or phrase?
   a. squalid
   b. inscrutable
   c. reflective
   d. viable

The next question is based on the following passage:

> The idea of cutting down the ancient forest was met with vehement opposition from the environmentalists; to them, it was __________. Destroying such a vital ecosystem went against their core beliefs and values.

7. Which choice completes the text with the most logical and precise word or phrase?
   a. bothersome
   b. anathema
   c. doctrine
   d. alacrity

The next question is based on the following passage:

> The Angakkuit, or Inuit spiritual leaders, are believed to communicate with the spirit world. This includes animals and humans. They may perform intricate rituals that call upon guidance from the

spirit world to heal the mental, physical, and spiritual ailments of the living. Their pivotal place in the community means that they are also teachers who pass down traditions to younger generations and preserve Inuit culture.

8. Which choice best states the main purpose of the text?
   a. To describe the importance of keeping cultural practices alive through every generation
   b. To prove that the spirit world is real and communicative
   c. To educate readers about the role of the Angakkuit in Inuit culture
   d. To promote spiritual practices that connect the living with spirits

While researching a topic, a student has taken the following notes:

> There are three major shapes of galaxies: elliptical, spiral, and irregular.
> Spiral galaxies are flat, rotating disks, and elliptical galaxies are round or oval.
> Irregular galaxies can be any shape, such as ring shaped.
> They were defined by Edwin Hubble in 1936.
> Elliptical galaxies are the largest.
> More than 60 percent of nearby galaxies are spirals.
> The Milky Way is a spiral galaxy.

9. The student wants to emphasize the most common type of galaxy that humans observe. Which choice most effectively uses relevant information from the notes to accomplish this goal?
   a. Elliptical galaxies are larger than spiral galaxies and are therefore easier to observe.
   b. Our own Milky Way galaxy is a spiral galaxy, meaning that it is a flat, rotating disk.
   c. Edwin Hubble determined that elliptical galaxies are the most abundant.
   d. Spiral galaxies, such as the Milky Way, are the most common type of observable galaxy.

The next question is based on the following passage from Henry VI Part 1 *by William Shakespeare. The speaking character, Joan, has been accused of witchcraft:*

> JOAN: First, let me tell you whom you have condemn'd:
> Not me begotten of a shepherd swain,
> But issued from the progeny of kings;
> Virtuous and holy; chosen from above,
> By inspiration of celestial grace,
> To work exceeding miracles on earth.
> I never had to do with wicked spirits:
> But you, that are polluted with your lusts,
> Stain'd with the guiltless blood of innocents,
> Corrupt and tainted with a thousand vices,
> Because you want the grace that others have,
> You judge it straight a thing impossible
> To compass wonders but by help of devils.
> No, misconceived! Joan of Arc hath been
> A virgin from her tender infancy,
> Chaste and immaculate in very thought;
> Whose maiden blood, thus rigorously effused,
> Will cry for vengeance at the gates of heaven.

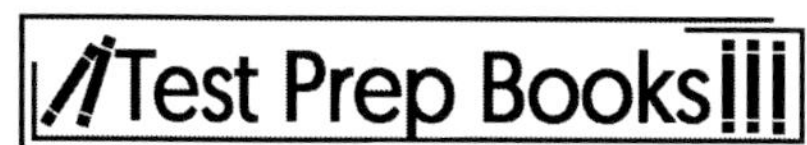

10. Which choice best describes the way Joan defends herself in this monologue?
    a. She argues that she has been possessed by a wicked spirit.
    b. She states that she is virtuous and chaste, therefore innocent.
    c. She claims that only God is allowed to judge her, not her abusers.
    d. She condemns her accusers for being bloodthirsty against women.

The next question is based on the following passage:

> Clustered Regularly Interspaced Short Palindromic Repeats (CRISPR) is a revolutionary technology that has the potential to change biotechnology research, agriculture, and medicine forever. The CRISPR process mimics the process in which bacteria defend themselves against viruses by using their genomes to memorize viral DNA. This could enable scientists to correct genetic mutation diseases such as sickle cell anemia or muscular dystrophy. It may also be used to research cancer treatment in new ways. Aside from medicine, CRISPR can be used to create more desirable crops that are resistant to disease and environmental stresses. This could be beneficial for addressing food insecurity in certain parts of the world. However, some question the ethicality of CRISPR tools being used for the genetic editing of embryos for favorable traits.

11. Which choice best states the main purpose of the text?
    a. To explain how CRISPR technology functions
    b. To draw attention to the quick-paced development of CRISPR
    c. To discuss the future potentialities of CRISPR
    d. To question the use of CRISPR tools in reproduction

The next question is based on the following passage:

> Fair river! in thy bright, clear flow
> Of crystal, wandering water,
> Thou art an emblem of the glow
> Of beauty, the unhidden heart,
> The playful maziness of art
> In old Alberto's daughter;
>
> But when within thy wave she looks,
> Which glistens then, and trembles,
> Why, then, the prettiest of brooks
> Her worshiper resembles;
> For in his heart, as in thy stream,
> Her image deeply lies,
> His heart which trembles at the beam
> Of her soul-searching eyes.

12. Which choice best states the main purpose of the text?
    a. To celebrate the beauty of a river undisturbed by humans
    b. To show that humans are not so different from their environment
    c. To illustrate the beauty of the goddess of nature
    d. To describe the poet's feelings for a beautiful young woman

The next question is based on the following passage from Meditations *by Marcus Aurelius:*

> It is the part of a man endowed with a good understanding faculty, to consider what they themselves are in very deed, from whose bare conceits and voices, honor and credit do proceed: as also what it is to die, and how if a man shall consider this by itself alone, to die, and separate from it in his mind all those things which with it usually represent themselves unto us, he can conceive of it no otherwise, than as of a work of nature, and he that fears any work of nature, is a very child. Now death, it is not only a work of nature, but also conducing to nature.

13. Which choice best summarizes what the author is saying in this passage?
    a. Nature does not discriminate against those who have honor and those who do not.
    b. Once men strip themselves of the superficial aspects that create misunderstanding with death, they do not fear it.
    c. Only mankind dwells on the nature of death due to our good understanding faculty.
    d. Children fear death because they have not considered that it is a work of nature and that it will come for everyone one day.

While researching a topic, a student has taken the following notes:

> There are two main types of Abstract Expressionism: action painting and color field painting.
> Action painting is when the physical act of painting is emphasized.
> Action painting can include pouring or splattering paint expressively.
> Certain patterns may convey aggression or balance.
> Color field painting focuses on the expressive effects of the paint colors.
> Some colors may make the viewer feel sadness while others inspire happiness.

14. The student wishes to explain how the two types of Abstract Expressionism differ from one another. Which choice most effectively uses relevant information from the notes to accomplish this goal?
    a. Action and color field painting both aim to evoke strong emotion, but action painting is focused on the physical act of painting, while color field uses expressive color choice.
    b. Action painting is meant to evoke a physical response in the person viewing, whereas color field painting aims to convey emotions that the person viewing may already be feeling.
    c. Action painting and color field painting are different ways to paint in the Abstract Expressionism style.
    d. Action painting is an aggressive art form, whereas color field painting is inspiring.

The next question is based on the following passage:

> Mycroft Holmes was a much larger and stouter man than Sherlock. His body was absolutely corpulent, but his face, though massive, had preserved something of the sharpness of expression which was so remarkable in that of his brother. His eyes, which were of a __________ seemed always to retain that far-away, introspective look which I had only observed in Sherlock's when he was exerting his full powers.

15. Which choice completes the text so that it conforms to the conventions of Standard English?
    a. peculiar light, watery grey,
    b. peculiarly light, watery grey,
    c. peculiarest light, watery grey,
    d. peculiarly light watery grey,

The next question is based on the following passage:

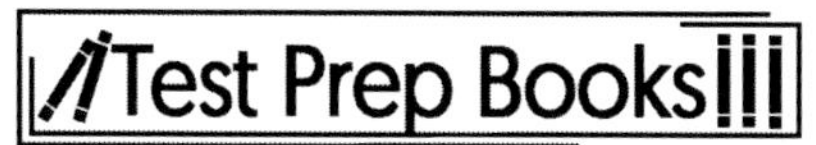

"Didn't I tell you __________ Flask; "Yes, you'll soon see this right whale's head hoisted up opposite that parmacetti's."

In good time, Flask's saying proved true. As before, the Pequod steeply leaned over towards the sperm whale's head; now, by the counterpoise of both heads, she regained her even keel, though sorely strained, you may well believe.

16. Which choice completes the text so that it conforms to the conventions of Standard English?
    a. so?", said
    b. so?," said
    c. so," said
    d. so?" said

The next question is based on the following passage:

This policy and reverence of age makes the world bitter to the best of our times; keeps our fortunes from us till our oldness cannot relish them. __________ to find an idle and fond bondage in the oppression of aged tyranny, who sways, not as it hath power, but as it is suffered. Come to me, that of this I may speak more.

17. Which choice completes the text so that it conforms to the conventions of Standard English?
    a. I begin
    b. I began
    c. We begin
    d. He began

The next question is based on the following passage:

Echoing the cry, Pallantides wheeled and rushed back into the pavilion. He cried out again as he saw Conan's powerful frame stretched out on the carpet. The king's great two-handed sword lay near his hand, and a shattered tent-pole seemed to show where his stroke had fallen. __________ was out, and he glared about the tent, but nothing met his gaze. Save for the king and himself, it was empty, as it had been when he left it.

18. Which choice completes the text so that it conforms to the conventions of Standard English?
    a. Pallantides's sword
    b. Conan's sword
    c. Pallantides' sword
    d. His sword

The next question is based on the following passage:

In the quest of her whom I had lost, __________ at length to the shores of Lethe, under the vault of an immense, empty, ebon sky, from which all the stars had vanished one by one. Proceeding I knew not whence, a pale, elusive light as of the waning moon, or the phantasmal phosphorescence of a dead sun, lay dimly and without luster on the sable stream and on the black, flowerless meadows.

19. Which choice completes the text so that it conforms to the conventions of Standard English?
    a. she came
    b. she were

c. I come
d. I came

The next question is based on the following passage:

> No Australians could be seen. Suddenly he came right to the edge of an enormous crater, and as suddenly stopped. He tried to reverse, but he could not change gear. __________ was absolutely motionless. He held out for some time, and then the Germans brought up a gun and began to shell the tank.

20. Which choice completes the text so that it conforms to the conventions of Standard English?
   a. The tank
   b. Those tanks
   c. A tank
   d. Some tanks

The next question is based on the following passage:

> As quickly as he could, Ben reported the situation to his superior, and received orders to divide his company, leaving a part __________ so that no Americans might drink from it. The rest of the company should go and hunt up the water barrel. Gilbert was detailed to accompany Ben, and the girl was given to understand that she must take the soldiers to where the barrel had been set up.

21. Which choice completes the text so that it conforms to the conventions of Standard English?
   a. to guard the poisonous well
   b. to well-guard the poisoned
   c. to guard the poisoned well
   d. to poison the well-guarded

The next question is based on the following passage:

> Although the internal combustion engine is a relatively simple design, many variations and innovations of the basic design have gained prominence in recent years. _________, the big-block V8 engine has been all but abandoned in favor of the inline 6 and turbocharged inline 4 engine, which boast comparable power and superior fuel economy.

22. Which choice completes the text with the most logical transition?
   a. For example
   b. Now
   c. Peripherally
   d. However

The next question is based on the following passage:

> A turbocharger is a forced induction device that compresses and pressurizes intake air in order to increase engine power without increasing fuel consumption. _________ the turbocharger being invented in 1905, "turbo lag" prevented turbochargers from being used on most passenger cars until the 1980s.

23. Which choice completes the text with the most logical transition?
   a. On account of
   b. Despite

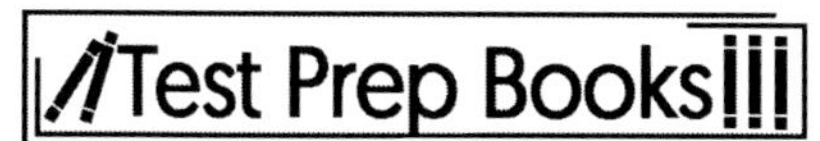

c. Following
d. Opposite to

While researching a topic, a student has taken the following notes:

> Ivan the Terrible was the first Russian tsar, who reigned as a part of the Rurikid Dynasty from 1547 to 1584.
> Ivan's conquest of the remaining khanates, which held large swathes of Russia, united the lands under the Grand Duchy of Moscow.
> Ivan modernized Russia by enacting legal reforms, establishing a police force, pursuing positive foreign relations with other European states, and colonizing Siberia.
> Ivan is best known for being a paranoid man who treated his family and nation with unmatched brutality, once killing his own son in a fit of rage.
> Ivan's close relationship with the Orthodox Church and his emphasis on his divine right to rule has influenced the Church's relations with the Russian head of state into the modern day.

24. The student wants to describe the changes that Ivan the Terrible brought to Russia. Which choice most effectively uses relevant information from the notes to accomplish this goal?

a. Ivan the Terrible was a paranoid man that presided over many wars and conflicts, leading to a crisis in Russia. He even killed his own son in a fit of rage which caused a succession crisis after his death.
b. Ivan the Terrible was an ambitious ruler that united Russia for the first time, colonized Siberia, created a police force to impose his will on the people, and established foreign relations with other European nations in pursuit of trade.
c. The Orthodox Church, which ordained Ivan the Terrible's divine right to rule and treat his subjects poorly, is still an active force in Russian politics today despite their suspicious connection to his son's untimely death.
d. After conquering all remaining khanate rump states and establishing a police force that terrorized the newly formed Russian Empire, Ivan the Terrible set his sights on colonizing all of Northern Asia and Eastern Europe.

The next question is based on the following passage:

> Agglomerated stone is a type of material made by combining finely crushed rocks with adhesive material. One of the most abundant uses of agglomerated stone is in kitchen countertops and stone flooring.

25. Which quote would best support the claim made in the passage?

a. "Agglomerated stone is created by mixing polymer resin with rocks, letting the composite harden, and then cutting it to size."
b. "Normally, a completed piece of agglomerated stone is about 90 percent rock and 10 percent adhesive material."
c. "The type of stone used for kitchen countertops is most commonly quartz, whereas flooring utilizes marble."
d. "Agglomerated stone is a cheaper alternative to solid pieces of rock, as sourcing large enough pieces to cut is as easy as creating them beforehand."

The next question is based on the following passage:

> In the American legal system, criminal and civil trials carry various differences. _________, a criminal trial is held to determine whether a person should be penalized for committing a crime, whereas a civil trial is held to determine if a monetary judgment should be awarded for a non-criminal act.

26. Which choice completes the text with the most logical transition?
    a. To clarify
    b. Lastly
    c. For example
    d. Primarily

While researching a topic, a student has taken the following notes:

> The 1920s saw an unprecedented increase in economic activity in the United States.
> Speculative asset trading created an inflationary bubble in the American economy.
> Many European countries defaulted on the loans they had been given during World War I.
> The bubble, alongside these loans going into default, caused a massive sell-off in the stock market.
> This sell-off, marking the beginning of the Great Depression, came to be known as "Black Tuesday."

27. The student wants to identify the causes of the Great Depression. Which choice most effectively uses relevant information from the notes to accomplish this goal?
    a. A massive stock sell-off known as "Black Tuesday" caused the Great Depression.
    b. The unprecedented increase in economic activity during the 1920s eventually caused a speculative asset bubble known as the Great Depression.
    c. A speculative asset bubble, alongside many European countries defaulting on their wartime loans, caused the Great Depression to be kicked off by a massive sell-off known as "Black Tuesday."
    d. The Great Depression led to a speculative asset bubble that caused many European countries to default on their wartime loans, which culminated in an event known as "Black Tuesday."

Reading and Writing: Module 2

The next question is based on the following passages:

> **Text 1:** Although the American public once had a fascination for the latest and greatest in architectural achievement, increasing new home prices combined with a nostalgia for a bygone era have led many new homeowners to opt to restore historic houses. Instead of tearing down old houses, many restoration specialists will use materials from dilapidated homes to create a new one for their clients less expensively.

> **Text 2:** As of 2024, the average home price in the United States is considered to be "unaffordable" for America's mean income bracket due to high interest rates and the lack of a supply of available homes. This is leading to an increasing number of Americans who rent, live with family, or refuse to move out of their current house due to economic anxiety.

1. What advice from Text 1 can an American take who finds themselves in a situation as described by Text 2 but still wants to purchase a house?
    a. Move back in with their parents.
    b. Arrange a rent-to-own agreement with their current landlord.
    c. Purchase a historic house and have it restored.
    d. Improve their credit score so they qualify for a mortgage on a new home.

The next question is based on the following passage:

> When designing a weightlifting routine, it is important to schedule at least one rest day in which the lifter __________. This important gap in training allows the body to maximize the muscle stimulus presented to it by the training.

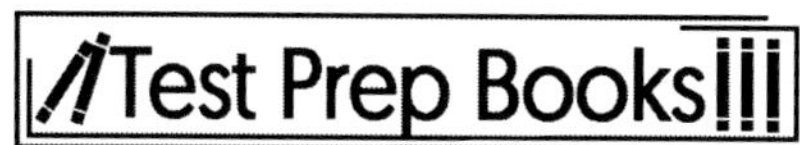

2. Which choice completes the text with the most logical and precise word or phrase?
   a. avoids physical activity
   b. makes up for any training that was missed
   c. works any weak spots in their physique
   d. applies heat to any sore muscles

The next question is based on the following passage from the poem "Recurrence" by Dorothy Parker:

> We shall have our little day.
> Take my hand and travel still
> Round and round the little way,
> Up and down the little hill.
> It is good to love again;
> Scan the renovated skies,
> Dip and drive the idling pen,
> Sweetly tint the paling lies.
> Trace the dripping, piercèd heart,
> Speak the fair, insistent verse,
> Vow to God, and slip apart,
> Little better, little worse.
> Would we need not know before
> How shall end this prettiness;
> One of us must love the more,
> One of us shall love the less.
> Thus it is, and so it goes;
> We shall have our day, my dear.
> Where, unwilling, dies the rose
> Buds the new, another year.

3. What is the main idea of the text?
   a. Life and love both follow cycles of good and bad, growth and diminishment.
   b. The most important relationships are the ones that survive in spite of obstacles and challenges.
   c. Human emotions are unpredictable, and romantic relationships never last.
   d. Commitment is the key to successful relationships.

The next question is based on the following passage:

> The palm is for friendship, hospitality, and good will; the fist is to smite the enemies of truth and justice.
>
> How many men are like the clenched fist—pugnacious, disputatious, quarrelsome, always spoiling for a fight; a verbal fisticuff, if not a physical one, is their delight. Others are more conciliatory and peace-loving, not forgetting that a soft answer turneth away wrath. Roosevelt was the man of the clenched fist; not one to stir up strife, but a merciless hitter in what he believed a just cause. He always had the fighting edge, yet could be as tender and sympathetic as any one. This latter side of him is clearly shown in his recently published "Letters to His Children." Lincoln was, in contrast, the man with the open palm, tempering justice with kindness, and punishment with leniency.

4. What is the main idea of the text?
   a. Men like Roosevelt and Lincoln should be remembered and admired for their aggression and ambition.

b. It is important to be willing to fight for just causes, no matter the danger involved.
c. Humans hold the capacity for tackling conflict with both loving tenderness and aggression.
d. A man's capacity to fight is the best judge of his character.

The next question is based on the following passage:

> How are we to reconcile the obvious hit-and-miss method of Nature with the reign of law, or with a world of design? Consider the seeds of a plant or a tree, as sown by the wind. It is a matter of chance where they alight; it is hit or miss with them always. <u>Yet the seeds, say, of the cat-tail flag always find the wet or the marshy places.</u> If they had a topographical map of the country and a hundred eyes they could not succeed better. Of course, there are vastly more failures than successes with them, but one success in ten thousand trials is enough. They go to all points of the compass with the wind, and sooner or later hit the mark. Chance decides where the seed shall fall, but it was not chance that gave wings to this and other seeds. The hooks and wings and springs and parachutes that wind-sown seeds possess are not matters of chance: they all show design. So here is design working in a hit-and-miss world.

5. Which choice best describes the function of the underlined sentence in the passage as a whole?
    a. It provides a contrast between theories of randomness and theories of intentional design.
    b. It provides an example that supports the author's beliefs about chance and design in nature.
    c. It refutes the author's beliefs about chance and design in nature.
    d. It emphasizes the importance of luck in the natural world.

The next question is based on the following passage:

> Despite her initial reservations, Sarah ultimately _____ her friend's suggestion of trying the new sushi place downtown. As they sat at the table, Sarah found herself pleasantly surprised by the exotic flavors and innovative dishes, grateful for her friend's persuasive powers.

6. Which choice completes the text with the most logical and precise word or phrase?
    a. acquiesced to
    b. implicated in
    c. alluded to
    d. participated in

The next question is based on the following passage:

> Despite her significant wealth, Emily led a(n) _____ lifestyle, avoiding excessive spending on luxury items or extravagant experiences. Her frugal habits allowed her to prioritize financial stability and long-term goals over immediate indulgence.

7. Which choice completes the text with the most logical and precise word or phrase?
    a. abstemious
    b. aesthetic
    c. benign
    d. munificent

The next question is based on the following passage, a poem titled "The Ghost" by Charles Baudelaire:

> Just like an angel with evil eye,
> I shall return to thee silently,

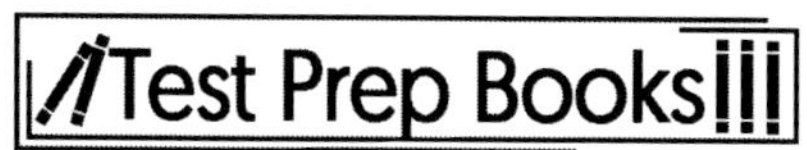

Upon thy bower I'll alight,
With falling shadows of the night.

With thee, my brownie, I'll commune,
And give thee kisses cold as the moon,
And with a serpent's moist embrace,
I'll crawl around thy resting-place.

And when the livid morning falls,
Thou'lt find alone the empty walls,
And till the evening, cold 'twill be.

As others with their tenderness,
Upon thy life and youthfulness,
I'll reign alone with dread o'er thee.

8. Which choice best states the purpose of this poem?
   a. The speaker is comparing angelic flowers with evil serpents.
   b. The speaker is describing their desire to be young again.
   c. The speaker is promising to return to a loved one after death.
   d. The speaker is hoping for winter to end, as they find it dreadful.

The next question is based on the following passage from Hamlet *by William Shakespeare:*

> HAMLET: I have of late (but wherefore I know not) lost all my mirth, forgone all custom of exercises; and, indeed, it goes so heavily with my disposition, that this goodly frame, the earth, seems to me a sterile promontory; this most excellent canopy, the air, look you, this brave o'erhanging firmament, this majestical roof fretted with golden fire, why, it appears no other thing to me than a foul and pestilent congregation of vapors. What a piece of work is man! How noble in reason! how infinite in faculties! in form and moving how express and admirable! in action how like an angel! in apprehension how like a god! the beauty of the world! the paragon of animals! And yet, to me, what is this quintessence of dust? man delights not me,—nor woman neither, though by your smiling you seem to say so.

9. What is Hamlet expressing in this soliloquy?
   a. Hamlet expresses his disappointment with humanity's foulness and disrespect towards nature.
   b. Hamlet laments that he is not living a life of greatness like other men and women.
   c. Hamlet argues with himself about the nature of humanity and if people are inherently noble.
   d. Hamlet contrasts the greatness of humanity with the lack of fulfillment in his own life.

The next question is based on the following passage from A Midsummer Night's Dream *by William Shakespeare:*

THESEUS: More strange than true. I never may believe
These antique fables, nor these fairy toys.
Lovers and madmen have such seething brains,
Such shaping fantasies, that apprehend
More than cool reason ever comprehends.
The lunatic, the lover, and the poet
Are of imagination all compact:
One sees more devils than vast hell can hold;

That is the madman: the lover, all as frantic,
Sees Helen's beauty in a brow of Egypt:
The poet's eye, in a fine frenzy rolling,
Doth glance from heaven to earth, from earth to heaven;
And as imagination bodies forth
The forms of things unknown, the poet's pen
Turns them to shapes, and gives to airy nothing
A local habitation and a name.
Such tricks hath strong imagination,
That if it would but apprehend some joy,
It comprehends some bringer of that joy.
Or in the night, imagining some fear,
How easy is a bush supposed a bear?

10. What is Theseus claiming about imagination in this passage?
    a. Imagination is necessary to be prepared against tricks and deception.
    b. Everyone has a form of imagination that fits their position in life.
    c. Imagination can create irrational ideas and fears that do not align with reality.
    d. There is no joy to be had in the world without the use of a strong imagination.

The next question is based on the following passage:

I met a traveler from an antique land,
Who said—"Two vast and trunkless legs of stone
Stand in the desert. . . . Near them, on the sand,
Half sunk a shattered visage lies, whose frown,
And wrinkled lip, and sneer of cold command,
Tell that its sculptor well those passions read
Which yet survive, stamped on these lifeless things,
The hand that mocked them, and the heart that fed;
And on the pedestal, these words appear:
My name is Ozymandias, King of Kings;
Look on my Works, ye Mighty, and despair!
Nothing beside remains. Round the decay
Of that colossal Wreck, boundless and bare
The lone and level sands stretch far away."

11. What is the main purpose of this poem?
    a. To show the impermanence of human power
    b. To express sadness at forgotten history
    c. To condemn past rulers who were unfair
    d. To celebrate the immortality of human achievement

The next question is based on the following passage:

The subject of pigeons' homing instincts perplexes scientists. Pigeons were once used as mail carriers due to their ability to return to their home location. It is unknown how pigeons are able to find their way home after traveling long distances. Scientists have tested various methods, including visual, magnetic, and olfactory cues. However, when scientists limit these cues—by

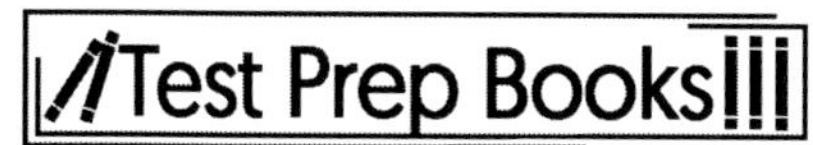

blindfolding the bird, for example—the pigeon can still find its way home! Scientists have determined that _________

12. Which choice most logically completes the text?
    a. pigeons should continue to be used as mail carriers for this reason.
    b. the pigeon is more advanced than many other species of animals.
    c. pigeons either use a variety of cues together or have methods that have not yet been discovered.
    d. they will never understand how the pigeon has evolved to find its way home.

The next question is based on the following passage:

Country	Estimated # of Casualties	Date Joined
The Soviet Union	24 million	June 22, 1941
Germany	6.5 million+	September 1, 1939
United States	418,000+	December 7, 1941
Japan	2.6 million+	September 22, 1940

A student is comparing the number of casualties during World War II for various countries that were involved in the war. They suspect that there may be a correlation with the number of casualties and how long the country was involved in the war. They determined that __________

13. Which choice most effectively uses data from the table to complete the text?
    a. the countries that were in the war for the shortest amount of time suffered just as many casualties as those that were in the war for longer.
    b. the countries that were in the war the longest ultimately suffered the most casualties.
    c. the correlation between time in the war and number of casualties is inconsistent.
    d. the countries that joined the war around the same time have similar numbers of casualties.

The next question is based on the following passage from Oliver Twist *by Charles Dickens:*

As Oliver accompanied his master in most of his adult expeditions too, in order that he might acquire that equanimity of demeanor and full command of nerve which was essential to a finished undertaker, he had many opportunities of observing the beautiful resignation and fortitude with which some strong-minded people bear their trials and losses.

14. What is the main purpose of this passage?
    a. To describe Oliver's undertaker adventures with his master
    b. To highlight Oliver's lack of understanding for what he should be learning
    c. To show Oliver's appreciation for having such a skilled master
    d. To explain Oliver's role as a companion and how it contributes to his education

The next question is based on the following passage:

That same night, Max fell fast asleep as soon as he was in bed. Never in his career had he used his muscles so much in one day. His rest was dreamless, but he awoke as the clock struck six, and lay thinking. It was a glorious morning, for his window was illumined by the sunshine, and he felt warm and comfortable. __________ the same, he shivered.

15. Which choice completes the text so that it conforms to the conventions of Standard English?
    a. For all
    b. But all

c. To all
d. At all

The next question is based on the following passage:

> The best editing tip I've ever heard is to cut 10% of the total words when crafting the second draft. This shouldn't trim content—don't cut scenes, characters, and so on. __________ draft ought to tighten sentences by pruning excess words.

16. Which choice completes the text so that it conforms to the conventions of Standard English?
    a. Rather, these
    b. Rather, that
    c. Rather, the
    d. Rather, this

The next question is based on the following passage:

> The lapwing is very intolerant of any trespass on his breeding territory on the part of his neighbors. As soon as the intruder is sighted, the owner of the territory charges. The two then mount up into the air, often to a great height, each striving to get above the other for a downward swoop. As the one "stoops" __________ the lower bird dodges, and so rapidly are the wings moved that they are often brought smartly together over the back, producing a clapping noise.

17. Which choice completes the text so that it conforms to the conventions of Standard English?
    a. at the other
    b. at the other,
    c. at it,
    d. for the other,

The next question is based on the following passage:

> Mr. Asquith had intended to speak on April 14th, evening, but the portentous and prolix Courtney had shut him out, and he had to wait till the following evening. __________ for Mr. Asquith had thus the opportunity of addressing the House when it was fresh, vital, and impressionable. In these long debates, the evenings usually became intolerably dull and oppressive.

18. Which choice completes the text so that it conforms to the conventions of Standard English?
    a. The change was perhaps desirable
    b. The change was, perhaps, desirable
    c. The change was perhaps, desirable,
    d. The change was, perhaps, desirable,

The next question is based on the following passage:

> Looking at it from the road, the walls hide all but two of the great towers which gave it its name, only four of which are now standing. Two Corinthian columns indicate the ancient Golden Gate through which Heraclius and Narsetes made their triumphal entry; according to legend common to Turk and Greek __________ this gate that the Christians will come on that day when they once more take possession of the City of Constantine.

19. Which choice completes the text so that it conforms to the conventions of Standard English?
    a. alike it is thorough

b. alike, it is through
c. a like, it is through
d. alike it is, thru

The next question is based on the following passage:

Shortly before Luther's departure to Worms, John Bugenhagen of Pomerania had appeared at Wittenberg—a man only two years younger than Luther. Bugenhagen was well trained in theology and humanistic learning, and already won over to __________ writings, and more especially by his work on the Babylonian Captivity. He had made friends with Luther and Melancthon, and soon began to teach with them at the university. John Agricola from Eisleben had already taken part in the biblical lectures at the university, which was then the chief place for the exposition of evangelical doctrine. This man, born in 1494, had lived at Wittenberg since 1516.

20. Which choice completes the text so that it conforms to the conventions of Standard English?
    a. Luther's doctrines by his
    b. Luther's doctrine's by his
    c. Luther's doctrines' by their
    d. Luther's doctrine, by his

The next question is based on the following passage:

The resentment of injury is regarded even by good men as entirely justified when injury to the person involves the rights of social order. Force is regarded by persons of the highest amiability __________ defense of society. The Church applauds the punishments inflicted by the civil magistrate, and even hastens to bless the banners and baptize the deadly weapons of the warrior.

21. Which choice completes the text so that it conforms to the conventions of Standard English?
    a. as necessary to the
    b. when necessary a
    c. as necessary as the
    d. as necessary, with the

The next question is based on the following passage:

Although experimentation with artificial fabrics has reached a fever pitch in the age of athleisure fashion, many animal products are still used in weather-resistant apparel. _________, sheep's wool and goose down are still used in thermal blankets, jackets, and winter boots.

22. Which choice completes the text with the most logical transition?
    a. For example
    b. Consequently
    c. Granted
    d. Likewise

The next question is based on the following passage:

King George V was the King of the British Empire from 1910 until 1936. George presided over pivotal events in British history such as the Empire's territorial zenith, the establishment of the House of Windsor, and the First World War, in which George's cousins, Kaiser Wilhelm II of Germany and Tsar Nicolas II of Russia, also participated. _________ Nicolas was overthrown in a coup and taken prisoner by Bolshevik forces by the end of the war, George refused to give him and his family asylum in Britain due to their extreme unpopularity.

23. Which choice completes the text with the most logical transition?
   a. Although
   b. To demonstrate that
   c. After
   d. Since

The next question is based on the following passage:

> The Russian Revolution is a highly complicated event that spans many years and is marked by several cataclysmic turning points. The February Revolution in 1917 ended with the establishment of the Provisional Government and the overthrow of Tsar Nicolas II. _________ Nicolas's removal, the October Revolution occurred later in the year in which the Bolsheviks seized power from the Provisional Government and took Nicolas and his family prisoner.

24. Which choice completes the text with the most logical transition?
   a. Following
   b. On account of
   c. Simultaneously with
   d. Despite

While researching a topic, a student has taken the following notes:

> The American Civil Rights Movement was a social and political movement that sought to grant equal rights to black Americans and to end legal racial discrimination and segregation.
> Two of the most notable leaders of this movement were Martin Luther King Jr. and Malcolm X.
> Martin Luther King Jr. advocated for a Christian model of nonviolent resistance via sit-ins and boycotts, whereas Malcolm X championed black separatism and the adoption of Islam by black Americans.
> King's ideals were most effective, culminating in the March on Washington in 1963. Malcolm X became embroiled in controversy with the Nation of Islam, a black separatist group with whom he was aligned.
> Malcolm X was assassinated by members of the Nation in 1965, whereas King was assassinated by a white supremacist in 1968.

25. The student wants to compare and contrast King's and Malcolm X's contributions to the Civil Rights Movement. Which choice most effectively uses relevant information from the notes to accomplish this goal?
   a. King championed Christian nonviolent resistance, whereas Malcolm X advocated for black separatism and black Americans' separation from Christianity. King led the March on Washington while Malcolm X experienced fracturing within the Nation of Islam.
   b. Malcolm X's actions and positions were highly controversial and, as a result, he was assassinated by members of the Nation of Islam in 1965. Three years later, in 1968, Martin Luther King Jr. was assassinated by a white supremacist who opposed his advocacy for racial integration.
   c. Martin Luther King Jr. held a PhD in Divinity and was a Christian pastor by trade before he engaged in a life of activism. Malcolm X, on the other hand, became a Muslim while serving a prison sentence for burglary and eventually established several temples on behalf of the Nation of Islam.
   d. King's model of nonviolent resistance was a Christian one that emphasized a peaceful response to the violence of segregationists. In contrast to Malcolm X's pro-segregationist stance, King's message was said to be diametrically opposed to Islamic ideals, and he was often accused of being anti-Muslim.

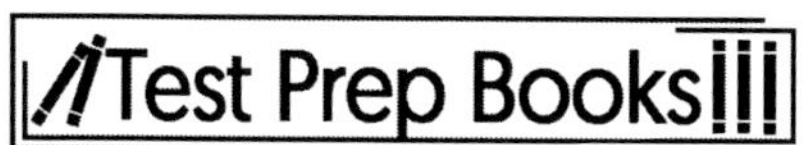

The next question is based on the following passage:

> Despite the dramatic increase in productivity from American workers that has been occurring since the 1970s, real wages adjusting for inflation have failed to catch up. Since 1979, productivity has grown eight times faster than the wage paid for a typical hour of work. Worker satisfaction, _________, has plummeted in recent years.

26. Which choice completes the text with the most logical transition?
   a. in other words
   b. for instance
   c. for this reason
   d. however

The next question is based on the following passage:

> Lessening the spread of agricultural pollution from animal waste is a critical concern when it comes to reducing industrial farming's environmental impact. Preventing runoff from contaminating soil is a vital step to preserving public health. _________, preventing runoff from contaminating drinking water is crucial when it comes to protecting the wellbeing of a farming community's inhabitants.

27. Which choice completes the text with the most logical transition?
   a. Subsequently
   b. Moreover
   c. On the contrary
   d. Most importantly

Math: Module 1

1. If a car can travel 300 miles in four hours, how far can it go in an hour and a half?
   a. 100 miles
   b. 112.5 miles
   c. 135.5 miles
   d. 150 miles

2. At the store, Jan spends \$90 on apples and oranges. Apples cost \$1 each and oranges cost \$2 each. If Jan buys the same number of apples as oranges, how many oranges did she buy?

3. What is the volume of a box with rectangular sides 5 feet long, 6 feet wide, and 3 feet high?
   a. 60 cubic feet
   b. 75 cubic feet
   c. 90 cubic feet
   d. 14 cubic feet

4. A train traveling 50 miles per hour takes a trip lasting 3 hours. If a map has a scale of 1 inch per 10 miles, how many inches apart are the train's starting point and ending point on the map if it traveled in a straight line?
   a. 14 inches
   b. 12 inches
   c. 13 inches
   d. 15 inches

5. A traveler takes an hour to drive to a museum, spends three hours and 30 minutes there, and takes half an hour to drive home. What percentage of their time was spent driving?
   a. 15%
   b. 30%
   c. 40%
   d. 60%

6. A truck is carrying three cylindrical barrels. Each barrel has a diameter of 2 feet and a height of 3 feet. What is the total volume of the three barrels in cubic feet?
   a. 3π
   b. 9π
   c. 12π
   d. 15π

7. Greg buys a $10 lunch with 5% sales tax. He leaves a $2 tip after his bill (which is not taxed). How much money does he spend?
   a. $12.50
   b. $12.00
   c. $13.00
   d. $13.25

8. Marty wishes to save $150 over a 4-day period. How much must Marty save each day on average?
   a. $37.50
   b. $35.00
   c. $45.50
   d. $41.00

9. Bernard can make $80 per day. If he needs to make $300 and only works full days, how many days will this take?

10. A couple buys a house for $150,000. They sell it for $165,000. By what percentage did the house's value increase?
   a. 10%
   b. 13%
   c. 15%
   d. 17%

11. A school has 15 teachers and 20 teaching assistants. They have 200 students. What is the ratio of faculty to students?
   a. $3:20$
   b. $4:17$
   c. $5:54$
   d. $7:40$

12. A map has a scale of 1 inch per 5 miles. A car can travel 60 miles per hour. If the distance from the start to the destination is 3 inches on the map, how long will it take the car to make the trip?
   a. 12 minutes
   b. 15 minutes
   c. 17 minutes
   d. 20 minutes

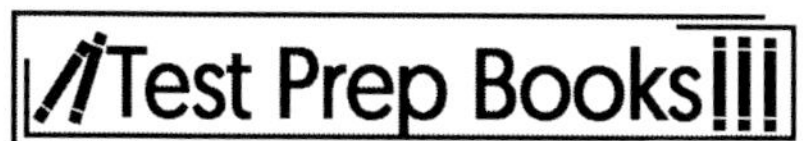

13. Taylor works two jobs. The first pays $20,000 per year. The second pays $10,000 per year. She donates 15% of her income to charity. How much does she donate each year?
    a. $4,500
    b. $5,000
    c. $5,500
    d. $6,000

14. A box with rectangular sides is 24 inches wide, 18 inches deep, and 12 inches high. What is the volume of the box in cubic feet?
    a. 2 cubic feet
    b. 3 cubic feet
    c. 4 cubic feet
    d. 5 cubic feet

15. Kristen purchased $100 worth of CDs and DVDs. The CDs cost $10 each and the DVDs cost $15 each. If she bought 4 DVDs, how many CDs did she buy?
    a. 5
    b. 6
    c. 3
    d. 4

16. What is the solution to $4\frac{1}{3} + 3\frac{3}{4}$?
    a. $6\frac{5}{12}$
    b. $8\frac{1}{12}$
    c. $8\frac{2}{3}$
    d. $7\frac{7}{12}$

17. Suppose the function $y = \frac{1}{8}x^3 + 2x - 21$ approximates the population of a given city between the years 1900 and 2000, with x representing the year (where 1900 is $x = 0$) and y representing the population (in thousands). Which of the following domains are relevant for the scenario?
    a. $(-\infty, \infty)$
    b. [1900, 2000]
    c. [0, 100]
    d. [0, 0]

18. What is the equation of a circle whose center is (0, 0) and whose radius is 5?
    a. $(x-5)^2 + (y-5)^2 = 25$
    b. $(x)^2 + (y)^2 = 5$
    c. $(x)^2 + (y)^2 = 25$
    d. $(x+5)^2 + (y+5)^2 = 25$

19. Which of the following equations best represents the problem below?

> The width of a rectangle is 2 centimeters less than the length. If the perimeter of the rectangle is 44 centimeters, then what are the dimensions of the rectangle?

a. $2l + 2(l - 2) = 44$
b. $(l + 2) + (l + 2) + l = 48$
c. $l \times (l - 2) = 44$
d. $(l + 2) + (l + 2) + l = 44$

20. How will the following algebraic expression be simplified: $(5x^2 - 3x + 4) - (2x^2 - 7)$?
a. x^5
b. $3x^2 - 3x + 11$
c. $3x^2 - 3x - 3$
d. $x - 3$

21. A family purchases a vehicle in 2005 for $20,000. In 2010, they decide to sell it for a newer model. They are able to sell the car for $8,000. By what percentage did the value of the family's car drop?
a. 40%
b. 68%
c. 60%
d. 33%

22. If the sine of $30° = x$, the cosine of what angle, in degrees, also equals x?

Math: Module 2

1. If Sarah reads at an average rate of 21 pages in 4 nights, how long will it take her to read 140 pages?
a. 6 nights
b. 26 nights
c. 8 nights
d. 27 nights

2. Sarah's car drove 72 miles in 90 minutes. There are 5,280 feet per mile. How fast did she drive in feet per second?
a. 0.8 feet per second
b. 48.9 feet per second
c. 0.009 feet per second
d. 70.4 feet per second

3. This chart indicates how many sales of CDs, vinyl records, and MP3 downloads occurred over the last year. Approximately what percentage of the total sales was from CDs?

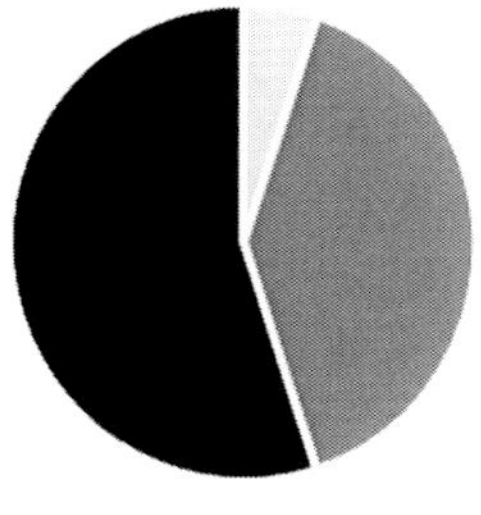

a. 55%
b. 25%
c. 40%
d. 5%

4. After a 20% sale discount, Frank purchased a new refrigerator for $850. How much money did he save off of the original price?

a. $170
b. $212.50
c. $105.75
d. $200

5. Which of the following is NOT a way to write 40 percent of N?

a. $(0.4)N$
b. $\frac{2}{5}N$
c. $40N$
d. $\frac{4}{10}N$

6. The graph of which function has an x-intercept of -2?

a. $y = 2x - 3$
b. $y = 4x + 2$
c. $y = x^2 + 5x + 6$
d. $y = 2x^2 + 3x - 1$

7. The table below displays the number of three-year-olds at Kids First Daycare who are potty-trained and those who still wear diapers.

	Potty-trained	Wear diapers	Sum
Boys	26	22	48
Girls	34	18	52
Total	60	40	

If a three-year-old girl is randomly selected from this school, what is the probability that she is potty-trained?

a. 52%
b. 34%
c. 65%
d. 57%

8. A clothing company with a target market of US boys surveys 2,000 twelve-year-old boys to find their height. The average height of the boys is 61 inches. For the above scenario, 61 inches represents which of the following?

a. Sample statistic
b. Population parameter
c. Confidence interval
d. Measurement error

9. A government agency is researching the average consumer cost of gasoline throughout the United States. Which data collection method would produce the most valid results?

a. Randomly choosing one hundred gas stations in the state of New York
b. Randomly choosing ten gas stations from each of the fifty states
c. Randomly choosing five hundred gas stations from across all fifty states with the number chosen proportional to the population of the state
d. All three methods would each produce equally valid results.

10. Suppose an investor deposits $1,200 into a bank account that accrues 1 percent interest per month. Assuming x represents the number of months since the deposit and y represents the money in the account, which of the following exponential functions models the scenario?

a. $y = (0.01)(1200^x)$
b. $y = (1200)(0.01^x)$
c. $y = (1.01)(1200^x)$
d. $y = (1200)(1.01^x)$

11. A student gets an 85% on a test with 20 questions. How many questions did the student solve correctly?

12. Four people split a bill. The first person pays for $\frac{1}{5}$, the second person pays for $\frac{1}{4}$, and the third person pays for $\frac{1}{3}$. What fraction of the bill does the fourth person pay?

a. $\frac{13}{60}$
b. $\frac{47}{60}$
c. $\frac{1}{4}$
d. $\frac{4}{15}$

13. Which of the following fractions is equal to 9.3?
    a. $9\frac{3}{7}$
    b. $\frac{903}{1{,}000}$
    c. $\frac{9.03}{100}$
    d. $9\frac{3}{10}$

14. What is the solution to $3\frac{2}{3} - 1\frac{4}{5}$?
    a. $1\frac{13}{15}$
    b. $\frac{14}{15}$
    c. $2\frac{2}{3}$
    d. $\frac{4}{5}$

15. What is $\frac{420}{98}$ rounded to the nearest integer?

16. What is the equation of a circle whose center is (1, 5) and whole radius is 4?
    a. $(x-1)^2 + (y-25)^2 = 4$
    b. $(x-1)^2 + (y-25)^2 = 16$
    c. $(x+1)^2 + (y+5)^2 = 16$
    d. $(x-1)^2 + (y-5)^2 = 16$

17. Where does the point $(-3, -4)$ lie on the circle with the equation $(x)^2 + (y)^2 = 25$?
    a. Inside of the circle
    b. Outside of the circle
    c. On the circle
    d. There is not enough information to tell.

18. What is the perimeter of the figure below? Note that the solid outer line is the perimeter.

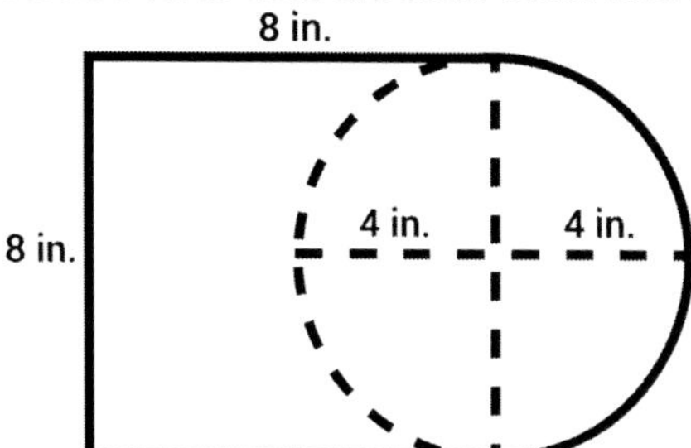

    a. 48.565 ft
    b. 36.565 ft
    c. 19.78 ft
    d. 30.565 ft

19. What is the volume of a cylinder, in terms of π, with a radius of 6 centimeters and a height of 2 centimeters?
   a. $36\,\pi\ \text{cm}^3$
   b. $24\,\pi\ \text{cm}^3$
   c. $72\,\pi\ \text{cm}^3$
   d. $48\,\pi\ \text{cm}^3$

20. What is the length of the hypotenuse of a right triangle with one leg equal to 3 centimeters and the other leg equal to 4 centimeters?
   a. 7 cm
   b. 5 cm
   c. 25 cm
   d. 12 cm

21. The perimeter of a 6-sided polygon is 56 cm. The lengths of 3 sides are 9 cm each. The lengths of 2 other sides are 8 cm each. What is the length of the missing side?

22. Keith's bakery had 252 customers go through its doors last week. This week, that number increased to 378. By what percentage did his customer volume increase?
   a. 26%
   b. 50%
   c. 35%
   d. 12%

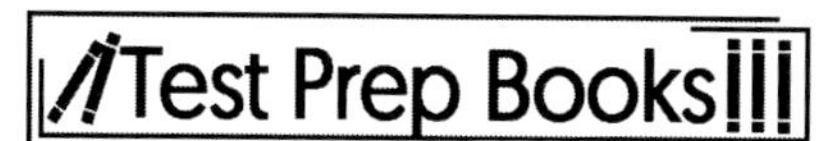

Answers Explanation

Reading and Writing: Module 1

1. B: Although Benny initially talks himself out of feeling any fear, he eventually does become afraid when confronted with the reality of his perilous situation. However, heeding the situation at hand, he puts his fear aside to help whoever is hurt despite the risk.

2. C: The Roman style, according to Text 2, was designed to appeal to the masses. The Romans dumbed down the sophisticated tones of the Greek epics, which were presented in a literary style that only those familiar with the theater could fully appreciate.

3. B: In this passage, Aramis expresses his difficulty in reading the thoughts or emotions of his companion, due to the darkness and the prince's reticence. He admits to having trouble *wresting* a "sincere declaration" from the prince. Choice *B* is the best synonym for *wresting*, as *eliciting* means drawing out or evoking something from someone. In this case, Aramis knows he will have trouble evoking a response or confession from the prince. Therefore, Choice *B* is the best answer.

4. A: The passage describes the opulence of M. de Beaufort's estate in Paris, which is reminiscent of the grandeur seen during the reign of Henry III, when some nobles were even wealthier than the king himself. Since that time, however, nobles were often targeted for execution because of the wealth they had accumulated. M. de Beaufort, however, was born into royalty and was able to safely maintain his opulent lifestyle. Choice *A* is the best answer, since his life is very different from the shortened lives of the nobles who came before him.

5. C: Choice *C* is the correct answer because the sonnet emphasizes the limitations of artistic expression, specifically writing and speaking, in capturing the true essence of individuals. The poet claims that despite people's attempts to convey their inner worlds through artistic expression, those inner identities remain inaccessible and incomprehensible to others. Therefore, Choice *C* most accurately reflects the main message of the poem. Choice *A* is incorrect because the poem states the difficulty of expressing oneself authentically through art. Choice *B* is incorrect because the poem does not qualify writing as a superior method of expression. Finally, Choice *D* is incorrect because the poem does not claim art or poetry distracts from more important matters.

6. D: Choice *D* is the best answer, as *viable* means feasible or capable of working successfully. The research team concluded the proposed solution was too expensive and held no guarantee of success; therefore, it was not viable. *Squalid* means dirty or impure, so Choice *A* does not make sense in context. Choice *B* is inappropriate because *inscrutable* means impossible to understand; the proposed solution was undesirable but not difficult to comprehend. Finally, Choice *C* does not work because *reflective* means thoughtful or meditative and does not make sense here.

7. B: Choice *B* is best because it conveys the weight of the situation. The environmentalists show intense opposition to the proposal of destroying the ancient forest; in fact, doing so goes against their foundational ethics. *Anathema* is something intensely disliked or loathed, so this choice reflects the gravity of their reaction. *Bothersome* implies a mild annoyance, which makes Choice *A* incorrect. If something is doctrine, it is to be followed without question; therefore, Choice *C* does not make sense in context. Choice *D* is incorrect because *alacrity* means cheerful readiness and does not make sense in context.

8. C: Choice *C* is the correct answer because it correctly identifies the main purpose of the passage. The passage is focused on the tasks of the Angakkuit. This includes rituals and teaching. Choice *A* is incorrect because although the cultural practices described are important to pass on, that is not why the text mentions them. It mentions them to describe another role of the Angakkuit. Choice *B* is incorrect because there is no evidence in the text to prove that the spiritual world is real, despite the Angakkuit's role as spiritual leaders. Choice *D* is incorrect because the text is not trying to convince the reader to partake in any of the activities mentioned.

9. D: Choice *D* is the correct answer because it uses the notes to emphasize what the student wishes to convey. The Milky Way is a galaxy that is immediately recognizable to most people, while the notes also specify that most galaxies nearby are spiral shaped. Choice *D* combines both of these points into a well-structured sentence that the student can use. Choice *A* is incorrect because it does not point out that spiral galaxies are the most common. Just because elliptical galaxies are bigger does not mean they are the most common. Choice *B* is incorrect because although it describes the Milky Way as being spiral, it does not specify that it is the most common type. Choice *C* is incorrect because the notes do not state that elliptical galaxies are most abundant near Earth.

10. B: Choice *B* is the correct answer because it is Joan's primary defense for herself when she is accused of witchcraft. This is primarily apparent in the last five lines of the monologue. She states that she is virginal, chaste, and immaculate. These are traits that would not have been applied to someone that was practicing witchcraft. They are the traits of an innocent, God-fearing person. Choice *A* is incorrect because when she mentions wicked spirits, it is to say that she has nothing to do with them. Choice *C* is incorrect because although Joan insults her accusers for judging others, that is not her primary defense. Choice *D* is incorrect because Joan condemns her accusers for lusting for blood; however, she does not specifically call out bloodthirst against women.

11. C: Choice *C* is the correct answer because it accurately describes the purpose of the passage. The passage is covering the ways CRISPR technology can be used in the future, including uses in medicine and agriculture. Choice *A* is incorrect because the passage does not go into detail about how CRISPR works. Choice *B* is incorrect because although the passage is aiming to educate about CRISPR's use, the actual process of its development is not discussed at length. Choice *D* is incorrect because only one line of the passage questions the ethicality of CRISPR in that specific field.

12. D: Choice *D* is the correct answer because it accurately identifies the main purpose of the text. The poet is discussing his feelings for "old Alberto's daughter" and her beauty. He is comparing her beauty to that of a river. Choice *A* is incorrect because he is using the river as a metaphor for the woman's beauty. It is not an actual river. Choice *B* is incorrect because the environment in this poem is for figurative language purposes. Choice *C* is incorrect because although the poet is speaking of the woman favorably, there is nothing to suggest that she is a goddess.

13. B: Choice *B* is the correct answer because it accurately summarizes what the author is saying in this passage. The author states that men with good understanding, who consider themselves without human superficiality, will understand that death is a work of nature and nothing to be feared. Choice *A* is incorrect because although the sentiment that nature does not discriminate is true per the passage, it is not the main point. The main point is focused on the processing and fear of death. Choice *C* is incorrect because other mammals and their conception of death are not mentioned. Choice *D* is incorrect because although children are mentioned in the end, it is not the main point to comment on their view of death.

14. A: Choice *A* is the correct answer because it uses information from the notes to compare action painting and color field painting. It first describes how they both evoke emotion and then describes how they do so in different ways. Choice *B* is incorrect because the original notes do not state that color field painting is focused on pre-existing emotions. It only aims to inspire feelings based on the imagery. Choice *C* is incorrect because it points out that both styles use emotion, yet it doesn't describe how they do that differently. Choice *D* is incorrect because although it may be true that the art styles convey different emotions, it does not describe the process for both.

15. B: Choice *B* is correct because it correctly uses the adverb *peculiarly* to modify the adjective *light* and uses a comma to separate the adjectives describing the color of Mycroft Holmes' eyes. Choice *A* is incorrect because the

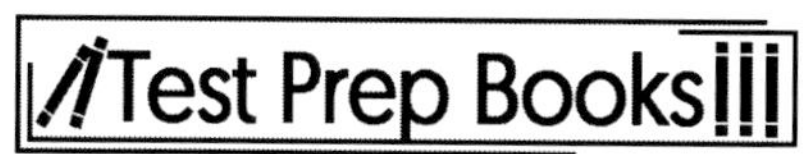

adverb form *peculiarly* better modifies the adjective *light.* Choice *C* is incorrect because *peculiarest* is an incorrect superlative; *most peculiar* would be the correct superlative form. Choice *D* is incorrect because commas are necessary in this list to divide up the specific attributes of Mycroft's eyes.

16. D: Choice *D* is correct because, in Standard English, a question in dialogue ends with the question mark followed by the ending quotation mark. Choices *A* and *B* are incorrect because Standard English does not add a comma after the question mark. Choice *C* is incorrect because a question mark is required to make the sentence a question.

17. A: We can infer from the following sentence's "Come to me" that this text must be completed with a singular first-person pronoun and a verb in the present tense. Thus, Choice *A* is correct. Choice *B* is incorrect because the verb is in the past tense. Choice *C* is incorrect because the subject pronoun is plural. Choice *D* is incorrect because the pronoun is in the third person, and the verb is in the past tense. While this is grammatically correct on its own, this formulation does not cohere with the rest of the passage and is therefore incorrect.

18. C: Choice *C* is correct because this answer correctly forms the possessive of a single individual whose name ends with an *s* using a single apostrophe, and it identifies the correct character acting during this sentence, who is introduced in the first sentence of the passage. Choice *A* is incorrect because the apostrophe is not typically followed by an *s* when forming a possessive for a name ending in *s* (the possessive is John Adams', not John Adams's). Choice *B* is incorrect because the other sentences in the passage indicate that Conan is the king, lying on the floor, and Pallantides is the one looking around. Choice *D* is incorrect because the use of a pronoun here references *the king* in the prior sentence, not Pallantides.

19. D: Choice *D* is correct because the past tense best matches this sentence's use of the past perfect (*I had lost*) and the use of the past tense throughout the passage. It also correctly identifies the narrator as the subject with *I*; the woman whom the narrator lost is not the one performing the action here. Choice *A* is incorrect because it incorrectly identifies the woman as the subject. Choice *B* is incorrect for the same reason and also because the verb *to be* does not fit with the proposition's sense of movement in the phrase "to the shores." Choice *C* is incorrect because the present tense does not fit with the tense of the sentence or the passage.

20. A: Choice *A* is correct because it correctly uses the definite article *the* and the singular form of *tank* to refer to the vehicle the previous sentence indicates the character is driving; it also matches the singular verb *was.* Choices *B* and *D* are incorrect because a plural noun does not work with the verb *was.* Choice *C* is incorrect because the indefinite article *a* does not make sense in the passage; this article could refer to any tank rather than the character's tank.

21. C: Choice *C* is correct because it correctly uses the infinitive *to guard*, the adjective *poisoned*, and the noun *well*, explaining what was done "so that no Americans might drink from" the well. Choice *A* is incorrect because *poisonous* is more ambiguous than *poisoned*, and the rest of the sentence suggests that the well being poisoned was a new development (as in, someone poisoned it) rather than a matter of the well being inherently poisonous. Choice *B* is incorrect because *poisoned* does not have a noun to modify. Choice *D* is incorrect because the adjective *well-guarded* likewise does not have a noun to modify.

22. A: Choice *A* is best as it sets up a noteworthy example of the change in engine design over time, which is the subject of the passage. Choice *B* is partially correct, as the example provided refers to the present day, but the lack of any chronological order of events in the first sentence makes Choice *A* better. Choice *C* is incorrect as it implies that the inline 6 and turbocharged inline 4 are present only on the fringes of engine design whereas the passage shows they have a central place. Choice *D* is incorrect as the example provided in the second sentence only reinforces the first sentence's assertion instead of contradicting it.

23. B: Choice *B* is best as it properly sets up the discussion as to why the turbocharger, a century-old invention, was not able to be used for the first eighty years of its life. Choice *A* is incorrect as it implies that the turbocharger was not able to be used on engines immediately because of when it was invented. Choice *C* is somewhat correct but places focus on the chronology of the turbocharger's history rather than the reasoning for its significant lag in popularity among engineers. Choice *D* is incorrect as it places the lack of turbocharger use in direct contrast with the timing of its invention rather than its technological limits at the time.

24. B: Choice *B* is best as it truthfully identifies the major changes that Ivan's rule brought to a newly united Russia. Choice *A*, although accurate, focuses more on Ivan's emotional demeanor and the consequences of his mental instability rather than the effect he had on Russia as a whole. Choice *C* is mainly focused on the effect that the Orthodox Church had on Ivan's rule and Russia today rather than Ivan's overall effect on Russian history. Choice *D* is technically true, although it incorrectly conflates Ivan's conquests inside Russia's modern borders with a desire to conquer other countries within Europe.

25. C: Choice *C* is best as it continues discussing the applications of agglomerated stone by detailing the various types that are used for the purposes already mentioned in the previous sentence. Choice *A* is correct but somewhat redundant as the process of creating agglomerated stone is already detailed in the passage's first sentence. Choice *B* contains accurate information but is unfocused, as it expands on information that the passage has already moved on from. Choice *D* could be correct, but the focus of the passage is on the application of agglomerated stone rather than the price itself.

26. D: Choice *D* is best as the second sentence communicates the most basic purposes for each kind of trial being held and the stakes found therein. Choice *A* is incorrect as there is no concrete statement to clarify but rather only the introduction of a survey of criminal and civil trials. Choice *B* is incorrect as no other descriptions of criminal and civil trials preceded the sentence it introduces. Choice *C* is somewhat correct, but *various differences* is not a statement that is typically exemplified with such non-specific information as found in the second sentence, which makes Choice *D* better.

27. C: Choice *C* is best as it identifies the two named causes of the Great Depression as speculative asset trading and European countries defaulting on wartime loans. It properly states that these two factors led to Black Tuesday, which marks the official beginning of the Great Depression. Although Choice *A* is partially correct, Black Tuesday did not cause the Great Depression; rather, it was a direct result of the symptoms that did and could be considered the first event of the Depression. Choice *B* is incorrect as it identifies the speculative asset bubble as the Depression itself. Choice *D* is incorrect as it implies that the Great Depression began before the factors that are stated to have caused it.

Reading and Writing: Module 2

1. C: According to Text 1, new home prices are higher than the price of purchasing a historic home and having it restored. Americans who find themselves unable to afford new homes could opt to buy an older house and restore it.

2. A: Since the passage is discussing rest days and mentions the importance of a gap in training, exercising more would not make sense in this context. Although applying heat to a sore muscle is a valid recovery technique, avoiding physical activity fits best with the general topic at hand.

3. A: Choice *A* is the best option because the poem emphasizes the cyclical nature of life and love, recognizing the temporary nature of experiences, including love, joy, and sorrow. The imagery of traveling "round and round" and "up and down," plus the reference to dying and budding roses, further emphasizes the theme of cycles of endings and beginnings in life and love. Choice *B* is incorrect because the poem does not define the most important types of

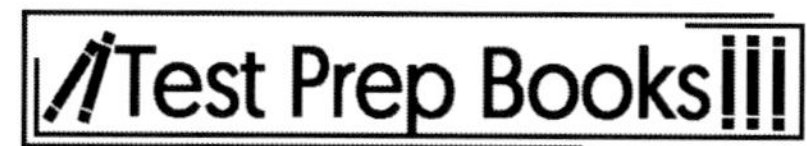

relationships. Similarly, Choice *C* is incorrect because the poem implies emotional experiences are fleeting but not necessarily unpredictable. Finally, Choice *D* is incorrect because the poem does not make a statement about the role of commitment.

4. C: The text contrasts two different approaches to tackling conflict: the open palm and the clenched fist. Choice *C* is the best answer because it expresses the dual nature of humanity and the potential for both love and violence. Choice *A* is incorrect, since Lincoln is named as a shining example of gentleness, not aggression. Choice *B* is incorrect because the passage meditates on the duality of human nature but does not make clear suggestions for how people should behave. Likewise, Choice *D* is incorrect because the passage describes men's capacity to fight but does not name this as an admirable or defining character trait.

5. B: Choice *B* is the correct answer because the underlined sentence illustrates how both design (or structure) of a natural element and chance (or luck) play a role in the successful continuation of life. In this example, the shape of the seeds of a cat-tail allows it to be picked up and carried by the wind, but an unseen force of luck seems to guide the seeds to places where they will grow. Choice *B* is correct because the example of wind-blown seeds serves to reinforce the author's belief that while chance may determine which seeds grow, the design of the seeds themselves suggests a deeper order or purpose in nature.

6. A: Choice A, *acquiesced to*, means to accept or comply reluctantly. This choice makes sense because at first, Sarah hesitated to join her friend at the sushi restaurant but eventually decided to give it a try. Choice *B* does not fit because *implicated in* means proven to be involved in a crime. Choice *C* is incorrect because *alluded to* means hinted at. Choice *D* is tempting since *participated in* means Sarah took part in the suggestion, but it falls short of conveying her initial hesitation and eventual cooperation. Choice *A* is the best fit.

7. A: Choice *A* is correct because it shows that Emily can afford opulence but chooses not to. *Abstemious* means marked by restraint. Emily has access to money but chooses to live modestly and prioritize saving her wealth for the future; therefore, she shows restraint in her spending. Choice *B*, *aesthetic*, does not make sense because that word means artistic or attractive and does not make sense in context. Choice *C*, *benign*, means harmless or mild. This choice may be tempting because Emily's spending habits cause no harm, but Choice *A* is still the stronger, more specific option. Choice *D* is incorrect because *munificent* means lavish or generous and actually expresses the opposite of the intended meaning.

8. C: Choice *C* is the correct answer because it is the choice that best states the purpose of the poem. The poem's speaker is writing about a loved one with whom they wish to visit even in death. This is evidenced by lines such as "I shall return to thee silently," which refers to the speaker coming back from beyond the grave. Choice *A* is incorrect because the flowers and serpents are not the main purpose of the poem; they are just forms of figurative language. Choice *B* is incorrect because the speaker doesn't mention a desire to be young again. Choice *D* is incorrect because winter is not the focus of this poem.

9. D: Choice *D* is the correct answer because it accurately describes what Hamlet is expressing in his soliloquy. He is impressed at how "infinite in faculties" man is. Yet he lacks delight in life, as he says in the last sentence. Choice *A* is incorrect because he mentions the words *foul* and *pestilent* to say that is how he currently sees the world in his state of disillusionment. It is not actually how he feels about the world. Choice *B* is incorrect because he is not comparing his life to others. He is speaking more generally about the capabilities of mankind. Choice *C* is incorrect because he is not contemplating how noble humans are. He believes that they are noble and admirable.

10. C: Choice *C* is the correct answer because it accurately states what Theseus is saying about imagination. He believes that imagination leads to deviations from reality that can be harmful. He says that lunatics, lovers, and poets see "more devils than vast hell can hold" to emphasize this point. Choice *A* is incorrect because he believes that tricks are a product of imagination. Choice *B* is incorrect because he does not mention that everybody has imagination. He seems to believe that imagination comes to those who wish to shape fantasies. Choice *D* is incorrect because the poet seems to think poorly of imagination.

11. A: Choice *A* is the correct answer because it accurately states the main purpose of the poem. The poem is observing a statue of a past ruler that is now in a state of decay. This shows that no matter how powerful and revered someone's power was, it is impermanent when faced with the continuation of time and history. Choice *B* is incorrect because the poem does not have a sad tone. The history is not forgotten, as the statue still stands; however, the ruler's power does not mean anything anymore. Choice *C* is incorrect because it is unclear if Ozymandias was a bad ruler. Choice *D* is incorrect because the poem is pointing out that human achievement is not immortal. The statue, the representation of achievement, will one day be gone.

12. C: Choice *C* is the correct answer because it is the most logical text to finish the sentence. Since scientists have eliminated cues and still not found the answer, it is reasonable to assume that pigeons are either using the cues in ways that scientists do not understand or they are using new methods entirely. Choice *A* is incorrect because although the text mentions that pigeons were used as mail carriers, it does not state that they should continue to be used as such. Choice *B* is incorrect because there is no comparison between other animals except to say that the pigeon is unique. Choice *D* is incorrect because scientists do not have the answers presently, but they may in the future.

13. C: Choice *C* is the correct answer because it is the best determination given the information provided in the table. The earliest country in the war, Germany, has fewer casualties than the second latest addition to the war, the Soviet Union. This shows that there is no correlation between time in the war and casualties. Choice *A* is incorrect because of the reason mentioned above. Choice *B* is incorrect because Germany was in the war the longest but did not have the most casualties. Choice *D* is incorrect because although the Soviet Union and the United States were only about six months apart in joining the war, they have vastly different casualty numbers.

14. D: Choice *D* is the correct answer because it accurately states the main purpose of the passage. In this passage, Oliver is following his master in order to learn his demeanor and strong qualities. This shows that observing his master's characteristics are a part of his training as an undertaker. Choice *A* is incorrect because there is no adventure being described except that Oliver is accompanying his master to an unknown location with an unknown objective. Choices B and C are incorrect because the passage doesn't give insight into Oliver's thoughts. It doesn't say whether Oliver understands what he should be learning or whether he appreciates his master.

15. B: Choice *B* is correct because the preposition *but* logically completes the sentence by providing a contrast between *warm* and *shivered.* Choice *A* is incorrect because *For* provides a sense of purpose, which does not create a contrast. Choice *C* is incorrect because *To* provides a sense of direction, which does not create a contrast. Choice *D* is incorrect because *At* provides a sense of place, which does not create a contrast.

16. D: Choice *D* is correct because *this* specifies that the speaker is discussing the same draft (the second draft) as mentioned in the first sentence. Choice *A* is incorrect because the plural *these* does not match the singular *draft.* Choice *B* is incorrect because, while *that* can point to a specific object like *this, this* more clearly refers to what was just discussed and aligns with *this* in the previous sentence. Choice *C* is incorrect because, while using the article *the* is not incorrect here, using *this* is more precise and thus preferable.

17. B: Choice *B* is correct because it correctly uses a comma to punctuate the end of the clause, uses the correct preposition indicating the target of the action, and correctly uses *the other* to make a distinction between the two birds. Choice *A* is incorrect because it does not have the necessary comma to separate the actions of each clause. Choice *C* is incorrect because, in Standard English, the pronoun *it* refers to a recently specified noun, and there is no singular noun before *it* that it clearly corresponds to. Choice *D* is incorrect because the preposition *for*, which indicates purpose, does not fit the context.

18. D: Choice *D* is correct because it uses the commas necessary to mark the aside *perhaps* indicating reluctance and the transition after *desirable* from one clause to the next. Choice *A* is incorrect because no punctuation is used to mark either element of the sentence. Choice *B* is incorrect because a comma is required before *for* when it connects two independent clauses. Choice *C* is incorrect because this answer's punctuation marks the word *desirable* as an aside rather than *perhaps*.

19. B: Choice *B* is correct because it correctly uses a comma to punctuate the transition from one clause to another. Choice *A* is incorrect because the answer lacks this comma and replaces *through* with the similarly spelled word *thorough*. Choice *C* is incorrect because the phrase *a like* does not have the same meaning as the word *alike* and does not make sense here. Choice *D* is incorrect because it places the comma after the wrong word, and the abbreviated spelling *thru* is not generally used for *through* in standard English.

20. A: Choice *A* is correct because it correctly uses the plural *doctrines* and the possessive pronoun *his* corresponding to Luther. Choices *B* and *C* are incorrect because both answers needlessly use the possessive form for the object being possessed, *doctrines.* In addition, Choice *C* incorrectly uses the plural possessive pronoun *their.* Choice *D* is incorrect because there is no grammatical need for a comma before *by*.

21. A: Choice *A* is correct because it correctly uses the preposition *as*, which corresponds to the verb *regarded* earlier in the sentence, and the preposition *to*, indicating purpose or direction (in this case, indicating what force is necessary for). It also correctly uses the definite article before *defense of society.* Choice *B* is incorrect because, without a preposition, the necessary relationship between *force* and *society* is unclear. Choice *C* is incorrect because *as necessary as* creates a comparison between *force* and *defense* rather indicating that defense is the purpose of force. Choice *D* is incorrect because the comma creates an aside, *with the defense of society*, which doesn't make sense here.

22. A: Choice *A* is best as it sets up the specific usage of sheep's wool and goose down as noteworthy examples of animal products that are used in weather-resistant apparel. Choice *B* is incorrect as the specification of which animal products are being used in clothing is not a consequence of the usage of the animal products themselves. Choice *C* is incorrect as it attempts to concede a point that is being expanded upon further. Choice *D* is somewhat correct as it attempts to agree with the assertion made in the first sentence, but it is implying that the usage of sheep's wool and goose down is *like* the animal products being used in clothing rather than being the products themselves.

23. C: Choice *C* is best as it communicates that George responded to Nicolas's capture after the fact with refusal, establishing a strong chronological order of events. Choice *A* is partially correct as it contrasts the dire nature of Nicolas's situation with George's refusal to help his cousin, but Choice *C* better demonstrates the sequence of events as presented due to George's reasoning already being detailed later in the sentence. Choice *B* is incorrect as George refusing to give Nicolas asylum is not an example of Nicolas's capture. Choice *D* is incorrect as George refused to give Nicolas asylum due to his unpopularity, not because he was captured.

24. A: Choice *A* is best as it establishes the October Revolution as having occurred later in 1917 than the February Revolution and Nicolas's removal from power. Choice *B* is incorrect as the October Revolution did not occur solely as a result of Nicolas's removal since he was never reinstated as Tsar. Choice *C* is incorrect because the October Revolution occurred after the February Revolution, hence its namesake. Choice *D* is partially correct as Nicolas's removal did not stop Russia from being engulfed in further turmoil, but the specific reasons for the October Revolution are not discussed and thus still make Choice *A* best.

25. A: Choice *A* is best as it describes King's and Malcolm X's positions on the racial issues they were fighting at the time while also detailing their accomplishments and differing trajectories within the peak of the civil rights movement. Despite containing true information, Choice *B* does not detail King and Malcolm X's contributions to the civil rights movement but rather contrasts their assassinations. Choice *C* also contains true information but does not address their contributions to the civil rights movement and is thus incorrect. Choice *D* is based upon conjecture from the notes, assuming that King was anti-Muslim due to his faith and implying that Malcolm X was pro-segregationist because of his black separatist views.

26. C: Choice *C* is best as it sets up the disparity between productivity and wages paid as the impetus for the plummeting of worker satisfaction in recent years. Choice *A* is incorrect because it implies that plummeting worker satisfaction is an alternative phrasing for the gap between productivity and wages. Choice *B* is incorrect because it implies that there is an example of a concept being illustrated rather than a cause-and-effect relationship between low wages and decreasing worker satisfaction. Choice *D* makes sense but turns the sentence into a contradictory statement attempting to refute the previous sentence rather than adding additional supporting information.

27. D: Choice *D* is best as it communicates the importance of preventing drinking water contamination over all other pollution concerns listed in the passage. Choice *A* is incorrect because it implies that reducing drinking water contamination is a step that can only come after the prevention of soil contamination. Choice *B* is somewhat correct, as a list of concerns does exist, but the passage works better when the second sentence is set up as a topic of greater importance than the previous one. Choice *C* is incorrect because it implies that preventing drinking water contamination is markedly different from preventing soil contamination.

Math: Module 1

1. B: 300 miles in four hours is $\frac{300}{4} = 75$ miles per hour. In 1.5 hours, the car will go 1.5×75 miles, or 112.5 miles.

2. 30: The best way to solve this problem is by using a system of equations. We know that Jan bought $90 worth of apples ($a$) and oranges ($o$) at $1 and $2, respectively. That means our first equation is:

$$1(a) + 2(o) = 90$$

We also know that she bought an equal number of apples and oranges, which gives us our second equation: $a = o$. We can then replace a with o in the first equation to give:

$$1(o) + 2(o) = 90 \text{ or } 3(o) = 90$$

Which yields,

$$o = 30$$

Thus, Jan bought 30 oranges (and 30 apples).

3. C: The formula for the volume of a box with rectangular sides is the length times width times height, so $5 \times 6 \times 3 = 90$ cubic feet.

4. D: First, the train's journey in the real word is $3 \times 50 = 150$ miles. On the map, 1 inch corresponds to 10 miles, so that is equivalent to $\frac{150}{10} = 15$ inches on the map.

5. B: The total trip time is $1 + 3.5 + 0.5 = 5$ hours. The total time driving is $1 + 0.5 = 1.5$ hours. So, the fraction of time spent driving is $\frac{1.5}{5}$ or $\frac{3}{10}$.

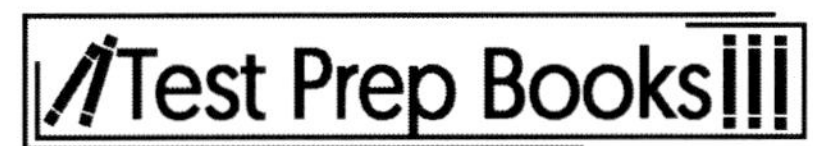

To convert this to a percentage, multiply the top and bottom by 10 to make the denominator 100. We find $\frac{3}{10} \times \frac{10}{10} = \frac{30}{100}$. Since the denominator is 100, the numerator is our percentage: 30%.

6. B: The formula for the volume of a cylinder is $\pi r^2 h$, where r is the radius and h is the height. The diameter is twice the radius, so these barrels have a radius of 1 foot. That means each barrel has a volume of:

$$\pi \times (1 \text{ ft})^2 \times 3 \text{ ft} = 3\pi \text{ ft}^3$$

Since there are three of them, the total is:

$$3 \times 3\pi \text{ ft}^3 = 9\pi \text{ ft}^3$$

7. A: The tip is not taxed, so he pays 5% tax only on the $10. To find 5% of $10, calculate $0.05 \times \$10 = \$0.50$. Add up $\$10 + \$0.50 + \$2$ to get $12.50.

8. A: Divide the total amount by the number of days: $\frac{150}{4} = 37.5$. She needs to save an average of $37.50 per day.

9. 4: The number of days can be found by taking the total amount Bernard needs to make and dividing it by the amount he earns per day:

$$\frac{300}{80} = \frac{30}{8} = \frac{15}{4} = 3.75$$

But Bernard is only working full days, so he will need to work 4 days, since 3 days is not enough time.

10. A: The value went up by $\$165{,}000 - \$150{,}000 = \$15{,}000$.

Out of $150,000, this is $\frac{15{,}000}{150{,}000} = \frac{1}{10}$ or 0.1. To get the percentage, multiply 0.1 by 100 to get 10%.

11. D: The total faculty is:

$$15 + 20 = 35$$

So, the ratio is $35 : 200$. Then, divide both of these numbers by 5, since 5 is a common factor to both, which results in $7 : 40$.

12. B: The journey will be $5 \times 3 = 15$ miles. A car traveling at 60 miles per hour is traveling at 1 mile per minute. The resulting equation would be:

$$\frac{15 \text{ mi}}{1 \text{ mi/min}} = 15 \text{ min}$$

Therefore, it will take 15 minutes to make the journey.

13. A: Taylor's total income is $\$20,000 + \$10,000 = \$30,000$. 15 percent as a fraction is $\frac{15}{100} = \frac{3}{20}$. So:

$$\frac{3}{20} \times \$30,000 = \frac{\$90,000}{20} = \frac{\$9,000}{2}$$

$$\frac{\$9,000}{2} = \$4,500$$

14. B: Since the answer will be in cubic feet rather than inches, the first step is to convert from inches to feet for the dimensions of the box. There are 12 inches per foot, so the box is $24 \div 12 = 2$ feet wide, $18 \div 12 = 1.5$ feet deep, and $12 \div 12 = 1$ foot high. The volume is the product of these three together:

$$2 \times 1.5 \times 1 = 3 \text{ cubic feet}$$

15. D: Kristen bought four DVDs, which would cost a total of $4 \times \$15 = \$60$. She spent a total of $100, so she spent $\$100 - \$60 = \$40$ on CDs. Since they cost $10 each, she must have purchased $\frac{\$40}{\$10} = 4 \text{ CDs}$.

16. B: First, separate out and add the whole numbers from the mixed fractions:

$$4\frac{1}{3} + 3\frac{3}{4}$$

$$4 + 3 + \frac{1}{3} + \frac{3}{4}$$

$$7 + \frac{1}{3} + \frac{3}{4}$$

Adding the fractions gives:

$$\frac{1}{3} + \frac{3}{4}$$

$$\frac{4}{12} + \frac{9}{12}$$

$$\frac{13}{12}$$

$$1 + \frac{1}{12}$$

Thus,

$$7 + \frac{1}{3} + \frac{3}{4} = 7 + 1 + \frac{1}{12} = 8\frac{1}{12}$$

17. C: The domain consists of all possible inputs, or x-values. The scenario states that the function approximates the population between the years 1900 and 2000. It also states that $x = 0$ represents the year 1900, with x representing the year (where 1900 is $x = 0$) and y representing the population (in thousands). Therefore, the year 2000 would be represented by $x = 100$. Only inputs between 0 and 100 are relevant in this case.

18. C: The equation for a circle is $(x-h)^2+(y-k)^2=r^2$, where (h,k) is the center of the circle. Nothing is added to x and y since the center is (0,0) and 5^2 is 25. Choice *A* is not the correct answer because you do not subtract the radius from x and y. Choice *B* is not the correct answer because you must square the radius on the right side of the equation. Choice *D* is not the correct answer because you do not add the radius to x and y in the equation.

19. A: The first step is to determine the unknown, which is in terms of the length, l.

The second step is to translate the problem into the equation for the perimeter of a rectangle:

$$P=2l+2w$$

The width is the length minus 2 centimeters. The resulting equation is:

$$2l+2(l-2)=44$$

The equation can be solved as follows:

$2l+2l-4=44$	Apply the distributive property on the left side of the equation.
$4l-4=44$	Combine like terms on the left side of the equation.
$4l=48$	Add 4 to both sides of the equation.
$l=12$	Divide both sides of the equation by 4.

The length of the rectangle is 12 centimeters. The width is the length minus 2 centimeters, which is 10 centimeters. Checking the answers for length and width forms the following equation:

$$44=2(12)+2(10)$$

The equation can be solved using the order of operations to form a true statement: $44=44$.

20. B: By distributing the implied 1 in front of the first set of parentheses and the -1 in front of the second set of parentheses, the parentheses can be eliminated:

$$1(5x^2-3x+4)-1(2x^2-7)$$

$$5x^2-3x+4-2x^2+7$$

Next, like terms are combined by adding the coefficients of the same variables with the same exponents, while keeping the variables and their powers unchanged:

$$5x^2-3x+4-2x^2+7=3x^2-3x+11$$

21. C: In order to find the percentage by which the value of the car has been reduced, the current cash value should be subtracted from the initial value and then the difference divided by the initial value. The result should be multiplied by 100 to find the percentage decrease.

$$\frac{20{,}000-8{,}000}{20{,}000}=0.6$$

$$(0.6)\times 100=60\%$$

22. 60: When x and y are complementary angles, the sine of x is equal to the cosine of y. The complementary angle of 30 is $90 - 30 = 60$ degrees. Therefore, the answer is 60 degrees.

Math: Module 2

1. D: This problem can be solved by setting up a proportion involving the given information and the unknown value. The proportion is:

$$\frac{21 \text{ pages}}{4 \text{ nights}} = \frac{140 \text{ pages}}{x \text{ nights}}$$

We can cross-multiply to get $21x = 4 \times 140$. Solving this, we find $x \approx 26.67$. Since this is not an integer, we round up to 27 nights because 26 nights would not give Sarah enough time to finish.

2. D: This problem can be solved by using unit conversion. The initial units are miles per minute. The final units need to be feet per second. Converting miles to feet uses the equivalence statement $1 \text{ mi} = 5{,}280 \text{ ft}$. Converting minutes to seconds uses the equivalence statement $1 \text{ min} = 60 \text{ s}$. Setting up the ratios to convert the units is shown in the following equation:

$$\frac{72 \text{ mi}}{90 \text{ min}} \times \frac{1 \text{ min}}{60 \text{ s}} \times \frac{5{,}280 \text{ ft}}{1 \text{ mi}} = 70.4 \frac{\text{ft}}{\text{s}}$$

The initial units cancel out, and the new units are left.

3. C: The total percentage of a pie chart equals 100%. We can see that CD sales make up less than half of the chart (50%) but more than a quarter (25%), and the only answer choice that meets these criteria is Choice *C*, 40%.

4. B: Since \$850 is the price after a 20% discount, \$850 represents 80% of the original price. To determine the original price, set up a proportion with the ratio of the sale price (850) to the original price (unknown) equal to the ratio of the sale percentage (where x represents the unknown original price):

$$\frac{850}{x} = \frac{80}{100}$$

To solve a proportion, cross multiply and set the products equal to each other:

$$(850)(100) = (80)(x)$$

Multiplying each side results in the equation:

$$85{,}000 = 80x$$

To solve for x, divide both sides by 80:

$$\frac{85{,}000}{80} = \frac{80x}{80}$$

$$x = 1{,}062.5$$

Remember that x represents the original price. Subtracting the sale price from the original price (\$1,062.50 − \$850) indicates that Frank saved \$212.50.

5. C: $40N$ would be 4,000% of N. All of the other coefficients are equivalent to $\frac{40}{100}$ or 40%.

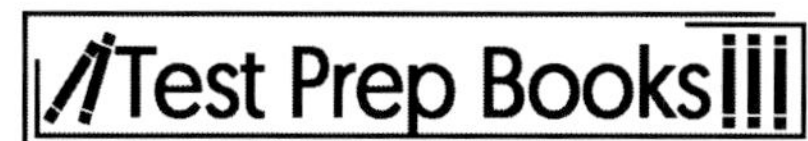

6. C: An x-intercept is the point where the graph crosses the x–axis. At this point, the value of y is 0. To determine if an equation has an x-intercept of −2, substitute −2 for x, and calculate the value of y. If the value of −2 for x corresponds with a y–value of 0, then the equation has an x-intercept of −2. The only answer choice that produces this result is Choice *C*.

$$0 = (-2)^2 + 5(-2) + 6$$

7. C: There are 34 girls who are potty-trained out of a total of 52 girls:

$$34 \div 52 \approx 0.65 = 65\%$$

8. A: A sample statistic indicates information about the data that was collected (in this case, the heights of those surveyed). A population parameter describes an aspect of the entire population (in this case, all twelve-year-old boys in the United States). A confidence interval would consist of a range of heights likely to include the actual population parameter. Measurement error relates to the validity of the data that was collected.

9. C: To ensure valid results, samples should be taken across the entire scope of the study. Since all states are not equally populated, representing each state proportionately would result in a more accurate statistic.

10. D: Exponential functions can be written in the form: $y = a \times b^x$. The equation for an exponential function can be written given the y-intercept (a) and the growth rate (b).

The y-intercept is the output (y) when the input (x) equals zero. It can be thought of as an "original value," or starting point. The value of b is the rate at which the original value increases ($b > 1$) or decreases ($b < 1$).

In this scenario, the y-intercept, a, would be $1200, and the growth rate, b, would be 1.01 (100% of the original value combined with 1% interest, or $100\% + 1\% = 101\% = 1.01$).

11. 17: To get 85% of a number, multiply it by 0.85.

$$\frac{17}{20} \times \frac{20}{1} = 17$$

12. A: To find the fraction of the bill that the first three people pay, the fractions need to be added, which means finding the common denominator. The common denominator will be 60:

$$\frac{1}{5} + \frac{1}{4} + \frac{1}{3} = \frac{12}{60} + \frac{15}{60} + \frac{20}{60} = \frac{47}{60}$$

The remainder of the bill is:

$$1 - \frac{47}{60} = \frac{60}{60} - \frac{47}{60} = \frac{13}{60}$$

13. D: To convert a decimal to a fraction, remember that any number to the left of the decimal point will be a whole number. Then, sense 0.3 goes to the tenths place, it can be placed over 10.

14. A: Convert the mixed fractions to improper fractions: $\frac{11}{3} - \frac{9}{5}$. Subtract using 15 as a common denominator and rewrite to get rid of the improper fraction:

$$\frac{11}{3} - \frac{9}{5} = \frac{55}{15} - \frac{27}{15} = \frac{28}{15} = 1\frac{13}{15}$$

15. 4: Dividing by 98 can be approximated by dividing by 100, which would mean shifting the decimal point of the numerator to the left two places. The result is 4.2, which rounds to 4.

16. D: Subtract the center from the x- and y-values of the equation and square the radius on the right side of the equation. Choice *A* is not the correct answer because the radius of the equation must be squared. Choice *B* is not the correct answer because you do not square the centers of the equation. Choice *C* is not the correct answer because you need to subtract (not add) the centers of the equation from x and y.

17. C: Plug in the values for x and y to discover that the solution works, which means the points are on the circle.

$$(-3)^2 + (-4)^2 = 25$$

$$9 + 16 = 25$$

Choices *A* and *B* are not the correct answers since the solution works. Choice *D* is not the correct answer because there is enough information to tell that the given point lies on the circle.

18. B: The figure is composed of three sides of a square and a semicircle. The sides of the square are simply added:

$$8 \text{ in} + 8 \text{ in} + 8 \text{ in} = 24 \text{ in}$$

The circumference of a circle is found by the equation $C = 2\pi r$. The radius is 4 in, so the circumference of the circle is 25.13 in. Only half of the circle makes up the outer border of the figure (part of the perimeter), and half of 25.13 in is 12.565 in. Therefore, the total perimeter is:

$$24 \text{ in} + 12.565 \text{ in} = 36.565 \text{ in}$$

19. C: The volume of a cylinder is $\pi r^2 h$, and $\pi \times 6^2 \times 2$ is 72 π cm^3. Choice *A* is not the correct answer because that is only $6^2 \times \pi$. Choice *B* is not the correct answer because that is $2^2 \times 6 \times \pi$. Choice *D* is not the correct answer because that is $2^3 \times 6 \times \pi$.

20. B: This answer is correct because the hypotenuse of a right triangle is the square root of the sum of squared legs, or $a^2 + b^2 = c^2$.

$$3^2 + 4^2 = 9 + 16$$

$$9 + 16 = 25$$

$$\sqrt{25} = 5$$

Choice *A* is not the correct answer because that is $3 + 4$. Choice *C* is not the correct answer because it neglects to take the square root of 25. Choice *D* is not the correct answer because that is 3×4.

21. 13: The perimeter is found by calculating the sum of all sides of the polygon:

$$9 + 9 + 9 + 8 + 8 + s = 56$$

Let s be the missing side length. Therefore, $43 + s = 56$. The missing side length is 13 cm.

22. B: The first step is to calculate the difference between the larger value and the smaller value:

$$378 - 252 = 126$$

To calculate this difference as a percentage of the original value, and thus calculate the percentage *increase*, 126 is divided by 252, and then this result is multiplied by 100 to find the percentage: 50%, or Choice *B*.

SAT Practice Tests #3, #4, #5, #6, and #7

To keep the size of this book manageable, save paper, and provide a digital test-taking experience, the 3rd - 7th practice tests can be found online. Scan the QR code or go to this link to access it:

testprepbooks.com/bonus/sat

The first time you access the tests, you will need to register as a "new user" and verify your email address.

If you have any issues, please email support@testprepbooks.com.

Dear SAT Test Taker,

Thank you for purchasing this study guide for your SAT exam. We hope that we exceeded your expectations.

Our goal in creating this study guide was to cover all of the topics that you will see on the test. We also strove to make our practice questions as similar as possible to what you will encounter on test day. With that being said, if you found something that you feel was not up to your standards, please send us an email and let us know.

We would also like to let you know about other books in our catalog that may interest you.

ACCUPLACER

This can be found on Amazon: amazon.com/dp/1637750250

TSI

amazon.com/dp/1637754434

We have study guides in a wide variety of fields. If the one you are looking for isn't listed above, then try searching for it on Amazon or send us an email.

Thanks Again and Happy Testing!
Product Development Team
info@studyguideteam.com

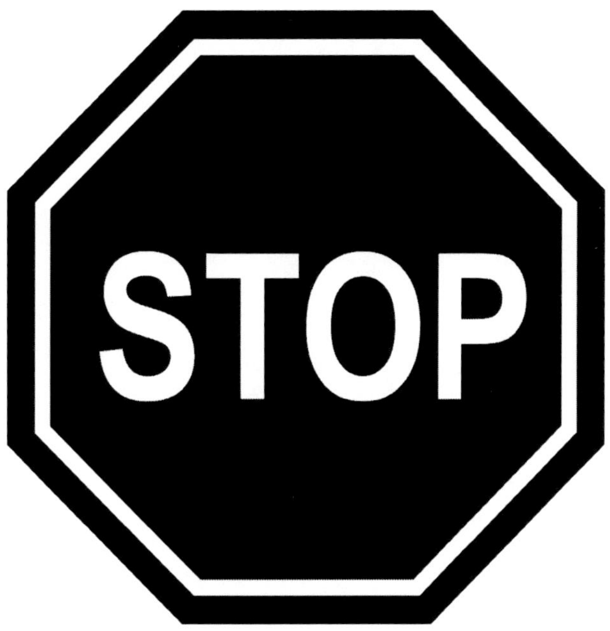

FREE Test Taking Tips Video/DVD Offer

To better serve you, we created videos covering test taking tips that we want to give you for FREE. **These videos cover world-class tips that will help you succeed on your test.**

We just ask that you send us feedback about this product. Please let us know what you thought about it—whether good, bad, or indifferent.

To get your **FREE videos**, you can use the QR code below or email freevideos@studyguideteam.com with "Free Videos" in the subject line and the following information in the body of the email:

a. The title of your product

b. Your product rating on a scale of 1-5, with 5 being the highest

c. Your feedback about the product

If you have any questions or concerns, please don't hesitate to contact us at info@studyguideteam.com.

Thank you!

Made in United States
North Haven, CT
27 January 2025

65033512R00124